Chican@ Power
and the
Struggle for Aztlán

Chican@ Power and the Struggle for Aztlán

by a MIM(Prisons) Study Group

MIM Distributors &
Kersplebedeb Publishing

Chican@ Power and the Struggle for Aztlán
by a MIM(Prisons) Study Group
2015

ISBN: 978-1-894946-74-2

MIM Distributors
PO Box 40799
San Francisco, CA 94140
email: mim@prisoncensorship.info
web: www.prisoncensorship.info
            www.abolishcontrolunits.com

Kersplebedeb Publishing and Distribution
CP 63560
CCCP Van Horne
Montreal, Quebec
Canada H3W 3H8
email: info@kersplebedeb.com
web: www.kersplebedeb.com
            www.leftwingbooks.net

This book is co-published by MIM(Prisons) and Kersplebedeb. Kersplebedeb considers this to be a thought-provoking intervention, and has respect for the work done by MIM(Prisons). That said, there is not theoretical unity on all points touched upon in this book, nor on each of MIM(Prisons)'s Six Main Points.

Printed in Canada

This project is dedicated to all those who lost their lives to brown-on-brown violence inside and outside of prisons.

Contents

Figures   4
Preface   6
On Rebuilding the Nation and Regional Divisions   8

Introduction   10
Who is a Chican@?   14
What is Aztlán? Who are la Raza?   15
Chican@ Nationalism, Revolutionary Nationalism,
Proletarian Feminism   17

**Part I: Chican@ Power and
the Struggle for Aztlán   20**

Section 1: History of Chican@s   22
The Birth of Mexico   22
Colonization, Development and the U.$. War on Mexico   25
Revolution in Mexico 1910   36
From Imperialist War to Braceros   42
The Brown Liberation Movement   45

**Section 2: Historical Basis of Aztlán
and the State of the Nation Today   56**
Territory   56
Language   58
Economy   61
Culture   65
The Border: Past, Present and Future   66
Aztlán is an Oppressed Internal Semi-Colony   68

Section 3: The Path Forward for Emancipation   71
Socialism and the Chican@ Nation   75
Incorrect Lines Toward Aztlán   79
Revolutionary Nationalism   84
Cell Structure, Barrio Committees,
and the need for a Vanguard Party   87

Section 4: Questions of Organizing   93
The First Nations and Aztlán   93
Chicanas: Wimmin Hold up Half the Sky   95
The Role of Chicanismo   98
Pandillas: Our Red Guards   99
Barrios Wrapped in Razor Wire   103

Contents, cont.

Part II: Further Research   108

Section 1: Obscured for Centuries,
the Nation is Bigger Than Ever   109
     A Rising, Vibrant Nation   110
     "Hispanics" and the Erasing of First Nations   119
     Measuring Assimilation   124
     Class Nature of the Internal Semi-Colonies   128
     Battling in the Realm of Ideas   129

Section 2: Real Lessons of the Chicano Moratorium
and the High Treason Against Maoism   131
     Three Views in Politics   134
     High Treason Against Maoism   136

Section 3: Why Revolutionary Proletarian Nationalism?   143

Section 4: Democratic Convention
Highlights Chicano Assimilationist   150

Section 5: Response to rcp=u$a's Opposition to Aztlán   154
     How Many Ways Can They Deny Our Right To Self-Determination?   156
     Nationalism is Bourgeois Anyway   164

Section 6: Murder of Chicano Youth Holds Lessons for
Revolutionaries   168

Section 7: Mexicans Targeted for Censorship   174

Contents, cont.

Part III: Chican@ Literature from a Maoist Perspective   176

Burning Chican@ Books   177

Occupied America   180

Mexico's Revolution Then and Now   183

The Chicanos: A History of Mexican Americans   186

Youth, Identity, Power   188

Chicano Liberation and Socialism   194

Labor, Family, Feminism and Revolution   202
    Class and Gender   203
    White Wimmin's Pseudo-Feminism   206
    Reproductive Rights   208
    Patriarchy in Revolutionary Organizations   209
    Distinctive National Culture   210
    Cultural Nationalism   210
    Intersections of Nation, Class and Gender   211

We Will Rise – Rebuilding the Mexikah Nation   214

Appendix   220
    1.a Brown Berets – Prison Chapter   221
    1.b United Struggle from Within   226
    1.c Maoist Internationalist Ministry of Prisons   229
    2.a Agreement to End Hostilities   233
    2.b United Front for Peace in Prisons   236
    3.a Class overview   238
    3.b Labor aristocracy   243
    3.c First World lumpen   255
    3.d Fascism and its class nature: A brief introduction   257
    4.a Why we use the word "migrant" and not "immigrant"   259
    4.b On Cesar Chavez and the Correct and Incorrect Handling of Contradictions Among the People   260
    5.a Cell Structure, Vanguard Parties and Mass Organizations   262
    5.b United Front   268
    5.c New Democracy and the Joint Dictatorship of the Proletariat of the Oppressed Nations   273

Glossary   291

Index   313

Figures

Figure 1.1.1 Camino Real   24

Figure 1.1.2 New Spain   26

Figure 1.1.3 Santa Fe Trail   28

Figure 1.2.1 Raza as Percent of Total U.$. Population   58

Figure 1.2.2 Raza population by county in the United $tates 2010   59

Figure 1.2.3 Linguistic Assimilation of Mexicans and Other Immigrants   60

Figure 1.2.4 Global Wealth Flow Under Imperialism   62

Figure 1.2.5 Wealth Flow in the First World   63

Figure 2.1.1 Foreign-Born Population of the
United $tates, by Region of Birth, 1960-2005   111

Figure 2.1.2 Reference map of present United $tates boundaries   112

Figure 2.1.3 Percent of Foreign-Born Population
from Mexico and Other Central America: 1960-2010   114

Figure 2.1.4 Raza as % of Population in 2010   115

Figure 2.1.5 Distribution of Largest Raza Populations Across the
Continental United $tates   116

Figure 2.1.6 % Living Below Federal Poverty Line
by Country of Origin   119

Figure 2.1.7 Economic Assimilation Indexes   120

Figure 2.1.8 Percentage of the Foreign-Born Population Who Are
Naturalized U.S. Citizens by Country of Birth: 2010   125

Figure 2.1.9 Percentage of Foreign-Born Population by Language Spoken
at Home and English-Speaking Ability by Country of Birth: 2010   126

Figure 2.1.10 % of Population with a Bachelor's Degree or Higher
Education by Nativity Status and Country of Birth: 2010   127

Figure 2.1.11 Median Earnings in the Past 12 Months
by Nativity Status and Country of Birth: 2010   127

Figure 2.3.1 Hispanic Ethnicity of U.$. Military   145

Figure 2.3.2 World Distribution of Household Wealth, GDP,
and Population in the year 2000   147

Preface

THIS BOOK WAS A COLLABORATIVE EFFORT written in a study group for U.$. prisoners, led by the Maoist Internationalist Ministry of Prisons, or MIM(Prisons) for short. While we all discussed, wrote and edited the material, MIM(Prisons) was the principal editor. Once we had a draft that was close to final, we sent advanced copies to a few other comrades inside and outside of prison for additional comments. We welcome readers to continue sending us feedback on this book, and we are eager to get it into the hands of those organizing for liberation in the belly of the beast! The greatest feedback will come in the form of advancements against oppression.

The two principal authors of this book are prime models of revolutionary leadership from behind prison walls. Ehecatl and cipactli are both long-time leaders in the anti-imperialist organization United Struggle from Within. Cipactli also writes on behalf of the Brown Berets – Prison Chapter, a more recent project cipactli helped initiate to push the Chican@ national liberation struggle forward. This book was a collaborative writing effort, rather than just a collection of essays with different perspectives.

Cipactli first inspired this project by putting together the central essay, which provided the framework for what became Part I of this book. Cipactli recognized the need for Maoist literature and leadership in the hotly contested struggle of Chican@s and migrants against Amerikan repression, especially in a new context of multiculturalism and widespread wealth throughout the United $tates. Coming together with a basic agreement around this need, and the line that needed to be presented, we assembled the material for this book.

The Maoist movement in Aztlán is still young. As such this book is somewhat preliminary and will not provide all the answers. In some aspects we did not all agree, but in the end, through unity-struggle-unity, we resolved most major disagreements to present a cohesive analysis. The core principles that we firmly put forth here are: 1) that a distinct Chican@ nation exists, 2) that it developed in dialectical relation to the oppressor nation of Amerika as a colony and later an internal semi-colony of the United $tates, and 3) that supporting and upholding the right to secession of the Chican@ nation and the territory of Aztlán is a must for anyone who struggles for an end to imperialism and oppression in today's world. We also firmly present that this contradiction between the oppressor nation and the oppressed nations is principal within U.$. borders and therefore deserves all the attention and energy of freedom-loving people.

A combination of repression and temptation threaten the liberation struggles of all the internal semi-colonies of the United $tates. These forces push for submission and assimilation into Amerika. It is for this reason that the essays in Part II of this book go deeper into the very question of the existence of and the need to liberate the Chican@ nation.

We close the book with some reviews of texts that we found either particularly useful or needing of critique in our research for this book. We hope that in doing so we provide a good jumping off point for others doing their own research. We also provide a number of appendices that go deeper into some of the political ideas mentioned in the book and a glossary of political terms as tools to better understand the message of this project.

One thing that distinguishes this book from all those we reviewed is its connection to organizers involved in the growing struggle today, and the clear framework that we provide via our organizations on what needs to be done. The appendix provides more information on the organizations we all represent and how to get plugged in to taking the next steps towards true liberation. We hope you will join us on that path.

MIM(Prisons)
May 2015

On Rebuilding the Nation and Regional Divisions

by cipactli

THE CHICAN@S WITHIN U.$. PRISONS are beginning to heal from the effects of hundreds of years of colonialism. One indicator of this is the historic Agreement to End Hostilities in prisons which was issued out of Pelican Bay State Prison's Security Housing Unit (long-term isolation) in 2012.[1] The fact that a war which lasted over 40 years between Chican@s in prisons has been stopped is huge. No longer will we allow the state to manipulate us into engaging in brown-on-brown crime, and conscious Chican@s will spend our imprisoned lives upholding this armistice. This step is a huge move in the direction of peace and consolidation for the nation. We revolutionary Chican@s will support this peace accord with our lives.

This book project is another indicator of a leap in consciousness in the imprisoned Chican@ population, which is a result of Chican@s on both ends of California coming together in unity despite Amerikkka's efforts to divide us. This is another first, where here we have Chican@ thought from the northern and southern regions of California uniting in this precious work. This is what re-building the nation looks like!

The Chican@ nation, like any other phenomenon, is not one static mass and it has many contradictions. The contradictions which arose in this project helped to shape and expand this book, and remain fluid in our search for truth and the path forward. Many forms of Chican@ thought (Chicanismo) exist within the nation and throughout the many regions of Aztlán. It is the people's interaction with reality and the material world wherever they reside which gives birth to their reaction in response. Our life experience tempers us and affects our growth and our challenges just as surely as it fuels our struggles. Chican@s exist in many different environments, some closer to Mexico, white communities, Black ghettos, or to reservations. Some are conscious and some are not. Understanding this social reality within the nation is perhaps just as important as dedicating one's life to healing the nation and rebuilding

Aztlán. Without understanding our current conditions, we cannot move forward.

The theme of this book can then best be summed up as how we analyze today's Chican@ nation and the historical developments coming out of the contemporary prisons. Our ability to overcome our historical state-provoked "divisions" as Chican@ prisoners can perhaps be a contribution to Chican@s outside of the pintas who may be divided by political contradictions and regionalism.

This project could not have been successful at this time without MIM(Prisons). Their hard work must be applauded because they helped to provide various means of assistance for this project when many groups have dismissed Chican@ prisoners as unworthy or incorrigible. MIM(Prisons) was extremely instrumental in facilitating this collaboration between Chican@s from both ends of California and the strengthening of our peace accords. *Chican@ Power and the Struggle for Aztlán* could only be made possible with their time, work, and ideological guidance.

Perhaps we will not live to see our work be victorious, but this is not why we do this. Someone once said "you don't win, you change the world" and I suppose with this project we don't expect to win today but we do expect to create change for the Chican@ nation, and, as a result, for the world.

As Chican@ communists we understand that petty regionalism and imperialist derived labels are poison to the nation. This project is but a prelude to what is to come from re-igniting the Chican@ movement.

Aztlán libre!

Introduction

"The nation, as a social and historical formation, exists in both objective and subjective reality. It is neither permanent, nor unchanging; both its overall existence in human society and its specific manifestations are subject to the laws of material development. The nation rises and falls, is born and dies, as determined by the motion of forces both internal and external to itself. Nations are not created solely by the drawing of state borders, any more than nation-states are the products of their official nations alone. Not all nations have developed nation-states, and not all states have been built around specific nations." - MC12 [1]

FOR REVOLUTIONARIES FROM THE OPPRESSED nations, this point speaks truth to power. All matter is in constant motion and change is the inviolable law of nature. In order for any national liberation movement to be successful, the emerging forces within the revolutionary movement must themselves move in accordance with the material laws of development. This is the only possible way we will ever accelerate the transformation of social progress and achieve our revolution. The Chican@ national liberation movement must embrace revolutionary science if it is ever to complete full emancipation from imperialist oppression and amalgamation. History has shown us that how oppressed nations organize is determinant of their struggles. How the Chican@ nation will decide to organize will be a matter of life and death to the nation; as correct tactics flow from correct strategies which in turn flow from correct political lines. Related to this point is the fact that there has been a renewal of discussion amongst the imprisoned Chican@ lumpen concerning the national-colonial question of the "Southwest United $tates," otherwise known as Aztlán. As such, and in recognition of the material laws of development, the Chican@ national liberation movement behind prison walls has begun to reconvene on a revolutionary-nationalist footing.

We should take into account what this effort means to Aztlán and to future Chican@s. Many of us already know and understand the bloody historical contradictions within the Chican@ nation. Most have come to understand that the pintas were battlegrounds where brown-on-brown crime was the normal program, but this was incorrect practice and fomented further divisions within our nation. For too long Raza have allowed the state to find ways to separate us. This is changing.

The authors of this book have provided us with the most current, correct and concise work out there with which to attract the Chican@ lumpen to our cause. Therefore in reading *Chican@ Power and the Struggle for Aztlán* we hope that one obtains a clear understanding of the nation and its need to be liberated. We also hope that this book challenges the imprisoned Chican@ lumpen to critically think about their place in history and the world. There is indeed a Chican@ national liberation movement that has begun to redevelop behind prison walls, and national liberation will become a real possibility for us as capitalist crisis continues to heighten. But before going into this subject any further it is essential that we build a foundation on which we can unite and push the movement forward. To do this we must address two widely held points of contention within the Chican@ community. First is the concept of Aztlán as a social and historical reality. Second is the very definition of Chican@ itself; "as words are another way of defining phenomenon, and the definition of any phenomenon is the first step to either controlling it or being controlled by it."[2] Thus we will begin by putting the term *Chicano* into its proper historical context.

The origins of the term *Chicano* are found in the word *Mexica*. Mexica was changed to Mechicano through Spanish mispronunciation, and was used to refer to people all over what would become Central America and the so-called "Southwest United States." Chicano and Chicana are just shortened versions of Mexica, and have long been considered acceptable variations on Mexica.[3]

The Spanish applied the gendered forms of their language to the people they conquered, with the masculine "o" being used to refer to both men and wimmin. This is an artifact of the Spanish language that evolved within a patriarchal society. Language is a part of our culture and we must revolutionize our culture to transform the nation. Therefore, we have chosen to use the gender neutral term *Chican@* to challenge the influence that patriarchy and machismo has had on our movement. We will only gain the full support of the people by challenging the oppression of *all* people.[4]

On a related note, the term *Mexican-American* should by no means be thought of as the next best available term used to describe Chican@s, as if Chican@s are as Amerikan as apple pie. This is an integrationist lie used by the imperialists and their coconut lackeys against the Chican@ people to provide false hopes of full assimilation into the Amerikan nation. Their intent is to distract us from real solutions to the problems of national oppression. To say that we are Mexican-American is to say that we have identified with our oppressor, thus disavowing our own and casting off into the abyss the oppressed people of the world. Instead we recognize that we are a nation separate from Amerika, with a separate history. Our nations do not intersect, rather they contradict via the oppressor/oppressed nation dynamic.

Activists before us refused the terms *Hispanic* and *Latino* as fully and concisely definitive of the Chican@ people. They correctly recognized the relationship of the general to the particular and saw that bourgeois academia was purposely jumbling these terms so as to keep us ignorant of our history. The activists further stated that: "We cannot coin terms for unity's sake when these terms fail to fully represent our diverse communities."[5] We fully agree. They also correctly saw the potential for the term Chican@ to fill the void left by the rejected terms and become backwards in its own right. Hence, the following was said perhaps as a safe-guard against potential national-chauvinist politicking on behalf of Chican@s:

> *"Chicanismo does not seek to use the word 'Chicano' as an umbrella term when describing all of 'La Familia de La Raza' (family of Latino nations). Rather, Chicanismo seeks to educate our barrios and campos about our history y culture to further create a movement of self-determination for the liberation of Aztlán. Something that Hispanic and Latino has yet to recognize."*[5]

Amerikans, through domestic colonialist policies in the field of education, are attempting to reduce the term *Chican@* to a philosophical conception that is firmly grounded within an individualist outlook. Some of our so-called "allies" within the Amerikan left, and even members of the nation itself, have taken the stance that Chican@s are not a nation, but are instead an ethnicity stripped and devoid of all the material criteria pertaining to nationhood. Our petty-bourgeois intellectuals have been the particular target audience of this ideological offensive. Many of them regurgitate such fallacious and reactionary ideas back to our people.

Most of these petty-bourgeois ideologues have served the imperialists as mouthpieces thru the means of film, literature and television, thus identifying with the oppressor and objectively becoming traitors to the nation. This erroneous reasoning is nothing but oppressor-nation politics, which are grounded in their desire to preserve their own material interests within a potentially revolutionary scenario.

Liberalism is a petty bourgeois philosophical outlook that rejects ideological struggle and stands for unprincipled peace. In particular, what is practiced within the university setting teaches students that everyone's opinion is equally valid and carries equal weight, thus burying the truth and discouraging students from reaching correct conclusions. Effective manipulation is owed in large part to various Liberal multiculturalist courses and so-called "ethnic studies" departments in Amerika's universities. The universities have been tasked with carrying out this virtual indoctrination of the Chican@ intelligentsia, who, along with the imperialists, have been greatly successful in erasing the national question of Chican@s in Aztlán. Within these university settings our culture is projected as quaint. "They teach us to celebrate culture while simultaneously offering workshops on how to manage 'diversity'; but within these workshops however conflict rarely arises, nor does it offend."[6]

Alongside this academic indoctrination are the very real material concessions made available to the Chican@ people in the form of superwages. These superwages are actually extracted and re-appropriated to Amerikans via stolen superprofits from the global periphery. Superprofits and other abundant goods are used to bribe Chican@s and ensure their loyalty to the oppressor nation. High living standards, due to the proximity and integration of the Chican@ nation with the empire, have resulted in the embourgeoisement of some Raza. This embourgeoisement is based materially on the enrichment of Chican@s through the forced impoverishment of the underdeveloped nations of the Third World, and ideologically in the identification of Chican@s with the Amerikan nation via the First World belief that they deserve to live whole levels above the rest of the oppressed world. Thus our attempts to rescue the nation are made that much more difficult, as many will see our struggle in complete opposition to their way of life. Indeed our struggle for an independent socialist Chican@ state *is* in complete opposition to the gross parasitism currently practiced by all Amerikans, whose privileged, decadent lifestyles are pre-supposed on the oppression and superexploitation of the

Third World. Or as the Communist International more eloquently put it when speaking of the European and Amerikan so-called proletariat in 1919, "At the expense of the plundered colonial peoples capital corrupted its wage slaves, created a community of interest between the exploited and the exploiters as against the oppressed colonies – the yellow, black and red colonial peoples – and chained the European and American working class to the imperialist 'fatherland.'"[7] This "chaining" of the Amerikan and European working class is more commonly known and firmly pronounced in the labor aristocracy theory, famously put forward by Friedrich Engels, V.I. Lenin and in more recent times the Maoist Internationalist Movement.[8]

The Chican@ nation is no exception to this bourgeoisification, like all other oppressed nations within the United $tates, except for perhaps undocumented migrants and the various First Nations who by and large still find themselves living in sub-humyn conditions. Indeed, even the Chican@ lumpen benefits from this oppressive relationship. However, due to the precarious stratification of the lumpen, and the imperialists' refusal to let us fully integrate into Amerika, our allegiance to the imperialists is more tenuous. As the lumpen experience oppression first hand here in Amerika, we are in a position to spearhead the revolutionary vehicle within U.$. borders.[9]

Who is a Chican@?

We define the Chican@ nation based on Stalin's scientific theory of nations. "A nation is a historically constituted, stable community of people, formed on the basis of a common language, territory, economic life, and psychological make-up manifested in a common culture."[10] Here we present a summary of who is a Chican@, and we will expand in detail on the criteria of nationhood in Part I Section 2.

Chican@s originated as people of Mexican descent residing on land that was to become part of the United $tates. While these people began to develop into a new nation, separate from Mexico, well before the invasion of the "Southwest," the development of the Chican@ nation was accelerated as generations living in the expanding Amerikan settler state developed distinct national characteristics. This nation has evolved to include many from Spanish-speaking Central and South America who have migrated to the United $tates and, living in Chican@ barrios, have become part of this nation in spite of their distinct national origin.

In general, people who were born outside the United $tates, but reside within U.$. borders, will be part of a national minority which identifies with their home country. They share the language and culture with their home country, and often they are sending much of their income there, perhaps even still planning to move back to their country of origin and considering that their territory. Often national minorities will live in a tight community within the United $tates, reinforcing their identification with their home country. This tie to their country of origin weakens in second and subsequent generations. As second-generation immigrants growing up in the United $tates, they are not given the opportunity to fully assimilate into the white nation, and so are likely to become part of an internal semi-colony. Similarly, people who migrate to the United $tates as youth often do not identify with their home country and grow up within an internal semi-colony.

We see the majority of youth immigrants and descendants of immigrants from Latin American countries assimilating into the Chican@ nation. While the factors which form their nationhood were not commonalities amongst their home countries, nor for the recent immigrants, imperialist Amerika creates conditions for these Latin American nationalities to come together.

There is the alternative that a minority of Latin American descendants take, which is full assimilation into the white nation. While not an option for most, those with lighter skin, no accent, and a wealthy family, as well as a few exceptions to this rule, have managed to gain the full benefits of the white nation and do not share a common territory, culture or economics with the Chican@ nation. People like George Zimmerman, who murdered 17-year-old New Afrikan Trayvon Martin for walking through his neighborhood, represent this group.

What is Aztlán? Who are la Raza?

Simply put, Aztlán is the name of the Chican@ nation's national territory, more commonly known as the "Southwest United $tates." Aztlán is also the word used to identify an internal semi-colony that has been and continues to be oppressed. The Chican@ nation of Aztlán developed in the territory of Aztlán during the Amerikan capitalist-imperialist stages of development.

Before the concept of Aztlán was ever used by Chican@ revolution-aries as representative of our struggle against imperialism, Aztlán was originally conceived in the 1960s as a propaganda tool used by cultural nationalists. We must move beyond such traditional and isolated celebra-tions of Mexican culture in which Aztlán is currently steeped.

The cultural nationalists envision Aztlán as a semi-indigenous, stateless society in which the Chican@ people (who they saw in the 1960s as distinctly Mexican in origin) could go back to living in pre-Columbian tradition free of Western influence. Indeed for the cultural nationalists, ridding the nation of European culture and thought (Marxism included), and even technology amongst the stricter adherents of "tradition," was itself principal. Their hate of the imperialist state was only relevant so far as they viewed the nation-state and imperialism as products of all things European.

There are still contradictions within Aztlán that must be resolved, none more important than the contradiction between those wanting to side with Empire and those wanting self-determination. For those seek-ing liberation from imperialism, we must recognize that this can only be accomplished via the Maoist road, as only the communists are capable of dealing with the principal contradiction in the world today. It is therefore the duty of communists from the Chican@ nation to begin constructing class, nation and gender alliances amongst Chican@s that advance the revolutionary interests of the nation to attack the very foundations of U.$. imperialism.

A related term that we will use throughout this book is *Raza*. Raza is the Spanish word for race, or people; Raza or la Raza is used as a catch-all term to describe the people of so-called "Latin America." While the con-cept of Latin America, and its derivatives Latino and Latina, are steeped in Spanish colonialism, Raza is a term that recognizes the indigenous roots of the majority of the nations south of the Rio Grande, as well as the Chican@ nation itself. We will get into this in detail in the chapter titled "Obscured for Centuries, the Nation is Bigger than Ever" in Part II of this book.

Chican@ Nationalism, Revolutionary Nationalism, Proletarian Feminism

We do not struggle because of unique aspects of our cultural identity; we struggle because of our relations to the economic system that we live in. Our struggle's class nature may be obscured by its national character, which at this point in the United $tates is determined by the principal contradiction of the oppressed nations versus the oppressor nation. Chican@ nationalism within the context of anti-imperialism and the struggle for Aztlán is revolutionary nationalism, nationalism of the oppressed, and applied internationalism. Our Chicanismo has a class character, and our liberation requires the leadership of class interests that are opposed to imperialism.

Just as all national liberation struggles in the Third World are directly connected to the emancipation of the proletariat and peasantry, so are those same class struggles nationalistic at their core in the era of dying imperialism. Their national characteristics might be obscured by the varying degrees of participation from the various classes within the nation. Just as they have their compradors and neo-colonial regimes, who are in the service of finance capital, so do we. But due to the different overall class makeup of the Chican@ nation compared to Third World nations, our struggle for national liberation is led by the lumpen class, as we will explain in more detail throughout this book.

While we see the liberation of our national territory of Aztlán as our principal cause, we also recognize that world proletarian revolution is necessary to end all forms of oppression. In any struggle for independence, the primary nation leading the charge never goes it alone. No national liberation struggle is ever pure in the nationalistic sense, but is made up of various oppressed people who are attracted to its cause. This oppression may be along lines of nation, class, and/or gender. As such it is only natural that some of our forces will be include Raza who are not Chican@s, as well as those who have come to identify as Chican@s, as many will see our struggle as their own. Our Chicanismo does not underestimate or undercut any other oppressed Raza from Latin America (or anywhere else) here in the United $tates that is equally striving to break from the yoke of imperialism. Chican@ nationalism must support the interests of other oppressed nations and national minorities, both from Latin@ nations and elsewhere in the world.

Our struggle is a revolutionary nationalist struggle and should be comprised of a united front between the Chican@ lumpen, the semi-proletariat, and the left-wing section of the petty bourgeoisie who are amiable towards the revolution, working in close alliance with the Mexican@ and other Raza national minority proletariat, semi-proletariat and petty bourgeoisie within U.$. borders. That said, national liberation is not enough in the age of imperialism. National liberation minus a socialist revolution is inextricably bound to bourgeois-democracy and neo-colonialism.

Along with class and nation, we must address gender as a third strand of oppression. Gender oppression is not distinct to the Chican@ nation; all who live in this society under U.$. imperialism experience the effects of gender oppression. As patriarchy still dominates gender relations in the world today, many Chicanos continue to be biased against Chicanas. They think there is no place for wimmin in the struggle.

What many of our Chicana predecessors knew long ago, and what most Chicanos are just catching up to, is that there is an interconnection between nation, class and gender, and that our struggles must also be interconnected in order to be successful. In our study of contradictions, we can see that feminism without a national struggle may lead to some benefits for some wimmin, but cannot lead to real wimmin's liberation and equality. This is especially true for oppressed nation wimmin. On the other hand, a national struggle without a feminist element will limit itself, never achieving communism. Historically, national struggles tend to resolve gender contradictions out of necessity, where gender struggles have never made this progress.[11]

For those who may still be confused or are new to the Chican@ struggle, it is not a matter of us allowing wimmin to be a part of the Chican@ struggle, as they have already been a part of the struggle giving their raw energy, sweat, blood and lives. It's a matter of everyone understanding that wimmin are a major component to our liberation movement. Without Chicanas and their full participation there will not be a liberated Aztlán! The emancipation of society relies also on the emancipation of everyone oppressed along gender lines.

So what then is the way out? The way out is a revolutionary national liberation struggle for self-determination that is guided by Marxism-Leninism-Maoism with the set goal of establishing a communist society by way of a joint dictatorship of the proletariat of the oppressed nations. We will get more into this path in Part I Section 4 of this book.

The Chican@ nation will either continue to develop and seek emancipation on behalf of all oppressed groups, or it will retrogress, stagnate and die – it is up to us! The Chican@ nation is an oppressed nation and it must be liberated!

Camaradas Unite! Long Live the People of Aztlán!

Long Live the Chican@ Nation! Down with Imperialism!

Part I:
Chican@ Power and the Struggle for Aztlán

THE PRODUCTION OF THIS ESSAY was the result of reflection on the body of work concerning the Chican@ liberation movement as well as looking at current conditions in today's world. Most of what has been already written on this topic was written decades ago, thus the need to write on the contemporary Chican@ struggle, which we hope adds to the body of work already in existence. Our main thrust in developing this book lies in Chican@ liberation.

The research put into this work drew from the history of theory and practice from the Chican@ movement, which we continue to delve into to gain more insight. This work is an attempt to contribute to the continued evolution of that revolutionary theory. Marx taught us that all matter is in motion and so with this motion we will continue to find new ways to apply the proper response to new phenomenon; new ideas and new actions will of course create new reaction.

We hope to develop new theory that breaks ground in political line, especially pertaining to the lumpen class. We are in a new phase in the Chican@ liberation movement where a fresh generation of Chican@s are rising to demand justice and self-determination in response to the repression Amerika unleashes on the barrios. Babies are literally ripped from their mothers' bosoms, families torn from their roots and separated because of the tools of white supremacy like the ICE raids and the injustice system. This repression is not new; rather it is refined and recycled from the oppressor nation tool box. We hope to develop, via brown youth, a new path to liberate Aztlán. This analysis will pick up where past revolutionaries left off to get to the heart of the Chican@ struggle and add to the theory that will move us forward. A step forward for Chican@s is a step forward for the international communist movement more broadly.

In putting together this writing we hope to provoke a new fervor of discussion in the Chican@ nation, vibrant debate in the Raza community, a hornets' nest in the Amerikan left circles and a grave thorn up into imperialism. But most of all we hope that it advances Chican@ thought and helps us achieve Chican@ independence. Recent attacks on Chican@ youth education in the United $tates and the banning of Chican@ literature in Arizona's schools have also compelled us to create more literature in the field of "Chican@ studies." These fascist actions will prod young Raza to become more conscious and revolutionary. The growing criminalization of Chican@s and other oppressed nations is also adding to this momentum. Chican@s fill U.$. concentration kamp control units in Aztlán more than any other nation. This repression will turn into its opposite as we continuously turn these dungeons into centers of development where we embrace and guide Chican@ youth who are ensnared in the same imperialist trap that caught us. We will churn out future Chican@ cadre from our cinder-block classrooms and create a new revolutionary culture that goes back to the barrios, fully conscious and stripped of oppressor-nation immorality or bourgeois ideology. The imperialist propaganda machine has waged an ideological offensive on our people for 500 years, seeking to capture our minds as they simultaneously capture our bodies. For this reason our existence depends on Chican@s to develop theory and flood the barrios and pintas with a Chican@ renaissance as seen through brown eyes, lest someone else develop a theory for us. This literature needs to be developed in order to counter what Amerika does and has done, to decolonize la Raza's minds. It is far easier to spread lies than to counter them, so we have much work ahead of us.

There are four sections to this essay - Section 1 deals with history of Chican@s from their emergence as a colonized nation to the Brown Power movement. Section 2 is on the exploitation of Aztlán and the early development of Chican@s. Section 3 tackles the path for Chican@ liberation. And Section 4 addresses our youth, Chicanas, and political line. In 1937, Mao wrote: "The vast majority of human beings have already prepared or are preparing to fight a war that will bring justice to the oppressed peoples of the world." Let us be amongst the majority as the oppressed nations build for war this time around.

Section 1:
History of Chican@s

The Birth of Mexico

Ancestors of the Chican@ people first stepped on the land that is now called the "Southwest United $tates," which we know as Aztlán, even before the Mayflower ship brought its horrors to these shores. Going back 50,000 years, civilizations existed on this continent, including the Aztecs, Olmecs, Zapotecs, Mayans, Incas and other indigenous peoples.[1] These cultures cultivated maize (corn) thousands of years ago and influenced life from the present-day Mississippi valley to the southern tip of Chile. Aztec influence has been discovered far away from the "Southwest":

"Far to the East, the mound builders of the Ohio and Mississippi basins also evidently received Mexican influence in their construction of serpent mounds and small pyramid-based temples as well as in pottery-making, agriculture, and other cultural elements. Clearly there was considerable early contact between the area of the southern U.S. and Mexico."[2]

The arrival of the European invader into the Americas in the 1500s was a formative event in future development of the Chican@ nation. Spanish conquistadors landed in what is now the Mexican state of Veracruz in 1519 and quickly moved in to colonize the Mexicas, or what is commonly called the Aztec Empire. Spaniards began mining the region's resources with the help of exploited native, and in later years Mestizo (mixed native/Spanish), labor.

The unquenchable thirst for gold drove the Spaniards to deeper territory, leading to the naming of their colony New Spain in 1521. New Spain covered a vast territory that today is considered the southern United $tates, Mexico and Central America. New Spain's capital was located on the conquered Aztec city of Tenochtitlan, located in the center of today's

Mexico City.

The increase in resource discovery fueled more and more mines, expanding into new land. The quest for more gold and silver led to the decimation of the indigenous populations. In the states that comprised northern New Spain at the time, such as California, the Spaniards had indigenous people (including Mestizos) working as "vaqueros, soap makers, tanners, shoemakers, carpenters, blacksmiths, bakers, cooks, servants, pages, fishermen, farmers as well as a host of other occupations."[3] The people were worked sometimes to death. This work pushed economic development across the region, which was a precursor to nationhood.

The Spanish colonizers started giving land grants in 1598 in an effort to stabilize their colony. Plots of land were given to families or villages to be used communally. Some grants were for single families to raise crops for the village or for commercial purposes. Some were given for workers in industries, such as builders, or in exchange for labor power. Some were meant to settle land or serve as a buffer zone against French or English encroachment. New Mexico was named by the Spanish colonialists after the Mexican@ peoples who originally inhabited the territory at that time, and was a major territory in the land grant campaign. Even then, New Mexico was a region which would develop significantly as part and parcel with the Chican@ nation.

The Spanish colonization expanded further with the expansion of the Camino Real de Tierra Adentro (The Royal Road of the Interior Land) which eventually reached from Mexico City to Spain's New Mexico. (See *Figure 1.1.1 Camino Real* on the next page) Along this route many villages were destroyed and families uprooted for its construction. With the expansion of Spanish plunder, indigenous people and Mestizos were forced into harsh work conditions, which led to some of the first workers' strikes in 1631.

New Spain operated as any other colonial power: on the sweat and blood of those it colonized. This brutalization led to the Pueblo Revolt of 1680. It was initiated by natives and Mestizos and soon spread and drove out the colonists until the 1690s. During the Pueblo Revolt, most of the records of the land grants that had been given out by the New Spain government were destroyed.

For most of the 1700s Spaniards used New Mexico as an outpost and frequently brought natives from as far south as Oaxaca to use alongside Mestizos as slave labor or exploited workers. Some of these natives

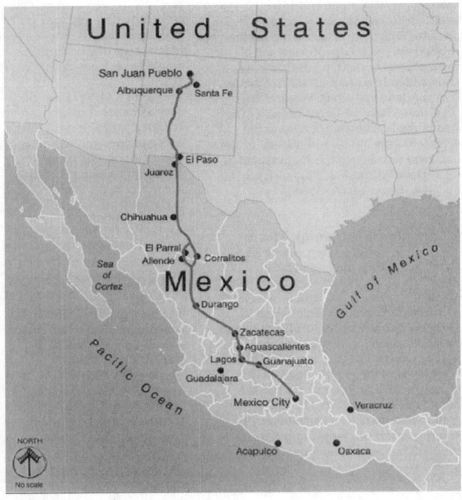

Figure 1.1.1 Camino Real

and Mestizos fled into the villages of New Mexico while others resisted with strikes and open revolt. At the time, the Mexican@ peasants were living communally as small farmers and artisans using barter systems. Their villages were self-sufficient and relied on fishing, agriculture, and hunting small game. The Spanish found it harder to colonize the territory that is now the Amerikan "Southwest" than it was to colonize the valley of Mexico.

The oppression faced by the natives and Mestizos in New Spain created the social conditions for an uprising there as well. On 16 September 1810 they rose up against the Spanish occupiers. The initial uprising was smothered, yet resistance continued in guerrilla warfare units all over New Spain, eventually leading to Mexico gaining independence from Spain in what would be dubbed the Mexican Revolution.

During the Mexican Revolution the frontier garrisons of Spanish troops were sent from the northern states back into the interior and in 1821, after a decade-long struggle, the people were victorious in the revolution. New Spain was toppled and the nation-state of Mexico was born. Although Mexico broke the colonial yoke of Spain it continued to suffer from inequality, exploitation and other residue from hundreds of years of colonialism. See *Figure 1.1.2 New Spain* on the following page.

Colonization, Development and the U.$. War on Mexico

The 1820s began to see Amerikan advances toward Texas, which was then part of the newly independent nation-state of Mexico. The white oppressor nation began to move in as immigrants into Texas, and the yankees came en masse. The Mexican government had "expelled all Spaniards, including Spanish missionaries, from its territories."[4] The gente living in these areas were essentially untethered from the government. At the same time mining opened up in the northern frontier, allowing a steady economy to continue.

After the Santa Fe Trail opened in 1822, linking Franklin, Missouri with Mexico's Santa Fe, New Mexico, the Chican@ nation really began to develop distinct characteristics from the rest of Mexico.(See *Figure 1.1.3*) The development of the Santa Fe trail helped to open up trade between Amerika and northern Mexico, making it cheaper to obtain goods from Amerikans than purchasing those same goods from the Mexican interior.[4] The injection of Amerikan capital led to a wider gap between the Chican@ nation and Mexico, and Chican@s began to develop their own classes. A bourgeoisie and petty bourgeoisie developed during this time which, for the most part, dealt with Amerikan markets and not Mexican capital. Chican@s were still being lynched, exploited and oppressed, but a Chican@ middle class began to arise.

The state of New Mexico spearheaded economic development, at a

Figure 1.1.2 New Spain

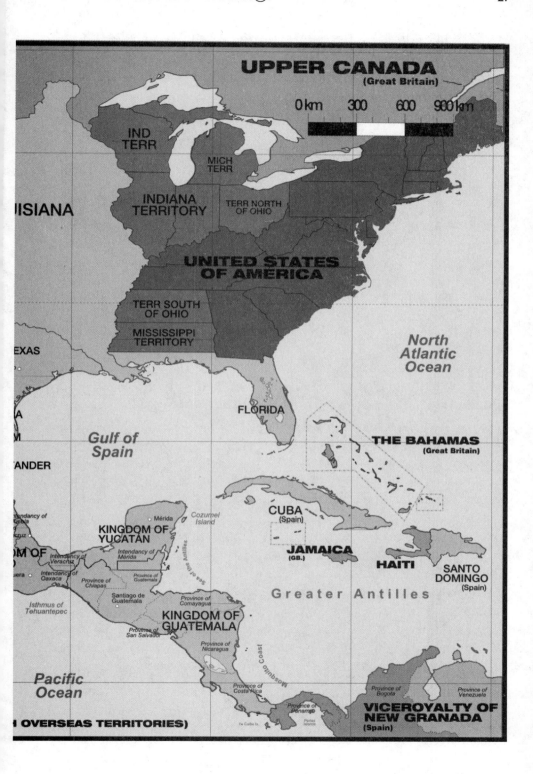

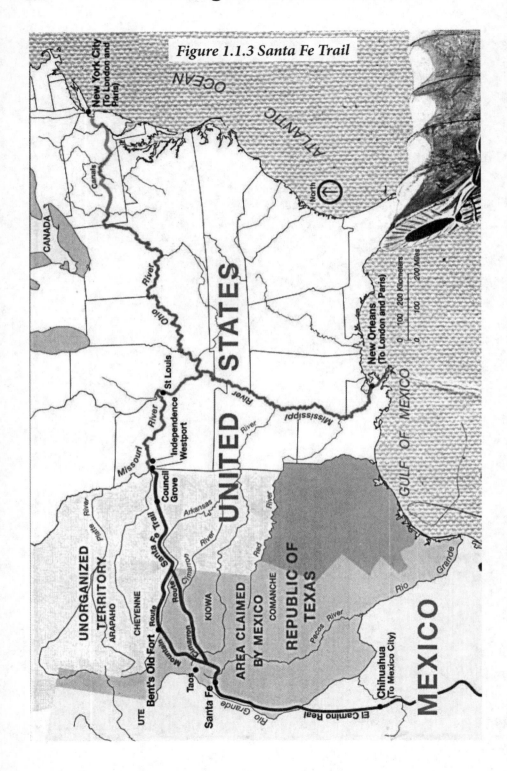

Figure 1.1.3 Santa Fe Trail

time when the majority of the population of New Mexico was Mestizos. This friction led to many uprisings in New Mexico when the Mexican government attempted to tighten control.

Class distinctions were more clearly developing in Alta California, where the Mexican government secularized all missions in the 1830s. Alta California was considered the area that is currently the states of California, Nevada, parts of Arizona, Utah, Colorado and Wyoming. Being such a large territory with now secularized missions, Chican@ culture began to develop independent of the rest of the country.[5]

"The more rigid and feudal patterns of Patrón and Peón never developed in California as in New Mexico, though there was a caste system. The Californians were divided into three classes. At the top were 'la gente de razón,' landowners who constituted roughly 10 percent of the population. Members of this group held the important social, economic, and political positions and maintained tight control of their privileged states by marrying predominantly within their class.

"The second group constituted the majority of the population – the artisans, small landowners, vaqueros, herders, soldiers, some servants and immigrant colonists. During the Mexican period the term 'cholo' was widely used for members of this class. Composed mostly of Mestizos and mulatos, they were generally illiterate as well as poor. At the bottom of the social ladder was the indian, who endured a condition of hardship under the supervision of the padres. Exploited by the mission system, the indian after secularization was reduced to a more desperate state – peonage."[6]

During this period the indigenous people were not solely from Alta California. Many indigenous people were transplanted from the Mexican interior into Alta California to work the mines and other occupations. These class developments, focused around agriculture and mining in the region, contributed to the development of Aztlán into a nation.[5]

The discovery of rich resources in Aztlán propelled Amerika to begin its imperialist land grab. The mining industry ripped the Chican@ peasants from the land they tilled and formed a Chican@ proletariat. This newly formed labor force for the many mines ensured a source of wealth for whoever possessed this resource-rich area. Feudal and semi-feudal relations that had kept people isolated economically and culturally to the *feudo* who they worked for were changing into a capitalist economy.

The influx of Amerikan settlers into Mexican territory included white supremacists like Stephen Austin, who was a psychotic racist, believing the white nation was sent by god and superior to other peoples. In reality Austin was a deranged slave holder and serial killer who hunted natives and Chican@s. Austin began organizing other white racist extremists to go to Texas "with a rifle." He pushed for Texas's independence from Mexico, using legal and illegal means to occupy Texas to promote white supremacy. It is thus no surprise that the city of Austin, Texas would be named after this maggot by Amerika. Although Texas was not ratified by the United $tates government as a state until 1845, in 1836 the Amerikan oppressor nation annexed the territory of Texas from Mexico. The national legend of The Alamo takes place during the Amerikkkan battles to annex Texas in 1835 and 1836:

> *"Probably the most widely circulated story was that of the last stand of the aging Davy Crockett, who fell 'fighting like a tiger' killing Mexicans with his bare hands. The truth: seven of the defenders surrendered, and Crockett was among them. The Mexican force executed them, and, one man, Louis Rose, escaped."*[7]

The U.$. War on Mexico (1846-1848) was one of the most vicious operations Mexican@s had faced since the Spanish arrival. The terrorism Mexican@s experienced was something only a barbarian could think of: babies slaughtered, children raped in front of parents, parents murdered in front of children, bodies mutilated, churches desecrated, elderly people raped and murdered in front of children. The atrocities were so gruesome and morally bankrupt that hundreds of Irish soldiers deserted the U.$. army to fight alongside Mexican@s against Amerikan soldiers. They were called the San Patricio Battalion (Saint Patrick Battalion).

U.$. President James Polk provoked this war on Mexico in order to expand the empire. He sent General Zachary Taylor to a contested area on the border and claimed Mexican@s fired on U.$. soldiers. This pretext lives on today in similar form. When Amerikan cops claim Chican@ youth reached for their waistband, they justify their authority to murder innocents. This same preemptive strike excuse is even still used on a broader scale for war today. In 1846 Mexican@s dealt with the terrorists Jim Bowie and Davy Crockett and today the Third World deals with SEAL Team 6, but it is this same performance, the same war crimes and crimes against humynity that we continue to fight and resist.

Although most of the yankees agreed with the taking of all of Mexico, employing a complete "saxonization" of Mexico, some were not so sure and felt that incorporating a large number of Mexicans into the United $tates would ultimately come back to haunt Amerika. Others were more blunt, as U.$. President Polk's Secretary of State James Buchanan put it, "How should we govern the mongrel race which inhabits Mexico?"[8] This was the general feeling from those in power in Amerika, and this is what Chican@s have been dealing with living as an occupied nation.

There were Mexican@ militias that rose up to fight against yankee imperialism. Juan "Cheno" Cortina, Francisco Barela, and Gregorio Cortez are some of our national heroes of this time period. Groups like Las Gorras Blancas (The White Caps) armed themselves to defend the people from white supremacy and oppression.[1] One such revolt was in New Mexico in January 1847, called the Taos Revolt, in which the Amerikan governor of New Mexico, Charles Bent, was assassinated. In fact, every one of the stolen states experienced revolts and many groups arose to defend the people.[5]

In 1848 the U.$. War on Mexico ended with the signing of the Treaty of Guadalupe Hildago. The United $tates acquired about 50% of Mexico's territory, including the territories that were to become the states of California, Arizona, Utah, Nevada, New Mexico, Texas and parts of Wyoming, Colorado and Oklahoma. This geographical area is what Chican@s today consider Aztlán, our ancestral homeland.

The initial proposal for the treaty included Article X, guaranteeing the protection of "all prior and pending titles to property of every description."

> *"The treaty thus afforded rights to Chicanos that extended well beyond their constitutional guarantees. ... [But] neither the sovereignty of Chicanos as a nation nor their right to occupy land as a people were recognized. Individual land titles were to be respected ostensibly, but the wording of the protocol cast doubt on the validity of these titles. ... The protocol stated that these grants 'preserve the legal value which they may possess; and the guarantees may cause their legitimate titles to be acknowledged before the American tribunals.' ... Not surprisingly, Chicanos did not fare very well before such American tribunals. Within two decades most were landless."[9]*

After the Treaty of Guadalupe Hildago was signed, people of Mexican descent were supposed to be treated with dignity here in the United $tates. The treaty claimed all land belonging to those of Mexican descent would be honored and people of Mexican descent would become full U.$. citizens within one year. This would ensure that the people would be free from oppression. The truth would soon become quite the opposite. Not only was a more brutal form of exploitation brought upon the people, but racism against Chican@s was now state sanctioned to promote this manifest destiny we have become all too familiar with.

Amerika began taking millions of acres of land owned by individual Chican@s or that had been owned communally by Chican@s for hundreds of years, dating back to the Aztec Empire and the Spanish land grants. This land grab was enforced by racist militia groups, white supremacists who flocked into Amerika's newly expanded territory. Paramilitary groups like the Texas Rangers were known as "Mexican killers" and hunted down defiant Chican@s and First Nations people. In this way terror was institutionalized in Chican@ and native communities. Of course some states within the "Southwest" had more repression than others. For example, the California gold rush of 1849 saw an influx in oppressor nation immigrants who swarmed California from all parts of North America in their obsessive search for gold. States like Texas seemed to draw the most vile and depraved of the oppressor nation. New Mexico was a little different with the oppressor nation focusing on opening up trade routes to the West Coast that could help capital flow freely from the West to the East Coast.[10,11] In New Mexico alone the federal government seized 1.7 million acres of communal land.[12]

This war and subsequent land theft has even been forgotten by many Amerikans who continue to occupy the Chican@ homeland. Today even Mexico downplays the land grab and the U.$. War on Mexico. The Chican@ bourgeoisie has conveniently white-washed this incident so as to secure their seat at the imperialist trough.

The land theft and oppression did not sit well with Chican@s, and it was a significant event in the formation of the Chican@ nation. Contrary to Amerikan propaganda and what is taught to our youth in Amerika's schools, Chican@s did not "melt" into Amerikan society, nor was the annexation a smooth process. Many Chican@s rose up, either on their own, or organized into militias and revolutionary armed groups to not just resist the oppression but also to fight for self-determination.

Repression of Chican@ prosperity was not limited to land theft but also to limitations on their ability to engage in work as free persons. In the early 1850s, the Foreign Miners Tax was enacted in California, targeting Chican@s as well as Chinese miners in the Gold Rush era. The tax started at $20 per month, was soon repealed, and reinstated in 1852 at $4 per month. Those who refused to pay the tax were not allowed to work, or harassed and robbed by tax collectors. Some Amerikans even pretended to be tax collectors just to steal from the non-English-speaking Chican@s and Chinese workers.

With this development came resistance from many. One such re-sister was Jaoquin Murrieta. A miner affected by the hysteria of the Foreign Miners Tax Law and Amerikan jingoism, Murrieta's brother was hanged and his wife raped by white supremacists. Murrieta then predict-ably dedicated his life to war on the oppressor nation. (13)

Chican@s were told by Amerika to use its court system to obtain justice. But courts always sided with Anglos on land disputes, and many Chican@s did not have money for expensive lawyers. Further, most did not speak English, or understand the tax laws themselves.

Years after the Treaty of Guadalupe Hidalgo, genocidal murder of Chican@s by the oppressor nation was used to clear people from land and ensure domination of the white nation. We know that thousands of Chican@s were lynched by Amerikans from 1848 to 1928, although the most thorough research on this topic documents only about 547 specific cases.(14) These occurred across Aztlán, but also in places like Nebraska and Wyoming, making Mexicans the second biggest target of white vio-lence, after New Afrikans, during this time period. The overall account of total lynchings is not accurately known because people were usually recorded as "black" or "white" in historical records from the time.

The conditions were for Chican@s what they are for all colonized people. As comrade Stalin stated:

> "Imperialism is the most barefaced exploitation and the most inhumane oppression of hundreds of millions of people inhabiting vast colonies and dependent countries. The purpose of this oppression is to squeeze out super-profits. But in exploiting these countries imperialism is compelled to build their railways, factories and mills, industrial and commercial centers. The appearance of a class of proletarians, the emergence of a na-tive intelligentsia, the awakening of national consciousness, the growth

of the liberation movement - such are the inevitable results of this 'policy.'
The growth of the revolutionary movement in all colonies and dependent
countries without exception clearly testifies to this fact."[15]

Many Chican@s rose in the defense of the people as national consciousness grew in opposition to Amerikan imperialism. Juan "Cheno"
Cortina led a resistance movement beginning in 1859, arming and mobilizing over a thousand people into a militia that fought white supremacy near Brownsville, Texas. Cortina waged war on those oppressing
Chican@s. Gregorio Cortez was another Chican@ hero who rose up in
Texas to resist white supremacy, eluding posses of racists and inspiring
many to join his militia. Catarino Garza was another such leader, also
in Texas. In California, Joaquin Murrieta formed a militia to fight the
oppressor nation and Tiburcio Vasquez led armed resistance to the occupation and oppression. Out of all the states in the "Southwest" after
1848, Texas experienced the most bloody armed resistance and New
Mexico served as the most organized resistance for Chican@s.

One of the more revolutionary groups was Las Gorras Blancas (The
White Caps) which rose in New Mexico in 1889 and initiated armed offensives on Amerika, including sabotage, destroying the railroads, cutting telegraph lines, torching oppressor nation ranches, and organizing
Chican@s in guerrilla warfare units. Most of their attacks were directed
at large landholders who had appropriated communal lands, and they
enjoyed the support of most of the Chican@ residents in San Miguel
County, New Mexico where they were active.[16]

La Mano Negra (The Black Hand) was another group to form at the
time in New Mexico and was active around the same time as Las Gorras
Blancas. This group eventually succumbed to brown bourgeois politicians.

The Mexican@ radicals Enrique and Ricardo Flores Magón would
further mobilize Chican@s in Aztlán. The Magóns led the Mexican political party Partido Liberal Mexicano (Mexican Liberal Party – PLM) which
was very active in Mexico and the United $tates in the early 1900s. Due
to the repression they faced and because of the bubbling social conditions in Mexico, they crossed into the United $tates to continue their
work of agitating and educating the people. It was the Magóns who created the slogan Emiliano Zapata would use: Tierra y Libertad (Land and
Liberty). When the brothers crossed into the United $tates they started
a newspaper, *Regeneración*, which served to build public opinion here in

Aztlán about the oppression Mexican@s faced from the Mexican tyrants in power as well as from Amerikans in the United $tates. *Regeneración* was probably the most revolutionary newspaper for Raza at that time. In the pages of *Regeneración* one learned of Raza being lynched by the oppressor nation, strikes that Chican@s were involved in, police brutality and other oppression.[17] The PLM provided the theoretical heartbeat of the social movement that would become the Mexican Revolution of 1910. It was in the pages of *Regeneración* that the Mexican Revolution of 1910 was explained as a battle between "capital and labor."[18]

Eventually the U.$. government decided to put a stop to their activism, arresting and sentencing the Magóns to prison in 1916, charging them with mailing obscene material (something we can all relate to with the modern censorship of nationalist literature in U.$. prisons). The Magóns and the PLM helped to raise the consciousness of Chican@s, Mexican@s and especially wimmin. Their efforts towards gender equality unleashed wimmin to organize political groups such as Hijas de Anahuac (Daughters of Anahuac).[19]

Revolution in Mexico 1910

The revolutionary struggle that occurred in Mexico with Pancho Villa in the north and Emiliano Zapata in the south was the most profound event thus far in the history of the Mexican people. Although this revolution did not culminate in socialism in Mexico, it was an advance in the struggle against oppression that brought agrarian reforms and toppled brutal tyrants of that era. The tangible progress gained did not last long in the physical sense, but in the ideological sense the mobilization of millions in Mexico, and especially wimmin who were active participants on all levels of the Mexican Revolution, gave a huge morale boost to generations of Mexican people. This is true for today's Chican@s, as many of our grandparents were participants in the Mexican revolution and we recall the struggle for liberation through persynal stories.

The oppressor nation would see the Mexican Revolution differently, calling Villa and Zapata monsters or bandits, etc. The oppressor will always paint a hero of the oppressed in this way. We need only look to current events in the corporate news media to see heroes of the oppressed such as Muammar Qadafi or Kim Il Sung dehumynized by the Amerikan propaganda media outlets, but their people love them.

In spite of the nominal liberation from Spain 90 years earlier, by 1910 almost 99% of the Mexican population was landless, suffering at the hands of hacendados and patrones in a feudal system dominated by a small Spanish elite. So the biggest contradiction that played out internally in the Mexican Revolution was the contradiction between those who used and depended on the land, and those who owned and controlled it.

The rise of U.$. imperialism that developed in the late nineteenth century exacerbated the class contradictions within Mexico by extracting wealth, as well as a section of the emerging proletariat itself, into newly expanded U.$. borders. The insatiable appetite for ever more resources led Amerika to sink its bloody fangs into Mexico's resource-rich land. This ravaging of Mexican land led many Mexican@s to migrate into the brutal work conditions in the Amerikan-owned mines. Amerikan capitalists bought Mexican mines, invested in textile mills, and created other industries in Mexico in order to exploit cheap labor. Mexico was used as Amerika's sweat shop, making Mexican people work themselves to injury, illness and death, while Amerikan capitalists increased their bank accounts and Amerikan settlers served as overseers and enforcers on their behalf. This stunted the development of the Mexican bourgeoisie, putting them in contradiction with the interests of Amerikan capital. Therefore a broad national unity in opposition to the forces of both feudalism and U.$. imperialism fueled the revolution of 1910.

In the end, land was finally given to those who had been working it for centuries. However, this was a bourgeois revolution that replaced one ruler out for power and profit for a few, with another seeking profit and power for their small privileged group. The Mexican bourgeoisie gained power and has been slowly reverting the gains from the revolution ever since. While land redistribution undercut the feudal class, the Mexican Revolution was also a blow to U.$. imperialism in that it nationalized the industries and mines of the north. These changes were embraced by the vast majority of Mexican people as was seen after the revolution, when Mexican@s en masse donated everything from jewelry to the few pesos they had to the new government in order to help rebuild the war torn country.

The author of *Mexico's Revolution Then and Now*, James Cockroft, asserts,

Four important lessons of the Revolution in 1910 - 1917 are:

- *The danger of handing over weapons prematurely and of trusting peace officers (the Zapatistas in Morelos in 1911);*
- *The importance of unity, and the trap of permitting the creation of an antagonistic division between the working class and the peasantry (the red batallions of the CASA DEL OBRERO MUNDIAL in 1915)[Red Battalions were workers (many communists and anarchists), who fought against Zapata and Villa's peasant movement. – Editor];*
- *The need to recognize and incorporate the demands and special needs of specific groups of the oppressed, such as women, the original peoples, and people of diverse sexual preferences;*
- *The importance of a genuine internationalism and anti-imperialism.* [20]

Another lesson to add to Cockroft's list is the need for a communist-led revolution. Without this component all the years of work will ultimately be reversed and reduced to a bourgeois nationalist revolution. Lenin's Russia was the first government to put this Marxist concept into practice. What many do not realize is that a dictatorship will exist one way or another, whether it is the rich dictating to the poor or the oppressed over the former oppressors. So long as classes exist, one class will wield power over another. The dictatorship of the proletariat occurs when historically-oppressed people are in command to keep the oppressors in check after a revolution so they don't restore capitalism. Mexico is an example of what happens when a dictatorship of the proletariat is not enacted and so the oppressors remain and can easily get back in power and reverse advances made by the revolution.

While fighting was contained mostly to Mexico's boundaries, there was a massive dispersal caused by the war which had a huge impact on the Chican@ nation. Most peasant families lost their homes in the chaos and destruction that ensued. At the time the war kicked off, most of Mexico was already in economic ruin due to the blend of prevailing feudal relations in the countryside and the phenomenon of rising capitalism. Together these conditions would ordinarily cause the peasant population to proletarianize by migration into the cities and industrial centers. However, Mexico was a neo-colony in the grips of early Amerikan imperialism with no industry of its own. The peasants naturally looked north over the border to greener pastures and the possibility of eking out an existence.

These conditions produced a huge wave of Mexican migration into Aztlán. The influx of labor increased the development of Amerikan capitalist production in the agricultural sector. Mining continued to develop as well but the greatest growth for Amerikan capitalism came in cotton production. Chican@s and new migrants from Mexico worked in Aztlán just like their New Afrikan counterparts. The vast majority of labor industries in the "Southwest United $tates" were using Chican@ and Mexican@ workers during this period.[21]

In the mines, where Chican@s experienced some of the most brutal work conditions, Chican@s organized the most. What Chairman Mao Zedong, who led communist China to victory over Japanese imperialism, said decades later about finding the most resistance where you find the most repression was being played out in the Chican@ nation. As Chican@s began organizing militant labor organizations throughout Aztlán, the oppressor nation was using racist militia and corporate henchmen (including police) to destroy these organizations. These militant labor organizations were forming because at this time many white unions would not allow Chican@s to join and thus Raza had to create their own labor unions.

Militant labor actions by the Chican@ nation culminated in what has come to be called the Ludlow Massacre, which some call the most significant labor strike in the history of the United $tates. Close to 10,000 workers (mostly Chican@s) decided to strike in Ludlow, Colorado in April 1914 to demand changes to the horrible work conditions. These workers were employed by Colorado Fuel and Iron Company, which was mostly owned by the Rockefellers. Fifty workers were killed when the National Guard was called in to attack the workers' camp, which also took the lives of family of these workers. It was without a doubt a horrible massacre, but to Chican@s even more brutal events were taking place concurrently in Arizona's labor struggles.

The pages of *Regeneración* reported on "a war of races in Arizona" and even *The Los Angeles Times* reported on this "race war."[22] In reality this was an oppressor nation war on Chican@s, and Chican@s resisting the oppression of white supremacy. Conditions for Chican@s in the mines were appalling. In the mines of Dawson, New Mexico 600 mostly Chican@ miners died in the three mine disasters of 1913, 1920 and 1923.[23]

There were conflicting currents in the United $tates in the early 1900s, with demand for cheap labor fueling immigration of Mexican@s, and white supremacist sentiments pushing to clear Mexican@s out of the country.

As Aviva Chomsky writes in her book *Undocumented: How Immigration Became Illegal,*

> *"When Congress passed the Literacy Act for immigrants in 1917, railroad, agricultural, and mining corporations raised a howl of protest and insisted that an open border was essential in order to obtain the labor they needed. In response, Congress quickly exempted Mexicans from the literacy require-ment. Migration ebbed and flowed directly in response to employment demands in the United States. When they needed workers, employers turned to Mexico. When they didn't – as in 1929, when Depression-era unemployment began to rise – the State Department instructed consular officers to increase their enforcement of the 'likely to become a public charge' restriction on would-be immigrants and refuse to grant entry visas to Mexicans unlikely to find work."[24]*

On the other hand, the Amerikan propaganda arm, like the Hearst newspapers, was fueling white supremacy by accusing Chican@s and migrating Mexican@s of everything from a revolution in the "Southwest" to an invasion of "Mexican Reds" and plotting with the German Nazis. The hysteria fueled Chican@ oppression with many Amerikan politicians wanting to enforce deportations of Raza. But at the same time Amerika was faced with a labor shortage due to World War I, with many workers going off to fight in the war, and thus the influx of Mexican workers was welcome.

What was common at the time in Aztlán was a form of serfdom where ranchers would "hire" migrant workers and enforce ridiculous terms to their working conditions. When the workers refused the ranchers, the local deputies would have the Chican@s charged with vagrancy and ensure they worked on this ranch to work off their "debt" to the boss. In this way, the ranchers kept Chican@ workers in debt peonage. This practice was also used for decades against New Afrikans in the "Southwest" states where slavery was illegal.

Up until the early part of the twentieth century Chican@s represented a colonial labor force for the most part. Even though a wide range of classes developed in the Chican@ nation, each class was still marginalized from white Amerika. Chican@s of different classes often were still restricted to the same barrios, where Chican@ merchants were restricted to selling to Chican@s, and Chican@ lawyers were restricted to representing Chican@s, etc. This does not imply of course that Chican@s are all motivated equally; political views come into play and class contradictions develop even within the internal colony.

Once more, as the oppression grew, so too did the resistance. One such form of resistance manifested in the Plan de San Diego and shortly thereafter, the Sediciosos. During the first decade of the 1900s a group of unidentified Mexican@s or Chican@s put out a document calling for armed resistance by Chican@s. The Plan de San Diego called for armed struggle against Amerika and proclaimed that upon victory the "Southwest United $tates" would become a Chican@ state, New Afrikans would form their own state and First Nations their own state. This was the first united front of the oppressed nations on these shores that sought independence for all oppressed nations upon victory; the Plan demonstrated true internationalism.

The most controversial part of the first version of the Plan de San Diego was its call to execute all white males in the "Southwest" over the age of 16, as well as anyone encountered with a gun who could not prove a right to bear arms. But it is not known whether this provision was actually in the original Spanish version, or was inserted by the government to justify violence against Chican@s. Basilio Ramos was arrested after he attempted to recruit a friend of the Sheriff's to the cause of the revolution. He was captured with the Spanish version of the Plan, but it did not survive his arrest.

A second version of the Plan was issued on the day the original Plan called for the revolution to start, titled *¡Manifesto a los Pueblos Oprimidos de América!*, which had none of the original signatories to the Plan de San Diego but had nine new signatories identifying themselves as The Revolutionary Congress Created by the Plan de San Diego. The second version dropped the call for execution of white males, and focused on the oppression and liberation of Chican@s.

> *"Whereas the document in Ramos's possession avoided mention of the land question or economic radicalism, the Manifesto openly proclaimed the movement's goal as 'Social Revolution' and called for the return of all arable land to the hands of 'proletarians' and combatants for the revolution, who could either keep the land in individual hands or proclaim 'complete communization' as they saw fit. All railroads and means of public transportation were to be collectivized, and the new nation would create 'Modern Schools' where 'Universal Love' would be taught to students without regard to their race or nationality. The document subsumed the provisions of the original plan, adding Utah and Nevada to the list of states to be liberated. This second version of the Plan ended with the hope that the struggle would spread beyond the new republic to 'all oppressed people of all despised races' who would one day overthrow their oppressors and join 'the concert of universal fraternity.'"[25]*

The Sediciosos, inspired by the Plan de San Diego, carried out raids and military actions throughout Texas before the uprising was ended in July 1916 by the U.$. military and vigilante response. Additional militant actions in Texas and elsewhere continued, inspired by the Plan in years to come.[26]

In response to these military actions by Chican@s there was an aggressive and violent counterstrike by the white nation, especially in Texas. Amerikans did not just strike back at Chican@s who were suspected of involvement; they seized the opportunity to punish any Chican@ against whom they held a grudge. Landowning Chican@s were at particular risk for violence. Chican@s were murdered, raped, run off their land, and kept from participating in any part of the political or legal system. In 1915-16 it is estimated that thousands of Chican@s were executed in south Texas in response to the Plan de San Diego. None of the guilty white supremacists were ever brought to justice and in many cases the crimes were perpetuated by the police or the Texas Rangers.[27]

From Imperialist War to Braceros

Chican@s began to be used in the U.$. military in record numbers in World War I (1914-1918). By the end of WWI, migrants spread to many Midwestern industrial cities, which were actively recruiting cheap Chican@ labor into the mines, steel plants, and other industries. Migrants would follow the seasonal harvests, and these workers' camps became permanent settlements for future Chican@ barrios.[28] The war in Europe helped improve the United $tates' position as an imperialist power causing its economy to grow.

Responding to the struggle in the barrios, and seeing the global exploitation bringing wealth into the United $tates, the Chican@ comprador bourgeoisie formed groups like League of United Latin American Citizens (LULAC), an organization open only to Mexican-American citizens of the United $tates which grew rapidly in the 1920s. Groups like LULAC worked to downplay the Chican@ national-colonial question, fighting to have Latinos accepted as "Americans." LULAC was not concerned with liberating the Chican@ nation, rather their battles were to get Raza a piece of the Amerikan pie, focusing on corralling all Latinos into bourgeois democratic politics.

In 1929, the Order of the Sons of America changed its name to the League of United Latin American Citizens (LULAC). The Order of the Sons of America's basic objective was to "enable Mexican-Americans to achieve acculturation and integration,"[29] demonstrates that it was indeed created by Tio Tacos.

LULAC did not represent everyone fighting on behalf of Chican@s, as this was a time of significant proletarian organizing in the United $tates. Chicana Luisa Moreno, a communist, was part of a movement to unite Spanish-speaking people against the often violent oppression they faced. She organized Chican@ workers in the factories in the 1920s and 30s, who were restricted to only the lowest paying jobs. She broke many stereotypes and was eventually targeted by the U.$. government and deported.

The authors of *The Chicanos: A History of Mexican Americans* summarized the effect of migrant labor in the United $tates in the 1900s, "The expanding prosperity of the South West in the first thirty years of this century was in large measure based on Mexican-American labor. This expansion could not have been achieved without the Mexican."[30] Yet after a period of prosperity following World War I, the 1929 stock market crash brought a capitalist crisis, and once more Chican@s were blamed for the decay of capitalism. During the Great Depression not only were Chican@s not able to acquire government assistance in the United $tates (even those who were U.$. citizens) but they were also excluded from the public works projects. The New Deal (1933-1938) was a deal between white capital and white labor, at a time when the militant proletariat of eastern European descent were newly integrated into the white nation. U.$. President Franklin D. Roosevelt used the National Guard to protect union strikers from police and vigilantes, rather than beat them into the submission as had been their practice in the past.[31]

The post-Depression 1930s enhanced the "white labor only" environment, similar to our present day. When capitalism cycles through its inherent periodic crises, Amerikans show their true colors by blaming the already oppressed. Almost a million Chican@s were repatriated to Mexico during this time; even those born in the United $tates were kicked out. An increasing offensive was directed against the Nationalist Party of Puerto Rico at this time, because "[u]nlike the settler workers, the liberation struggle of Puerto Rico was not seeking the reform of the U.S. Empire but its ouster from their nation."[31]

During the New Deal, the Communist International was criticizing social democracy in Europe as social fascism for appealing to the labor aristocracy interests in line with the rising fascist powers. In North America the fascist forces were not well developed, but social democracy still served to benefit the labor aristocracy to the exclusion of the oppressed nations.[32]

Chican@s participated in the hundreds of thousands in World War II (1939-1945). Chican@s were "allowed" to fight and die for Amerika, but returned home to find their friends and families could not even enter the same classrooms as white Amerikans. Some of the Chican@s, who were fighting for Amerika in other parts of the world would come back to the United $tates only to be attacked by sailors and the pigs. One example of this is what became known in the capitalist media as the Zoot Suit Riots. Still today Chican@s are sent to fight other oppressed people around the world, only to get a letter while in a foxhole somewhere saying their parents were deported or locked up in an immigrant concentration kamp.

As the oppressed nationals were sent off to fight in the imperialist war effort, wimmin were finally brought into the U.$. work force. But this new labor force was not enough to keep the domestic economy afloat. The hardest and dirtiest jobs, like those in the mines and in the fields, were empty as no one in Amerika wanted to do this back-breaking labor. Thus in 1942 Amerika initiated the Bracero Program, which basically contracted cheap labor from Mexico. The agreement was supposed to ensure that these rented workers would be treated humanely by the Amerikan companies, but what came was more exploitation and more oppression. These workers found themselves in bad conditions without the right to unionize, organize or protest. Many were cheated in various swindles over the years this program was in operation, totaling millions of dollars. From 1942 to 1945, 168,000 Braceros were sent to work in the United $tates.[33] The Bracero Program was meant to be temporary but seeing the profit squeezed out of the hardworking Mexican@s, in 1951 the U.$. Congress moved to make it permanent.[34] Yet, by 1964 the oppressor nation had decided to discontinue the Bracero Program after Chican@ militancy rose against the issue of exploiting the Bracero workers.

Even bourgeois integrationist groups like LULAC attracted repression from the state at this time. Effects of the Cold War ensured that anyone who did not agree with Amerikan laws 100% were looked at as communist or "anti-American." Red-baiting was common and the militant strikes of this time involving Chican@s were always met with violence. The war was not just with countries around the world but also with anyone in the United $tates not agreeing with the imperialist agenda.

In 1954 the Immigration and Naturalization Service (INS) initiated Operation Wetback, an all out attack on Chican@s and Mexican@s even worse than the ICE raids we see today. The Amerikan government allowed Chican@ communities to be terrorized and deported en masse. Between 1953 and 1956, two million Raza were deported. It's important to remember this was during the McCarthy era when there was an open witch hunt for communists in the United $tates. This hysteria was used to target Chican@ militants, Chican@ workers, organizers, activists and revolutionaries and deport them to Mexico – even though many were born and raised in the United $tates. The Amerikan government, and specifically the Federal Bureau of Investigation (FBI) under Director J. Edgar Hoover, used Operation Wetback as a vehicle to get rid of Chican@ radicals in the same way that the events of September 11, 2001 were used as a vehicle to make war on Afghanistan and further diminish so-called "rights" of Amerikan citizens by enforcing new policies like the Patriot Act. Amerikan intelligence agencies saw the rise in Chican@ resistance and hoped to nip the bubbling Chican@ movement in the bud. As always Amerika underestimated the people's will and determination to overcome.

The Brown Liberation Movement

The 1960s brought an explosion of resistance in the Chican@ community, and the barrios came alive with militancy. Raza were in the streets protesting and organizing the gente. Raza groups were coming out of the woodwork along with new programs, newspapers, and muralists, all adding to what was playing out in the other oppressed communities of the internal semi-colonies in the United $tates. This fervor ran deep through the nation, and there were even several Chican@ prisoner publications circulating in the 1960s: *El Chino*, *La Voz del Chicano* and *Aztlán*.[35]

The struggles during this time period were inspired by the events happening internationally. The Vietnamese people were giving Amerikan imperialism a shellacking in the jungles of Southeast Asia. Northern Korea gave Amerika a thrashing years earlier. The imperialist-backed regime in Cuba was toppled. And of course Mao's China was making unprecedented leaps.

Chican@s were encouraged by the national liberation movements of Latin America, Africa and Asia, as well as the uprisings and struggles in the United $tates, especially from groups like the Black Panther Party for Self-Defense. This period was marked by a new generation defining who they were, and doing so by making a political statement.

At home, there were still signs hung up in front of businesses and in communities saying "No Mexicans Allowed" in states like Oregon and Texas.[36, 37] During this time only 49.7% of the Chican@ population had plumbing in their homes, whereas 94% of white people had indoor plumbing.[38] The inequality and oppression faced by Chican@s not only led to demanding civil rights and better education, but Raza also began to awaken to the idea of real revolution and thus the idea of Chican@s having real revolutionary power. Grappling with these possibilities led to a struggle for Brown Power, and Chican@ Power specifically. Chican@s were no longer satisfied with a march or voting for a Chican@-friendly bourgeois politician. We began to see there was no such thing as justice within Amerikan politics, and that imperialism itself is the problem that is oppressing the people here and internationally.

The farmworker struggle added to the general fervor with its energy and efforts to fight oppressive conditions for field workers. These efforts helped bring even more people into the struggle for humyn rights for Raza, and this often led them into the broader movement for anti-imperialism. The teatro campesino, plays and improvised theater by and for farmworkers out in the agricultural fields, showed that Chican@s were taking on agribusiness and added to the resistance of the times and development of a distinct Chican@ culture.[39]

It's important to point out that the farmworker struggle was a reformist effort that worked within the confines of the Amerikan political system. Chican@ revolutionaries understood the farmworker struggle would not lead to the liberation of the Chican@ nation, but this effort did bring many into demanding humyn rights who would have otherwise been excluded. Those who could not read or write or speak English, who often lived in the shadows, were being mobilized to demand justice and basic rights, standing up to agribusiness and corporate power, learning how their exploitation was linked to others' exploitation and protesting, often with their blood and lives on the line.[40]

A strong Chican@ youth movement began to develop in Colorado as well as California. Carlos Muñoz, Jr., the author of *Youth, Identity, Power: The Chicano Movement* was a leader of the Chican@ movement of the 1960s. His activism began with the anti-war movement during the U.$. War on Vietnam. As a college student, Muñoz was president of the United Mexican American Students (UMAS). He was one of the organizers of the high school student walkouts in Los Angeles in 1968. These walkouts were organized because of racist teachers and poor education that the predominantly-Chican@ student population was forced to endure.

The first major college student strike in the 1960s occurred at San

Francisco State University and was led by New Afrikan and Chican@ students.[41] On 3 March 1968, students all over Aztlán (over ten thousand in California alone) staged a walkout to protest the white supremacist brainwash education in schools. The students held signs with slogans such as "Chicano Power" and "Viva la Revolución." This was unprecedented for Chican@ youth and invigorated Chican@ adults enormously. The action electrified Aztlán. *The Los Angeles Times* published a headline of "Brown Power" over this student action.[42] The very next day on 4 March 1968, FBI Director J. Edgar Hoover issued a memo to pigs across Amerika to "place top priority on political intelligence work to prevent the development of nationalist movements in minority communities."[43] The state saw very quickly the threat of the Chican@ movement, and like the Black liberation movement the state would move to disrupt it at all costs.

The pigs called the student action "The Brown Power Strike" and about 90 days later thirteen Chican@s were rounded up and arrested for organizing the strike. Those arrested belonged to different Chican@ organizations, including four members of the Brown Berets and Muñoz himself. They were indicted for "conspiracy to violate the educational code of California" and "disturbing the peace and quiet of neighborhoods." Known as the East Los Angeles 13, they all faced sixty-six years in prison if found guilty. This case was overturned by an appellate court and is known as *People v. Castro, et al.*

Muñoz was also one of the organizers of a conference in Santa Barbara, California in 1969 involving Chican@ student leaders and faculty from throughout the state. This conference introduced proposals for the creation of Chican@ studies departments in all California colleges, which did not exist at that time. The conference approved a document titled "El Plan de Santa Barbara" which attempted to organize the Chican@ student movement. This conference was also the founding of El Movimiento Estudiantil Chicano de Aztlán (The Chicano Student Movement of Aztlán – MEChA). MEChA to this day remains the largest Chican@ student organization in the United $tates. It has direct links to the movement of the 1960s, which is good, however MEChA relies more on a cultural nationalist approach to struggle even though this recalcitrant approach has helped to stunt any real advances toward liberating the Chican@ nation.[44]

Some of those who took a revolutionary nationalist approach went on to split with MEChA to form El Comité Estudiantil del Pueblo (The

Student Committee of the People). The two-line struggle between MEChA and El Comité is broken down:

> "*Some Chicano movement activists obsessively continue to hold on to the view that we must struggle against exploitation, racism, repression and for self-determination, guided by the spiritual, cultural and moral values of our indian ancestors. ... [T]hey also hold the view that since the white European Invader is our oppressor, we must reject any ideas ... that come from white people. ... But the problems our people face today ... require concrete solutions. ... Cultural practices, spiritual beliefs, love ... Chicanismo ... do not teach us how to organize a workers strike, how to organize and struggle against police brutality, how to stop the dragnet raids and mass deportations of our people, how to organize a student movement. ... It does not teach us how to create a society free of exploitation, how as part of the working class we can take power. ... Our children should not feel proud that they are Mexicanos only because of their color. The strongest national consciousness comes from a knowledge that the masses of our people have made great contributions to the progress and development of organized society, industry and agriculture [and] led ... great struggles to organize workers against exploitation. ... Teaching history in this manner ... creates strong pride in our heritage. But it also recognizes and respects the role of other nationalities as workers and ... teaches our people true internationalism. It exposes the class nature of US society [and] ... imperialist as the bloodiest, most brutal exploiter ... responsible for the underdevelopment of the Third World. ... [W]e also learn the true nature of racism as having an economic base. ... [R]evolutionary nationalism entails working class solidarity which knows no borders. A concept especially important to us who exist divided from our people by the border established by the imperialist US powers. True revolutionary nationalism can only be developed in this context. Un Pueblo sin fronteras [a people without borders].*"[45]

El Comité felt that rather than form an independent Chican@ nation that Chican@s should struggle to re-merge the "Southwest" with Mexico.

At this time another revolutionary organization emerged called the August 29th Movement (ATM). ATM was more of a Maoist group and seems to have had the most correct line to come out of the Chican@ movement. ATM upheld the theory of Marx, Lenin, Mao and Stalin.

They opposed El Comité and anyone else who denied the existence of Chican@s as an independent nation. ATM used comrade Stalin's line on the national question in order to develop a line that outlines the necessity of establishing a Chican@ nation in what is currently the Amerikan Southwest.[46] Although ATM agreed with El Comité that MEChA had become watered down, it differed in that ATM believed it was the duty of the more advanced revolutionary elements within the Chican@ movement to raise MEChA's consciousness to a higher level rather than abandon it. Unfortunately ATM's answer was to call for a multinational communist party in the United $tates. This ultimate reliance on the white nation leftists seems to explain ATM's demise. Solidarity and united front efforts must be promoted with all revolutionaries in North America but ultimately Aztlán's national liberation must be built by Chican@s.[47]

Another legendary leader in the Chican@ power movement was Reies Lopez Tijerina. Tijerina was taught very early on what it meant to be Chican@ in the United $tates. The son of a sharecropper, Tijerina worked the fields alongside his father starting as a child. His grandfather was lynched by Texas Rangers so that a white farmer could take his farmland. This was something that happened to many of the original Chican@s after the U.$. War on Mexico of 1848. The audacity of the ruling class to expect peace from Chican@s is remarkable, when the harvest of its land holdings were tilled in the ashes of our ancestors, and its machinery oiled with our blood! This horrific event would live on in the memories of Tijerina and would no doubt fuel his drive for liberation. Most of Tijerina's activity centered around land grants that were documented since the Spanish occupation which showed that Chican@s owned land for hundreds of years. Tijerina created the Alianza Federal de Mercedes (Federal Alliance of Land Grants), which fought for land and was armed for self-defense. Amerika's repressive agencies targeted the Alianza and Tijerina, as any Chican@ teaching other Chican@s how to struggle was just too much. But before the state was able to carry out any operation to neutralize Tijerina, he and some members of his group occupied the county courthouse at Tierra Amarilla, New Mexico in 1966. Tijerina and Alianza members performed a citizens arrest on the District Attorney and put him on trial in a people's court for not enforcing the land grant laws. Forestry workers were also arrested and tried for trespassing on Chican@ land, and their vehicles were commandeered. A gun battle ensued and Tijerina was captured and sent to prison.

Many Chican@s were inspired by the militancy of this time, caus-ing more Chican@ groups to spring up. One such group was the Young Citizens for Community Action (YCCA) which a year later formed the Brown Berets. The Brown Berets rose as the militant arm of the Brown Power movement, setting up programs feeding the children, free health clinics, and other services. Their newspaper *La Causa* (*The Cause*) was the voice of the barrio. The Brown Berets set up schools for Chican@ youth to teach Chican@ history in place of the watered-down imperialist propaganda fed to our youth in Amerikan schools. The Brown Berets of the 1960s inspired many Chican@ revolutionaries who today continue the struggle to liberate the Chican@ nation. Out of the Brown Berets legacy formed another politically advanced group, La Junta (The Meeting).

The influence of the feminist movement was felt in the Chican@ struggle as well, from leaders such as Elizabeth "Betita" Martinez. Betita was active in the civil rights movement, she was involved in the Student Nonviolent Coordinating Committee (SNCC), and she became coordina-tor of SNCC's New York office. In the 1960s Martinez, like many other Chican@s, focused on the Chican@ nation, but continued to work with groups like the Black Panthers on mutual projects. Martinez moved to New Mexico, the heart of the Chican@ nation, where she co-founded and edited the newspaper *El Grito del Norte* (*The Call of the North*), while continuing to organize in the barrios. She took part in publishing many books including *Viva La Raza* and *500 Years of Chican@ History in Pictures*, which is one of the best examples of Chican@ photo journalism and historical accounts ever created. The newspaper *El Grito* was ground-breaking as the first revolutionary nationalist Chican@ newspaper pub-lished and nearly totally staffed by wimmin. *El Grito* was anti-capitalist, anti-imperialist, anti-religious and denounced "gringo society." Betita's columns were often revolutionary-feminist and battled patriarchy even within the Chican@ struggle. She no doubt helped to develop the con-sciousness of the Chican@ nation in many ways.

Rodolfo "Corky" Gonzalez was a former Golden Gloves boxer turned Chican@ revolutionary who published his own newspaper *El Gallo: a Voz de la Justicia* (*The Rooster: The Voice of Justice*) which served as an organizing tool and news source for Chican@s and Raza in general. Corky went on to form Crusade for Justice, an organization to politicize and revolutionize Raza. Crusade for Justice ran a bookstore, a school for kindergarten to college age youth, a community center, and was responsible for organizing and hosting the first annual Chicano Youth Liberation Conference in Denver, Colorado in 1969. Crusade for Justice faced significant surveillance and repression from the FBI.

It was at the Youth Liberation Conference that Chican@s came together like they never had before. It was here that the concept of "Aztlán" and Chican@ independence was brought to the Raza like never before. At the conference a preamble and three point plan was adopted. It is here that the participants adopted *El Plan Espiritual de Aztlán* which accepted the term *Chicano* as a symbol of resistance.[48] *El Plan Espiritual de Aztlán* brought to the forefront the necessity of Chican@ self-determination, as they described:

> *"A nation autonomous and free, culturally, socially, economically and politically will make its own decisions on the usage of our lands, the taxation of our goods, the utilization of our bodies for war, the determination of justice (reward and punishment) and the profit of our sweat."*[49]

This document was a leap forward in Chican@ political line, moving from thinking in terms of struggling for reforms within Amerikan bourgeois politics to the idea of fighting for Chican@ independence and liberation of the ancestral homeland, Aztlán.

While certainly a remarkable step in the development of our national consciousness, this conference also had some shortcomings. *El Plan Espiritual de Aztlán* was steeped in patriarchal tone with talk about "brotherhood" of Chicanos and our "forefathers" in Aztlán. There is no talk of the First Nations who exist within many parts of the land base we call Aztlán.[50] The program speaks of nationalism, self-determination, independence and total liberation from the oppression and exploitation, but not of socialism or communism. For the Chicano Youth Liberation Conference, the Chican@ struggle was simply about breaking from the "gringo" (i.e. national oppression).

Proposals at the conference were generally progressive, such as "capitalist economic institutions were to be replaced by people's cooperatives," but it was not clear what the organizers thought would enable this to happen. History proves that only a socialist revolution will topple capitalism and make space for national liberation. To believe anything less will do is to succumb to idealism. The cultural nationalist trend that some subscribe to in the Chican@ movement often times has claimed to want to do away with capitalism or obtain equality and a classless society, but falls short of declaring the path of a socialist revolution. While Corky and the Crusaders were guiding the Chican@ movement onto the anti-imperialist road, the leaders were not communists, meaning that they did not thoroughly attack oppression in all its forms.[50]

One group that was an offshoot of Crusade for Justice was la Raza Unida Party (RUP). RUP was originally comprised of petty-bourgeois members, and initially formed as a reaction against the Democratic Party which had refused to open up to Chican@s. Even though RUP developed from the leadership of the Crusaders, they rejected national liberation and self-determination at the first Chican@ conference held in Denver in 1969. Chicana activists, including Martha Cotera, Betita Martinez, Bernice Zamora and Francisca Flores, saw this as a huge blow to the Chican@ national liberation struggle.

Still other groups arose at this time, like the Chican@ group Revolutionary Caucus, who released a statement that was even more politically advanced than the Crusade statement:

> "We, a non-conquered people living in a conquered land, come together hoping that a plan of liberation, a concrete revolutionary program acceptable to the entire Southwest will come from this conference. Subjected to a system that has denied our human dignity, our rights are also being denied under a constitution which we had no part in formulating and more fundamentally the rights protected under the Treaty of Guadalupe Hidalgo... has been violated.

> "We are oppressed first because we are Chicanos, because our skin is dark. But we are also exploited as workers by a system which feeds like a vulture off the work of our people only to enrich a few who own and control this entire country. We suffer double oppression. We catch double hell.

> "We will not attain what's rightfully ours, or our democratic right of self-determination without having to overturn the entire system."[51]

As the above statement explains, Chican@ revolutionaries in the 1960s began to realize that it was Amerikan imperialism that stood in the way of Chican@ liberation. Like all oppressed people at this time, Chican@s began to really study the achievements of liberated nations and the works of Marx, Lenin and Mao. Marxism-Leninism-Maoism (MLM) was a tool that allowed the oppressed to address all forms of oppression in a coherent analysis and get at the root of their causes. Some of the most advanced applications of MLM in the United $tates came in the form of the Black Panther Party for Self-Defense and the Young Lords Party.

The Young Lords started as a lumpen organization in Chicago, evolving from street activity to a political party under the influence of the conditions of the day. Their recruiting base was youth, mostly 16 to 26 years old, from first generation, Spanish-speaking families. Primarily Puerto Rican, they also had many Cuban, Dominican and Mexican members, and about 20 percent were Black. They saw themselves as part of a larger movement to change the system, seeing allies in the people of Vietnam, Cuba and China and the internationalist struggle of the Third World in general.[52] For us they are of particular interest in the example they set of transforming a street organization into a revolutionary party. There are also lessons to be learned in how they handled the national question, and how they united people of various national backgrounds into a Puerto Rican nationalist organization.

The Young Lords Party (YLP) in New York combined revolutionary feminism and nationalism in a campaign against genocidal conditions in relation to Puerto Rican wimmin's reproductive health. The influence of wimmin on the ideological line of the YLP led to a broad program for reproductive rights, including the right to an abortion, which has been opposed by the vast majority of nationalist organizations in the United $tates. While no group can escape the patriarchy without destroying it, YLP was truly a feminist revolutionary nationalist organization.

El Centro de Acción Social Autonoma (The Center of Action and Social Autonomy – CASA) was a Chican@ Marxist organization that emerged in 1975 and tried to get in where they fit in within the still strong Chican@ liberation movement of the time. The history of CASA is offered by Laura Pulido in her book *Black, Brown, Yellow, & Left*, where she looks at the battle for reproductive rights as one case where CASA took a strong stance on gender issues paralleling the Young Lords.[53] From 1968 to 1970 there was a surge in hysterectomies and tubal ligations in Los Angeles County General Hospital, primarily affecting Chicana and New Afrikan wimmin. Pulido credits CASA's strong stance to the fact that the target was the genocidal state and not gender relations internal to the nation.

Half the organization was wimmin, but they mostly played a sub-ordinate role. The exceptions were those few with strong theoretical/academic backgrounds. The accessibility of theory to wimmin has long been a problem in a society where wimmin are taught to be intimidated by it. Overcoming the gender divide in the theoretical realm is crucial. *Black, Brown, Yellow, & Left* also documents the different ways men talked about wimmin when wimmin weren't around, another problem not unique to CASA.

Pulido compares CASA to other similar organizations in Los Angeles, specifically the Japanese-led East Wind and the Black Panther Party for Self-Defense (BPP). There was a class difference between the BPP and CASA, with Panthers coming from single-mother households and more lumpen backgrounds and Chican@s having two working parents (and often more adults in the house) in a patriarchal family structure. These differences in family life were gender differences that seem to be largely determined by class, though there are also cultural explanations, including the strong Catholic influence in Chican@ homes. The class difference is pronounced even in where people are today, with former Panthers being much more likely to be homeless, in jail, on public as-sistance, or just impossible to track down. This class difference likely had something to do with the politics these organizations took up in general.

While the BPP was struggling with patriarchy in the Party, there were many structural aspects of their organization that led to wimmin getting much more respect and power within the organization than in CASA. Most of these aspects reflected more left-leaning politics than those of other organizations, such as CASA, which arose after the BPP had mostly degenerated. Communal living and communal child care were both promoted within the BPP, while CASA relegated child care and home making to the realm of the persynal, or the "subjective" as Pulido puts it. This could be a product of the class nature of those in the BPP, and the weakened patriarchal family structure that resulted. Even in spite of these material influences, CASA should be expected to have taken up the most advanced revolutionary lines, including on gender. The military structure of the BPP meant that all people were expected to do chores in the shared houses, just as all people operated weapons when the pigs came knocking. Pulido acknowledges the sharing of these traditionally gendered tasks (though certainly not equally) allowed wimmin to stand as more equal in the BPP. She says the BPP's focus on community organizing was also easier for wimmin to excel in than the academic focus of CASA's theoretical debate sessions.

Essentially, the Chican@ movement began as a liberal reformist movement, which with time transformed into a cultural-nationalist movement, and finally took up "class-based politics," as explained by the historian Juan Gomez Quinones. It ultimately became mired in the cultural-nationalist psyche of the time, which is unfortunately still prevalent today, as well as the patriarchal ideology inherent within the cultural-nationalist train of thought and of the roadblocks it presented to the movement as a whole. What progress that couldn't be destroyed by our own shortcomings was attacked by the U.$. government using COINTELPRO-type tactics. The Brown Power movement was dissolved alongside the strong Black Power movement, and until now we have stagnated in building up our national struggle for independence once again.

Section 2:
Historical Basis of Aztlán and the State of the Nation Today

IN ORDER TO FULFILL THE definition of a nation a people must meet certain concrete historical conditions. It is not simply a matter of a group of people claiming to be a nation, as some have erroneously done with identity politics. The national question is a scientific development which comrade Stalin defined very well: "a nation is a historically evolved, stable community of language, territory, economic life, and psychological make up manifested in a community of culture."[1] In Section 1 we presented the historical development of the Chican@ nation's origins. In this section we will look more closely at the national characteristics of the Chican@ nation.

The material conditions that make up Aztlán are distinct from the material conditions of our Mexican@ ancestors. Our interaction and struggles under Amerikan imperialism have also been a major factor in our distinction as a people. Our existence, even through the repression that has been unleashed on our people by the oppressor nation since our birth, has also created contradictions that have both helped and hurt the development of our nation. While sections of our nation have been bought off, other sections have been severely repressed, imprisoned and even killed.

Territory

Aztlán was the land of origination that was said to be north of the valley of Mexico. It is well known that many indigenous peoples traveled throughout the Americas for many different reasons, intermarrying with other tribes and migrating seasonally in some cases. The large indigenous population on both sides of the Rio Bravo form the primary basis of the emerging Chican@ nation. Spanish colonization in the region mixed in Spanish and other Europeans, as well as African slaves.

The Aztecs are believed to be the first to stably occupy this region. Aztlán was the historic homeland of the Aztec people, who would become Mexican@s and later Chican@s. It was from Aztlán that the Aztecs migrated south to build the Aztec capital Tenochtitlan. Although the precise geographic location of historic Aztlán has not been located, most scholars and historians agree that Aztlán is in what today is called the "Southwest United $tates," territories that the United $tates stole from Mexico: California, Arizona, Utah, Nevada, New Mexico, Texas and parts of Wyoming, Colorado and Oklahoma. Evidence of Aztec culture is still being found today in states as far out as Kansas and Oklahoma.

In 1968 the Chican@ poet Alurista resuscitated the concept of Aztlán. And again, the Chicano Youth Liberation Conference of 1969 brought the concept to the people. The liberation of Aztlán, our homeland, is what Chican@s are currently struggling for.

Most recently an influx of Central/South American peoples have arrived into long-held Chican@ barrios. Initially arriving as part of national minorities, many of these people have also grown up identifying as Chican@s themselves.

According to the U.$. Census, Raza continue to be the fastest growing population in the United $tates because of migration and high birth rates.[2] The Raza population grew 53% from 1980 to 1990, 58% from 1990 to 2000 and 44% from 2000 to 2010. (See *Figure 1.2.1 Raza as Percent of Total U.$. Population* on the next page.)

The data from the 2010 Census confirms the growing population of Raza both in Aztlán and in the United $tates overall. According to the April 2010 Census, the total U.$. population at the time was 308.7 million, while the Raza population was 50.5 million. This is up from 44.6 million in 2006, and the 2010 Census predicted it will reach 133 million in 2050. One in four babies born in the United $tates today are Raza. One in two born in Texas and California are Raza. The highest concentration of Raza today remains in the "Southwest." States known to be the Chican@ homeland continue to have the highest number of Chican@s and continue to grow as every year we are replenished with new births and more waves of migrants ensuring the presence of the future of our nation. *Figure*

Figure 1.2.1 Raza as Percent of Total U.$. Population [2]

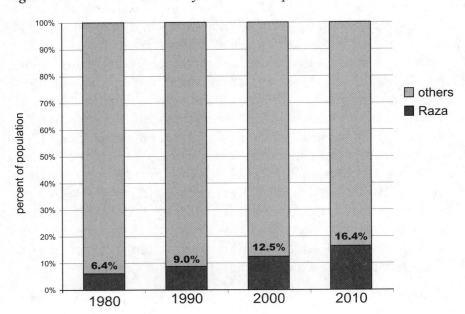

1.2.2 on the opposite page shows the percentage of the population that is Raza by county in the United $tates. The dark grey line indicates an approximate northern border for Aztlán.

Language

Stalin wrote "There is no nation which at one and the same time speaks several languages, but this does not mean that there cannot be two nations speaking the same language!"[3] In putting together this book, we looked at Spanish, English, and Spanglish as candidates for the national language of Aztlán. We have concluded that the common language for Aztlán is in fact English, as counterintuitive as that may be to some. Of course many Chican@s do speak Spanish, and many also speak Spanglish or Caló, but the only unifying language across all generations of Chican@s is English.

To include a few facts on this we're just going to talk about people of Mexican descent because they are most studied, and make up the vast majority of the Chican@ nation. It's possible people from other countries show very different patterns, but this seems unlikely.

Figure 1.2.2 Raza population by county in the United $tates 2010
Indicating the Mexico-U.$. border in 1836.   Source: Wikipedia user Yerevanci's own work

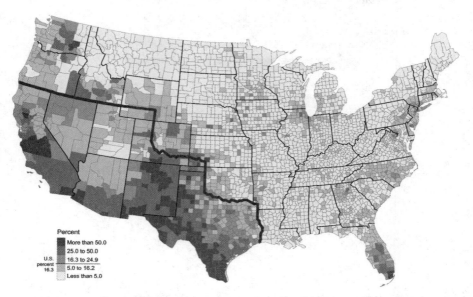

First generation Mexican migrants may not speak much English, but they still fall into the category of national minority. One doesn't become Chican@ simply by crossing the border. They are not yet assimilated into the Chican@ nation. As we wrote in Section 1, these Mexican nationals identify with their home country and are often sending money back to support their family who still lives abroad. In 2011, 35% of Mexican-origin people in the United $tates were foreign born. They virtually all spoke Spanish and only one-third of Mexican immigrants spoke English proficiently.[4]

On linguistic assimilation, Mexican nationals start off way behind among the foreign-born in the United States. But by the second generation, they catch up with Asians and Europeans.[5] See *Figure 1.2.3* on the next page. Third-generation Mexican migrants, on the other hand, are mostly speaking English only. "In 1990, 64 percent of third-generation Mexican-American children spoke only English at home; in 2000, the equivalent figure had risen to 71 percent."[6]

Youth born in Mexico who migrate with their parents at a young age do assimilate quickly into the Chican@ nation. These folks are disadvantaged in school but learn English quickly and end up not strongly identifying with their home country. Many even end up forgetting their Spanish as they assimilate.

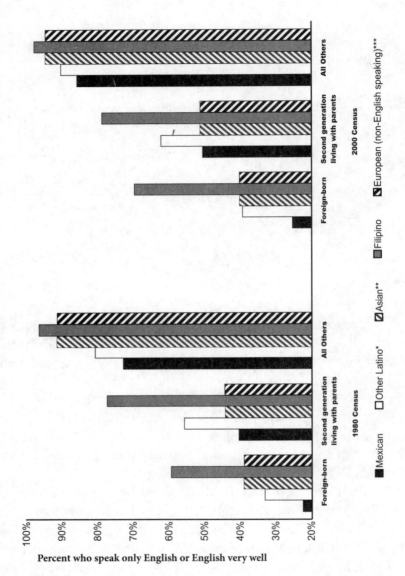

Figure 1.2.3 Linguistic Assimilation of Mexicans and Other Immigrants

Bars indicate the percentages who speak only English at home or who speak English "very well." "All Others" indicates all respondents of a given ancestry who are neither foreign-born nor of the second generation living with immigrant parents.

*Other Latino includes those of South American, Puerto Rican, and Cuban ancestry.

**Asian includes those of Chinese, Japanese, Korean, and Vietnamese ancestry. Indians were excluded due to the extremely high English proficiency among first-generation immigrants.

***European (non-English speaking) includes those of German, Italian, Polish, and Russian ancestry.

Source: Integrated Public Use Microdata Series, 1980 and 2000 Census 1% samples.

Economy

The economy of the Chican@ nation began to develop in the 1800s with the merchants, artisans and ranchers, many of whom were given land grants by the Spanish colonial government as part of the development of New Spain. This economic activity was further stimulated by the injection of Amerikan capital. The introduction of mines and agriculture, business and industries dramatically changed economic relationships. Opening up trade with the expanding United $tates ensured that this economic growth continued right up to the U.$. War on Mexico.

The revisionists will say the Chican@ nation did not develop economically because of the overbearing domination of U.$. imperialism, but this is an overestimation of the economic independence of the majority of the world's nations who live in a state of neo-colonialism today outside of U.$. borders. In his study of underdevelopment in "Latin America," Andre Gunder Frank demonstrated the dominance of those economies by Spain and later the United $tates, which led to no real national bourgeoisie, only a comprador class that exists as an enabler of imperialist plunder.[7] This is why today's rising bourgeois nationalism in Bolivia emerged from the likes of shoe-shine boys and cocaleros, and they face much resistance from the imperialists. Earlier we mentioned the failures of Mexico to take advantage of the land reform after the revolution as many feudal countries in Europe and Asia were able to do.[8] This had much to do with the influence of emerging U.$. imperialism to the north and its influence on the Mexican nation. So we should not mistake the nominal independence of Third World nations under imperialism as reason to deny the national existence of Aztlán.

The main classes of the Chican@ nation are the bourgeoisie, petty bourgeoisie, semi-proletariat, and the lumpen.[9] The bourgeoisie are firm supporters of U.$. imperialism, just as the bourgeoisie in power in most Third World countries today are. These are brown proud patriots of the United $tates, and many of these vendidos (sellouts) are part of the state apparatus. The Chican@ bourgeoisie are big business owners, corporate CEOs and many are included in the political and bureaucratic strata of U.$. imperialism. Their base of support lies in the Chican@ bourgeois intellectuals and politicians, military, capitalist and social bureaucracy, including many clergy. The bourgeoisie have a hand in not just keeping Chican@s and other Raza in a

Figure 1.2.4 Global Wealth Flow Under Imperialism

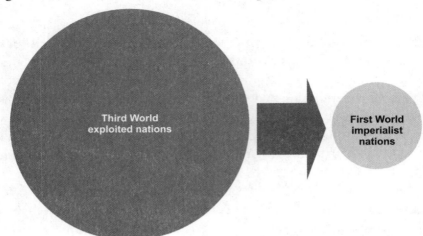

semi-colonial state, but also in the oppression and exploitation of Third World nations around the world. These compradors aid U.$. imperialism's neo-colonialism of the Chican@ nation by taking positions in the U.$. government to make it appear as if Chican@s are in positions of power, but a few compradors in government don't change the reality of Amerikan domination over the Chican@ nation. Boriqua (Puerto Ricans) also experience the same thing with the use of compradors to uphold U.$. imperialism within the colony.

The Mexican@ and other Raza national minorities are unique in the United $tates for the size of their proletariat and semi-proletariat workforces in a country where those with legal working status are paid exploiter-level wages. The proletariat are the national minority workers mostly working in agribusiness, those who toil in the fields across the United $tates in order to put vegetables and fruits on the plates of Amerikans, as well as those toiling in illegal garment and processing factories within U.$. borders. These workers are the most exploited in the United $tates today and are overwhelmingly Mexican@. Although they include child workers, and are often forced to work with no safety gear, cancerous pesticides, no insurance, and no restrooms, they are still paid significantly more today than the majority of Third World peoples.

The Chican@ nation's close proximity to these exploited and oppressed classes exerts a positive influence on the Chican@ nation, and preserves a national consciousness that is connected to Mexican@s and other exploited nations.

Figure 1.2.5 Wealth Flow in the First World

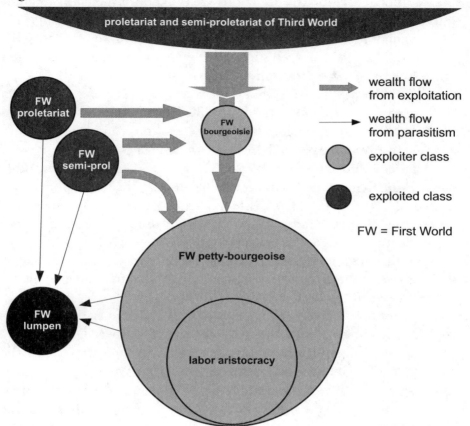

The semi-proletariat is just a small minority of the Chican@ nation. This class includes the marginally employed, such as former prisoners, street vendors and small business hustlers who barely scrape together an income each month. Most, but not all, have cars, live in homes with running water and electricity, and have made improvements in their working conditions due in part to militant Chican@ labor struggles from decades past.

By virtue of the vast stolen wealth hoarded within U.$. borders, even the Chican@ nation is dominated by a new petty bourgeoisie. Traditionally this class includes small business owners, merchants, intellectuals, small farmers, artisans and fishermen. In the modern U.$. economy, the petty bourgeoisie is dominated by small business owners and a well-payed technocratic class. The majority of Chican@s work in the service economy earning wages that make them a part of either the labor aristocracy or the traditional petty bourgeois. For this reason, the immediate economic interests of the majority of the Chican@ nation is tied to U.$. imperialism. Yet nation is still important, and when faced with questions of life and death, the petty bourgeoisie can line up strongly on the side of their oppressed nation in opposition to imperialism.

There now exists a vast labor aristocracy (as Lenin defined it), which includes a majority of people residing in the United $tates. The superprofits extracted by Amerikan imperialists by exploiting Third World nations are used to buy off the people here in the United $tates. U.S. citizens enjoy the luxuries afforded by Third World exploitation while demanding more crumbs and living parasitically as the most over-consuming population the world has seen. This labor aristocracy has actually developed beyond what Lenin described in his day as a layer of workers, into almost every worker in the United $tates receiving this privilege. The only exceptions are non-citizen migrant workers and some prisoners and released felons. For this reason there is only a very small proletariat in the United $tates at this time.

The First World lumpen includes the street elements, the marginalized, the unemployed, and the underclass in the imperialist countries. The Chican@ lumpen are those who are chronically unemployed or, to be specific, the "unemployables": those outside of the Amerikan economy, the "criminals," mentally ill, and prisoners. This includes most of those the state labels "gang members," including those living on welfare. In the Chican@ nation it is the lumpen and semi-proletariat, allied with the Mexican@ and other national minority proletariat and semi-proletariat, who will be the backbone of a revolution. It is these classes who are the least bought off by imperialism and who have the least to lose and the most to gain from the liberation of the Chican@ nation.

Today we should work to unite the lumpen of the Chican@ nation with Marxism-Leninism-Maoism in order to develop the vanguard of our national liberation movement that will one day be successful in bringing socialism to a liberated Chican@ nation. We will get more into this point in Part I Section 4.

Culture

Chican@ culture was not so much inherited as evolved due to Chican@s' distinct conditions living under U.$. imperialism. Chican@ culture is derived from many different influences on our ancestors living in the Americas; the culture of the Pueblo First Nations, various indigenous cultures of Mexico, the Mexican national culture and the Hispano-Iberic culture of Spain, which drew from the Moors and many Iberian peoples. Our psychological make up is seen in our culture. Chican@ literature and folk stories are distinctly Chican@. Much of our music is Chican@ in origin, not just Spanish songs native to Chican@s but new genres like Chican@ techno, Chican@ freestyle, R&B and most recently a genre called Chican@ rap. Chican@s have even entered the art world with what has come to be known as Chican@ art or the revolutionary art we call Aztlán realism. Our art is distinctly Chican@ and often depicts the struggles of the brown community living under imperialist oppression. All this has melded to create a Chican@ culture that is distinct from Mexico's.

The above points show the Chican@ nation meets all the characteristics of a nation laid out by Stalin. Should the Chican@ nation, or any other group, fail to meet any of these characteristics they will cease to be a nation. It is possible that at some point in the future Amerika will find it useful to assimilate the Chican@ nation as a whole. We must continuously evaluate the characteristics of the nation so that our analysis is based on a scientific assessment of current reality.

The Border: Past, Present and Future

The border that separates Mexico from the Chican@ nation is Amerika's "iron curtain." After the U.$. War on Mexico, Amerika eagerly allowed droves of Mexican@s to enter the newly expanded borders of the United $tates. As was discussed earlier in this book, the Bracero Program helped Mexican labor build Amerikan industries in the territory of Aztlán. This migration was welcomed at the time because it allowed Amerikan capitalists to appropriate surplus labor from Mexican@s.[10]

The border is still semi-porous as Amerika continues to use Mexico as a reserve labor force. In many cases Amerikan capitalists organize Raza to be brought over the border, packed like sardines in suffocating trucks. As with the slave ships, many don't survive the trip to the United $tates. The state has border patrol agents guarding and preventing Raza from entering the United $tates, and U.$. politicians speak of building electric fences along the border. Others support white supremacist militia groups that organize armed paramilitary units and camp out on the border to openly track (and often kill) migrants.

In regards to the border, the U.$. imperialists are damned if they do and damned if they don't. On the one hand they need Mexican@s and other Raza to continue to flow into the United $tates to provide cheap domestic labor for the benefit of Amerikans. Yet there is the very real threat of an ever-growing Raza population which will become a menace for the oppressor. The birth rate of Raza is higher than the birth rate of the white nation. What this means for the future of Amerika simply terrifies the oppressor nation. The thought of brown people one day being the majority of the U.$. population, and the possible political or revolutionary implications are just too much. So the imperialists are stuck between either protecting their dollars or protecting the white privilege that solidifies Amerikan support around the empire. They have clearly chosen to protect white privilege. This is seen in the crackdown on migrants by ICE, building a wall and using drones to seal off the border between the United $tates and Mexico, etc.

The imperialists see that what happens in Mexico is very relevant to Amerikan interests, but this is true for the Mexican government and people as well as Chican@s. It recently came out that U.$. agents were flooding Mexico with high-powered weapons under Operation Fast and Furious.[11] This was meant to help destabilize Mexico and give Amerika more influence and power over the country. We saw recently where a U.$. border agent shot a Mexican child of 14 years, Sergio Hernandez, as he played on the Mexican side of the border. This open season on the Raza enraged the people. It didn't matter that he wasn't Chican@ or that he was a Mexican citizen; every barrio in Aztlán felt this repression like so many other legal lynchings we have faced for hundreds of years by the predator.

We need to keep in mind the relations between state actions and capitalist interests. States exist to protect class interests. The efforts mentioned above are used in order to secure the interests of the capitalist class as a whole. Whether Mexican@s will be allowed to migrate and work in the United $tates, or not, and whether the border will be militarized or electrified, or not, depends on how it affects the power of the bourgeois class.

The notion of a "national border" is a bourgeois concept that was imposed on indigenous people in the Americas by European colonizers. The border is a product of capitalism's need to commodify everything as private property, and defend their imperialist power. In early capitalism, the border of the nation-state served to expand the influence of the state and unite across a large population. As capitalists began to look outward for capital accumulation, and the contradiction between oppressor and oppressed nations grew stronger, borders became more important as a means of keeping certain "inferior" nationalities out. In particular, for Amerika, the border is to keep the exploited out in order to concentrate the wealth accumulated by the superexploitation of other nations in the hands of Amerikans.

In order to affect lasting change around problems like migration and the border, capitalism must be demolished. We need to end capitalist relations of production that influence racist laws and pull the strings behind the scenes on policies such as the militarization of the border. This monopolization of the entire political process in the United $tates by the oppressor nation proves that the ballot box is not a viable avenue to truly liberate the Chican@ nation or any other oppressed nation. People who simply rely on protesting single issues like the border, environment, save the whales, etc., will never achieve true, lasting success under a capitalist system.

The southern border of the United $tates, imposed in the middle of Mexico, has blossomed into a militarized zone of concrete, drones, and armed patrol to keep Raza movement controlled. Chican@ communists understand that only a revolution that liberates Aztlán will solve the border question. All communists are internationalists who are for open borders, yet we know true internationalism can only be fully practiced when, as Lenin said, all nations are liberated and given the right to secede. This will only occur through a socialist revolution on these shores. Communists struggle to end deportations and the militarization of the border for capitalist interests. We work to educate and organize Mexican@ migrants in the United $tates and lead them to better their conditions while creating more allies in our struggle for an independent Chican@ nation. We show Raza that U.$. imperialism is behind their oppression here in the United $tates, thus guiding them to the anti-imperialist united front. As more and more Raza, not just Mexican@s but from all over what is called "Latin America," continue to migrate into Aztlán, many are beginning to recognize their affiliation to Aztlán. These Raza are replenishing the Chican@ nation daily with new and fresh hearts, minds and brown fists. So let us guide them into an effective solution to the border. There will never be a resolution to the border question without a resolution to the Chican@ national-colonial question.

Aztlán is an Oppressed Internal Semi-Colony

In imperialist countries exploitation and other forms of oppression lead to mass resistance of the oppressed peoples, who themselves are forged into nations. Through this process the Chican@ nation became a symbol of strength and resistance for the oppressed that the imperialists needed to take down. And taking on the more numerous and often larger oppressed nations head-on was not a safe bet for the oppressors. As a result, they developed a new form of colonialism: neo-colonialism. Kwame Nkrumah in his analysis of neo-colonialism in Africa defined it as: "The essence of neo-colonialism is that the state which is subject to it is, in theory, independent and has all the outward trappings of international sovereignty. In reality its economic system and thus its political policy is directed from outside."[12] Nkrumah stressed the importance of dividing the oppressed into smaller groups as part of this process of preventing effective resistance to imperialism as had already occurred in China, Vietnam, Korea, Cuba and elsewhere.

Neo-colonialism was first used by the British on what is referred to as "Latin America" in the early 1800s. Amerika followed in employing this method throughout "Latin America" and beyond soon after. Neo-colonialism has a devastating effect on the domestic economy of a nation. But colonialism is not strictly an economic phenomenon, it is also an expression of the oppressor nation and a formal promotion of white supremacy and its ideology. Colonialism itself is divided along national lines with one nation dominating another.

Traditionally, colonies were developed as a means of meeting the economic needs of ever-expanding capitalism in the conquering country. By stealing resources and people, exploiting labor and land and imposing their products and economic policies, the colonial power benefits greatly from the relationship. As Chican@s today enjoy the legal benefits of U.$. citizenship, they either earn the exploiter wages of the imperialists or don't work, and are not generally economically exploited. We use the term semi-colony to indicate this colonial relationship that lacks some of the characteristics of a traditional colony. Of course, the territory of Aztlán provides much wealth to the Amerikan nation, and as such there is a significant economic threat to Amerikans by Chican@ nationalism.

Here in the United $tates we experience what is called internal colonialism. Internal colonialism was defined by Chican@ teacher and author Mario Barrera: "Internal colonialism is a form of colonialism in which the dominant and subordinate populations are intermingled, so that there is no geographically distinct 'metropolis' separate from the 'colony.'"[13]

This is the condition of the United $tates today where there are no more areas with signs saying "white only." In most cases oppressed nations are allowed to live in multinational neighborhoods and shop in the stores of the oppressor nation but the white ruling class continues to be the white ruling class. Wall Street continues to control the political ideology of Amerikans today just as Britain did to the early colonists of yesterday. Chican@s continue to be ruled by the oppressor nation even if we are "intermingled." The colony is no longer surrounded by a fence, it is no longer marked by signs, but continues to be the dominant relationship in the United $tates. This is seen in the attacks on Raza throughout the United $tates in the form of murder, rape, etc., that go without justice, and the terror instituted on hard-working migrants who are raided by ICE and other agencies. We see signs of the occupation in families who are ripped apart, babies taken right out of the arms of mothers, and deported never to be seen again. This leaves thousands of brown children in Amerikan foster care where they will be vulnerable to further brutality. Finally, the occupation is seen in the criminalization of our youth turning Aztlán into one big prison house.

The recent banning of Chican@ studies and books by Chican@ authors also shows us we are still an internal colony, so don't be bamboozled just because some of us may be "intermingled." What we have experienced since our land was stolen in 1848 by Amerika has been structural discrimination expressed in the socio-political-economic relations of Chican@s and the oppressor nation. This is used by imperialism today in the United $tates to maintain its stranglehold on the Chican@ nation. Yet even progressive Euro-Amerikan people and white lumpen benefit from this internal colonialism through inherited white privilege. This is not saying they all think they deserve this benefit, some may hate it, but it is the reality nonetheless of living in the United $tates. The Chican@ nation, like other oppressed nations in the United $tates, continues to revolve around colonial divisions. Our job today is to educate our people to this complex layer of oppressive relations. Whether the lumpen can grasp this or not will determine our future and the future of class struggle in the United $tates.

Section 3:
The Path Forward for Emancipation

"OUR BELOVED SUN HAS DISAPPEARED and has left us in total darkness. But we know that it will again return, will again come out and will come anew to shine upon us. But while it stays in the underworld we should rapidly gather and embrace ourselves. And in the center of our hearts we will hide all that our heart appreciates and considers a treasure. And we know like a great jade we will destroy our houses of youth, our universities, our ball-courts, our houses of young men and our houses of song. That our roads may be deserted and that our homes may preserve us. For now we do not know until when our new sun will come out. That the fathers and the mothers may never forget to teach their children. The fathers with the boys, the mothers with the girls. And that they teach their children while they live precisely how good has been that which has been until today, our beloved Anahuac! The refuge, the protection and the care of our energies. And as a result of our customs and the behavior that our elders received and our parents with efforts sewed in our essence. Now we deliver the task to our children that they guard our writing and our knowledge. From now on our homes will be our houses of youth, our universities, our ball courts, our houses of young men, our houses of song. And don't forget to inform our children intensely how it will be. How we will rise! And exactly how its destiny will be realized and how it will fulfill its grand destiny. Our beloved motherland Anahuac!" - declaration delivered to the Mexica Nahuatl people by the last reigning Aztec prince Cuauhtemoc upon their final retreat from Tenochtitlan (Mexico City) and into the southern jungles of Mexico and Guatemala in their attempt to evade Spanish rule, August 1521

"All military laws and military theories which are in the nature of principles are the experiences of past wars summed up by people in former days, or in our own times. We should seriously study these lessons paid for in blood, which are a heritage of past wars. That is one part. But there is another. We should put these conclusions to the test of our own experience, assimilating what is useful, rejecting what is useless and adding what is specifically our own. The latter is very important for otherwise we cannot direct a war." - Mao Zedong, "Problems of Strategy in China's Revolutionary War," December 1936.

This quote from Mao Zedong is a summation of what he meant when he said that the living soul of Marxism is its ability to be applied to our particular and unique conditions. This understanding is exactly why Maoism as a philosophy, political ideology and as a military science has been so successful in addressing the plight of the oppressed worldwide. Maoism is a military science that is universal and applicable to all countries and all terrains.

The above speech by the Aztec prince Cuauhtemoc is at once part of a military directive, as well as an expression of hope and perseverance in the midst of a most horrific reality. Counterposing the quote by Cuauhtemoc to today's conditions, the outright barbaric actions of the conquistadors are a thing of the past, but national oppression continues in newer forms. Just as the Mexica-Nahuatl were a people unable to return home because of Spanish conquest and occupation, so are we, the Chican@ people, unable to reside independently within Aztlán due to Amerikan conquest and occupation. We should take heed of Cuauhtemoc's words and not lose hope of an Aztlán independent and free. Let us not forget what Chican@ revolutionaries, and the Raza sought and fought for during the last surge of national liberation struggles. Let us revive the spirit of rebellion that our predecessors projected so well when they dared to challenge the state; that same misdirected spirit of rebellion which our carnales on the block exemplify so well. Our youth act out for various reasons such as not knowing what the future can hold, or because they do not understand why our reality is the way it is. They do not understand the monster of imperialism and the oppression and alienation it engenders. They do not understand the Marxist theory of history, which is not just about the class struggle, but national struggles as well – and for the Chican@ people the national struggle has not ceased.

The class struggle today manifests itself as a struggle between nations. Before we can organize to defeat the parasitic bourgeoisie who feeds off the labor of the proletariat we must first organize to defeat the parasitic core capitalist centers that feed off the oppressed and exploited nations in the periphery. The class struggle is inextricably bound to the national struggles of the oppressed nations of the Third World as well as the struggles of the internal semi-colonies of the United $tates, i.e. Aztlán, New Afrika, Boricua and the First Nations. It is this contradiction that drives these national liberation struggles, the principal contradiction that must be untangled before we can make progress on the class struggle.

Today the Chican@ nation is at a crossroads. The Raza population is growing faster than any other, so that, according to the 2010 Census, Raza may be the largest population in the United $tates in a few decades. A large population of any people does not automatically translate to a progressive force. The possibility exists for Raza to be bought off by Amerikan imperialism and to become a reactionary force as a group, helping to uphold U.$. imperialism not just in Aztlán but throughout the world on a mass scale. One can see the importance of educating the Raza now before we get to be the largest population in the United $tates. This education must provoke a class consciousness in order for us to be successful.

In recent years we have seen oppression of Chican@s in all levels of society. The assault on migrants, ICE raids, incarceration, and the attacks on Chican@ studies in schools are just a few examples. States like Arizona are not just banning Chican@ studies in schools, but also banning books on Chican@ history, such as *Occupied America: a History of Chicanos* by Rodolfo F. Acuña. States like Alabama passed laws denying work, health care and other services to migrants and their children. This backfired when crops began rotting in the fields for lack of sufficient workers, because the Amerikans who went to work those fields found the job too hard and left for home after working a week or two. Alabama was sent scurrying to repeal some of these racist measures.

This increased repression may swing the Raza left when a decade ago some were flirting with bourgeois Republican ideas due in part to religious sentiment. In the Amerikan electoral system, we have the choice of voting for this oppressor or that oppressor, the smiling oppressor or the frowning oppressor, but our circumstances do not change. We will not stop the rape of our natural resources, terrorizing of our barrios, or denial of Chican@s' basic humyn rights through prayer, or through relying on Chican@ bourgeois politicians, or groups like LULAC who simply want to see more brown faces in high places. It is common sense that the ruling class and its compradors will not volunteer to give up their parasitic ways. Chican@ revolutionaries also know to not have hope in the supernatural (religion); we believe in people's power.

In order for Chican@s to get on the path for real liberation we need to politicize Chican@s and build public opinion for revolution and socialism. This is the first but most essential step at this stage because without doing this we will not find that path, and we will simply lose our way. In order to build public opinion in the Chican@ nation we need to educate Raza and create a new revolutionary culture in the barrios, in the pintas and wherever Raza are at. We need to really study our revolutionary history and grapple with political line surrounding the Chican@ nation. We need to educate our youth and allow Raza to see that another society is possible. Marx once said "once the inner connection is grasped, all theoretical belief in the permanent necessity of existing conditions breaks down before their collapse in practice."[1] This is a powerful statement and applies to what we have been talking about. Today Chican@s see the way things are and many can't even imagine a different society much less grapple with how we are going to get there. Yet once people grasp that, then this imaginary belief in the permanence of our situation dissolves. Before we dismantle our oppression we must first grasp the idea that it doesn't have to continue. Our job should thus be to help Raza realize that we do not have to live under a ruling class, a dictatorship of capital; the Chican@ nation demands liberation!

It is our job, those of us who seek to emancipate Aztlán, to begin now to educate the Raza. You can be in a cockroach infested barrio or in a steel cage in a dungeon, it does not matter. You must begin to educate the Raza about our situation today, our historia and where we want to go tomorrow. We need study guides and study groups to really take this seriously and engage all who can be engaged in learning more on what will emancipate Aztlán. The white supremacists are organizing and educating in militias and groups all over the United $tates – the time is now to be a part in determining the course Raza take in the future. When we educate Raza we are essentially transforming them, politicizing them, and revolutionizing them.

The situation in Mexico will always impact the Chican@ movement. Corruption has been building for decades and most of the apparent gains of the 1910 revolution have been reversed. The many conscious Raza who have been deported from the United $tates serve to replenish the ranks of the radical youth movement of Mexico and Central America. The devastation caused by the North American Free Trade Agreement (NAFTA) has fueled the rage in the rural peasantry. The Mexican proletariat may be moving towards a righteous battle, and the Chican@ nation should keep these events in mind as we work to push our own consciousness forward and join the fight against oppression and exploitation.

Chican@s are tired of being hoodwinked and sold snake oil by capitalist parasites. We want freedom and self-determination! The energy we see today in the streets in the protests over "immigration" issues has not been seen since the 1960s.[2] A new wave of resistance is here and Chican@s will use it to propel our struggle further than it has gone thus far. We refuse to be fooled by the Tio Tomás who the U.$. imperialists put in "public office" to show us brown faces in high places. No longer do we believe the lies of just "pulling ourselves up by our bootstraps." We know we are oppressed and we want freedom! Our freedom will come when Aztlán is liberated!

Socialism and the Chican@ Nation

Socialism is the transitional stage in a society between capitalism and communism. Communism marks the end of class society when a state or even a standing army is no longer necessary. It is a stage of humyn social development when oppression no longer exists, where no group oppresses any other group. This stage of communism will not develop so long as oppressive systems exist in the world.

Our current oppressive economic systems of imperialism and capitalism didn't always exist. Class divisions began thousands of years ago, but before that societies existed on a communal way of life; rather than everything being owned by individuals, things belonged to communities, or to no one at all. This way of communal living existed for thousands of years before class divisions arose. It was only when earlier humyn beings developed the tools to produce surplus sustenance that class divisions came about. When individuals began producing their own food rather

than hunting and gathering, those who were better at it benefited more. The larger the cultivation became, and the larger scale of domestication of animals, the greater the inequality. There developed owners and workers; rulers and those being ruled.[3]

During these early times, new class divisions took on many forms of conflict. Rebellions of all types sprang from the existing despair, and people created religions in hopes of finding a way out of the oppression. Monarchies came and went, masters and slaves were introduced, then feudalism developed to exploit the toiling masses.

These oppressive horrors continued in the world uninterrupted until 1871 in Paris, France when the people rose up and cast off the chains that bound them. The Paris Commune was established, and only lasted physically for two months. But it remains in the minds of all who struggle against an oppressive state as a major event in the annals of people's struggles everywhere. The thousands who were slaughtered in the first attempt to establish a new order of social relations free from class divisions live on in memories, as people would come to rise up all over the globe and remember those who first rose up in 1871. As good as the Paris Commune was, it lacked a vanguard leadership and thus was easily crushed. This can be seen as a microcosm of what a nation would be like simply having a revolution with a bunch of groups in a loose alliance with no vanguard. Yes, it may be temporarily successful at toppling an old order, but it will not last without a vanguard to lead the people not only in battle but also in rebuilding a new society (think Egypt in 2011).

Largely in response to the Paris Commune, Karl Marx and Frederich Engels produced a body of work surrounding a new society with new relations of production. The "Communist Manifesto" was amongst this work. Marx taught us that the class which owns the means of production (factories, machinery, technology, etc.) also controls the politics (including the state apparatus that is the prisons, military, legal system, etc.) and the overall ideology of a society. But Marx showed that class systems create the conditions in which a revolution will occur to change the production relations. He explained that this is a natural occurrence, a matter of the material world being in constant motion. Forces of oppression push toward reactions in society to modify production relations to be more appropriate for the developing productive forces.

Based on Marx's teachings, in 1917 the Russian revolution toppled the Tzar and then the capitalist class, creating the world's first socialist state led by V.I. Lenin. Leading up to the revolution, Lenin spent years leading a series of political struggles that drew clear distinctions between the proletarian line and others, and that developed the blueprint for how to build an effective communist party. By the time Lenin died, the Soviet Union had effectively won the ongoing civil war and defeated imperialist invasions that threatened the first socialist state. They had survived a period of compromise with various economic interests to rebuild the country from a combination of war and backwards feudal relations to build the first socialist economy run by the people and in the interests of the people. The world watched in awe, as the Soviet Union developed in leaps and bounds. Then capitalist crisis raised its head again, bringing another inter-imperialist war that would hit Russia even harder than the first. But under Stalin's leadership and foresight, the Soviets prepared for Nazi invasion for years before it happened, and their fighting spirit landed the majority of blows to the German fascist regime that led to its collapse. The Soviet Union lived on for some years after the war to continue to successfully build socialism in one country, but then rose to superpower status in the hands of the the capitalist-roaders who took over after Stalin's death.

While World War II brought great devastation to the Soviet Union and Europe, it created openings for more class struggle, especially in the colonized nations. During those years Mao Zedong became a leading figure in the communist-led national liberation struggle in China, gaining victory and liberating China in 1949. China's liberation from Japanese imperialism and capitalism went against the dominant theory at the time. Even the dominant theory from leadership of the Soviet Union believed that a socialist revolution could not occur in a non-capitalist country, and some went so far as to say peasants were not a revolutionary force. Mao's China gave us the highest advancement in socialism the world has yet to see. The Chinese revolution brought the Great Proletarian Cultural Revolution of 1966-76, which unleashed the masses to struggle with the leadership theoretically, challenging new oppressors who had arisen and were deviating from the path toward communism. Class struggle continues even during socialism, as a new bourgeoisie arises even within the party itself. This proved to be true after the death of Mao in 1976. Major advances in society were achieved in Mao's China and his leadership and political theory has yet to be surpassed in many areas.

Capitalist society has deformed the concept of what a people's hero is. Today we often find the "ballers" or those who hurt or oppress the people to be the most idolized. This is because many concepts are affected by living in a capitalist society. Even the idea of work has a whole different meaning today than it would under a socialist society. Today work in the imperialist countries means to get rich or earn money to accumulate "stuff" i.e. consumerism and "living large." All this is a perverted thought process that only creates an environment where nothing is good enough, producing a compulsion for accumulation.

Socialism is an economic system, enforced by a state, where the needs of the people are put at the forefront. Guarantees such as housing, work, land, food, and health care are universal. Society does not operate on who "comes up" more or the easiest, but rather a new ethos, a new culture where society looks to people who serve the people the most as the heroes. Socialism will help repair our communities and our ideas of what is really important in life and bring equality to our society.

The liberation of Aztlán under a socialist state would not just be an advance for the Chican@ nation, but for all Raza, as well as all oppressed nations in the United $tates and worldwide. Emancipating Aztlán should be the priority of all Raza in the United $tates. This objective, once ful-filled, would serve as a liberated zone for all Raza as well as a beacon for other oppressed nations. The creation of a socialist republic of Aztlán will advance the international communist movement by not only serving as a base but working as the vanguard in support of all national liberation struggles globally with our final aim of world communism. A socialist Aztlán will serve as a fountainhead of Pan-Latino unity.

Raza in the United $tates would be welcome in socialist Aztlán. Raza whose homeland was still under imperial control would be encour-aged and assisted to build a cadre to eventually liberate their homeland, wherever it is. In this way, the people's government of Aztlán would serve as a launching pad for revolutionaries of all oppressed nations to liberate their people. Thus it would be in the interest of all Raza to struggle for a liberated Aztlán. First Nations and other oppressed peoples should stand in solidarity with the Aztlán liberation movement as we stand with you.

Incorrect Lines Toward Aztlán

Although the gist of this essay highlights the principal contradiction facing the Chican@ nation, i.e. Aztlán vs. U.$. imperialism, there also ex-ist secondary contradictions within the nation that must be identified if we are ever to resolve them. Mao spoke of knowing who are our friends and who are our enemies. This not only means our principal enemy (U.$. imperialism) but even within the nation there will be those who practice enemy politics. Understanding this will be essential to the future of Aztlán. Even within the future vanguard party there will be struggle determining whether the revolution continues or whether we stagnate on the capitalist road. On these shores, the united front will take on a flavor distinct from historical examples in the Third World. To build this united front we must understand the peculiarities of our situation.

Amongst Chican@s many are seeking to free our people from the chains of capitalist-imperialism. But only a true revolutionary path will take us to this course. In the realm of theory there are many ideas, and as eccentric or frustrating as these lines may be it is important that Chican@s who are serious revolutionaries read up on these different lines and dis-cuss them with others. Grapple with them to see for yourself what is the most likely vehicle to push the movimiento forward to victory. There are probably too many different lines to list here so we will only discuss a few in this writing. In Parts II and III of this book we will look at specific examples of the different lines and what makes them useful or not.

One line put forward is that of **communalism**, which negates the importance of a party and even a state, whether socialist or otherwise. Communalists seek to restore Aztlán into a tribal society operating on a council of elders and communal way of life. Imperialism would never allow us to live harmoniously in a big commune. This ideology does not even believe in a standing army, so how would we protect a communal Aztlán? The Paris Commune is the best example of what can go wrong without a dictatorship of the proletariat. This line is idealist at best. The people will never achieve liberation using this line. It would not just waste the people's time, it would also do a lot of harm to the people in the process.

Many others put forward a **reformist bourgeois nationalist** way of struggle. Adherents of reforming the United $tates seek out what they call a "silent revolution" where somehow Chican@s will slowly grow in political power in the United $tates and work as a Trojan horse to Amerikan democracy. These people believe Aztlán can eventually be seized through a slow non-violent revolution. We can just look at what happens when Chican@s are even given high-paying union jobs; most pack up and leave the barrio for the mostly white suburbs never to be seen again. They can get a ten or twenty dollar raise and forget they even knew you, so what would happen if they got high power jobs within the Amerikan superstructure? Even if these sellouts' morality were improved prior to integration, U.$. imperialism would not allow anyone to come in and legally change things to significantly benefit the oppressed and exploited of the world.

Some point to a **multinational party**. The argument here is that we all got Lenin wrong and that there really aren't any nations in the United $tates besides maybe the New Afrikan nation. Even then, the existence of the New Afrikan nation does not give automatic grounds for secession into an independent nation-state. The revisionists of Marxism claim Chican@s or First Nations are merely oppressed minorities or nationalities, but not nations in themselves (see our response to the Revolutionary

Communist Party in Part II Section 5). These crypto-Trotskyists claim to have the oppressed nations in mind when they really wish to keep oppressed nations in a subservient state, even after a transition to socialism. They claim there is no need for the Chican@ nation to organize on its own because when their multinational party gains power Chican@s will be liberated and assimilated into the "new" Amerika built on socialism. This is a controversial question today in the United $tates. Some say the population of the United $tates is assimilated and thus there is no more need to build a single nation party. But as we have already demonstrated in previous sections, the Chican@ nation exists as an oppressed internal semi-colony, and we recognize that it has the right to self-determination. History has demonstrated that this battle is best undertaken with single nation parties.

There are multinational parties that should be supported such as those who promote self-determination for the internal semi-colonies up to and including the right to secede. But let's be clear, such parties are rare. The Maoist Internationalist Movement (MIM) was one such party, but it dissolved into separate cells in the mid-2000s. The problem and main obstacle in building a multinational party today lies in the obstacle that has remained firmly in place since the first settler stepped foot on the continent: white chauvinism. Oppressed nation people attempting to join a multinational party face this contradiction just like in joining white labor unions. Sakai gets at this when s/he states:

> "The organization of nationally oppressed workers into or allied with the trade-unions of the settler masses was only an effort to control and divide us."[4]

This method of undermining the nationally oppressed workers is used not just in the trade unions but in the political parties as well, where the oppressed can be better corralled into following the often white nation leadership while the interests of the oppressed nations are conveniently set aside. The crypto-Trotskyists maintain a thin veil of inclusion but when we get down to fundamental questions surrounding the internal semi-colonies, such as the liberation of Aztlán, the New Afrikan nation's right to secede, the First Nations' rights to control their resources, and Boriqua's right to be free from neo-colonialism, we get the same excuses and revisionist responses that ultimately uphold our oppression. These erroneous tendencies derive from a long lineage of white chauvinism that has calcified in the line of the old parties. Their reliance on the labor aristocracy is really a reliance on white nation labor which controls the labor unions in the United $tates. And this labor is not a proletarian force but rather a petty bourgeoisie. Thus it is no surprise when we hear the Trotskyists of all stripes deny a labor aristocracy exists, claiming that all those wealthy petty bourgeois workers are actually proletarian.

In some countries multinational parties are essential. As one comrade put it:

> "Those who cut down multinational organizing cut down the Chinese, Vietnamese, Eritrean, Tigrayan, Peruvian and Russian revolutions of this century. In other revolutions there was a single-nationality composed of various 'races,' as in the case of Cuba. Hence to oppose multinational organizing in all circumstances is to oppose communism. To oppose communism is to oppose all the genuine nationalism of the oppressed nations..."[5]

So there are circumstances where multinational parties are a positive thing. The challenge for this in the United $tates is that white supremacy is so deeply embedded in this society that it has saturated everyone's minds and created deep-seated divisions which were not felt in Third World countries. The reactionary nature of the white nation can be traced to earlier settlers who created the concept of "race" to justify their oppression of non-white peoples worldwide. They needed to keep the exploited peoples in their place by creating the idea that there are different races of humyns, some superior and some inferior. This idea of race has been a central ideology to support Amerikan imperialism to this day, even when wrapped in talk of "post-racialism." Racism also helped combat class contradictions that were developing between poor whites and the white bourgeoisie, so that poor whites were treated a bit better and were a peg higher than the oppressed nations. As whites embraced this role, nation became the principal contradiction early in the development of Amerikan society; a prelude to what was to come on a global scale.

With this privilege in a predominately white Amerika, a white leadership in a multinational party leaves little chance for a righteous revolutionary line. Our current society severely hinders this process from developing. It's not impossible, but certainly unlikely at this time and current concrete social conditions.

The oppressor nation continues to hunt down brown youth sending our people off to the morgue or prison, and our neighborhoods are still being flooded with drugs and liquor stores. Terrorizing our community, the oppressor has surely not assimilated our people, as our barrios continue to take a barrage of abuses and repression. The lynchings have simply turned to legal lynchings, such as life in prison, the death penalty, or murder by police.

It's important to remain open-minded to the changing conditions in society in order to determine the best way forward. It is up to the Chican@ nation whether Aztlán is liberated or not. This is not saying a united front is not necessary in the United $tates but ultimately it will be up to Chican@s to free our people.

While the bourgeois nationalists discussed above tend to be integrationist in nature, bourgeois ideas can also come in a more radical package in the form of **narrow nationalism**. Such groups might be appealing to more alienated youth who readily reject the multinational formation. Narrow nationalism often takes the form of **cultural nationalism**, which promotes a cultural form without any revolutionary content to address the economic substructure. Chican@ cultural nationalists focus on learning to speak Nahuatl rather than studying revolutionary theory. They will attend an event for Aztec dance rather than a protest against imperialism. But while there is certainly a lot to learn from the past, and a rich culture to derive a collective pride from, these things do not get us any closer to an independent and free Aztlán.

The cultural nationalists say that they are the authorities on how we should struggle to attain a better future because they are well-versed in the ways of the Mexica. They also say that the revolutionary nationalist doesn't know what s/he is talking about because we supposedly take our cues from a white man's ideology.

While most cultural nationalists are well intentioned, cultural nationalists have never liberated any nation from imperialism. Rejuvenating our heritage may inspire some to go further and take up revolutionary nationalism, but ultimately it leaves the imperialist state unchallenged and intact.

Narrow nationalism also emulates bourgeois politics in the form of Chican@ capitalism. The promoters of Chican@ capitalism are interested in having a Chican@ nation whose relations of production mirror that of the United $tates, only with Chican@s in power. These narrow nationalists tell Raza to "buy brown," that is spend their dollars in brown business thus "uplifting" la Raza economically. The ultimate goal for these narrow nationalists is brown capitalism. To them an exploiting class is okay so long as it's a brown exploiting class. This strategy omits internationalism and sells out the exploited people of the Third World.

Our cultural history is important but at some point we need to look past simply reading about pyramids or drawing the Aztec calendar and really study up on what will enable us to free our nation today. Learn about other oppressed nations that rose up in past revolutions fighting either imperialism or imperialist-backed regimes. How did socialism help advance society? How did the health care improve? Did literacy improve? How were things changed like food, housing, land or wimmin's rights? These are all things we need to look into to find out which nations improved society the most so that we can understand how we will rebuild Aztlán. Narrow nationalism many times becomes reactionary as it begins to turn on the Chican@ struggle and poison the people. We should always be wary of cultural nationalism in its many forms. These cultural nationalists blame "the gringo" for our oppression without looking into the capitalist-imperialist system that utilizes "the gringo" ruling class to enforce the oppression we suffer.

Some claim to be revolutionaries or even communists but instead exercise **Chican@ chauvinism**. In their eyes if Raza are not Chican@ or Mexican@ they are not worthy of being a Chican@ or part of the struggle for the Chican@ nation. This backwards thinking will never lead to real freedom for a people. If anything it slows down our ability to really free the people and upholds imperialism's lock on our oppression.

Revolutionary Nationalism

The idea of nationalism conjures up controversial images depending on what circles you frequent. For some, nationalism seems harmful and for others it is a positive phenomenon. Some even have different lines differentiating the "good nationalism" and "bad nationalism." As materialists, we don't choose ideologies based what we feel is good or what you feel is bad. We need to analyze circumstances based on how they really are, and determine what is correct.

As opposed to cultural nationalism or bourgeois nationalism, revolutionary nationalism is an unequivocally progressive ideology. Many people who have not really studied up often confuse these forms of nationalism or simply lump them together and paint them all as wrong. This is one of the major faults of present-day anarchism. Mao spoke on national liberation struggles and how this is the only way to achieve socialist revolution under imperialism, and he proved it in practice.[6]

All matter exists in motion, and without this constant motion which gives impetus to change, all things must come to an end. The end of a thing is the beginning of something new and an expression of perpetual motion. Therefore if the national movement isn't moving forward it will retrogress, stagnate and die.

As revolutionary nationalists our long-term goal is communism, but we know this will take many many years and can only occur on a world scale. Socialism however is our transition period where we will build world citizens, create a true proletarian morality and heal the people from centuries of oppression caused by capitalism and its effects. We understand that a communist world will not come about all at once. As oppressed nations break the chains of imperialism and become socialist, our international goal becomes closer to reality. Chican@s will do our part by freeing our nation, thus applying internationalism to our own liberation struggle.

Communists understand that a revolution's core essence includes self-determination: the right of nations to choose their future. Here in the United $tates there are many factors that are unique, like the many different peoples living together, the popularity of multiculturalism, the specificities of the oppressed internal semi-colonies, etc. Some will question whether secession of a single nation-state is really necessary or possible. This is a good question.

When socialism reaches the United $tates, it will become immediately imperative that the revolutionary vanguard of the various internal semi-colonies seize power. If the cultural nationalists or bourgeois nationalists step up to lead, it will only lead to our destruction. Revolutionary nationalists are struggling for a socialist state for their people, to organize society along socialist principles. Revolutionary nationalists want to improve the conditions for people in Aztlán and the entire world, not brown capitalist exploitation. This is why it is so important for Chican@ revolutionaries today to raise public opinion in the brown community to educate Raza on the correct path.

The awakening of Raza, especially due to Amerikan repression and ICE raids, is ironically helping us to raise consciousness. It is accelerating this process and bringing more Chican@s to our side and proving the so-called Amerikan dream has always been a nightmare.

Today the most important contradiction is between imperialism and oppressed nations. There are of course other contradictions but the main thing holding back the oppressed from being free from oppression is imperialism. In "On Contradiction," Mao discussed the temporary alliances between various classes in the course of a revolutionary struggle. Here in the United $tates we can temporarily ally with different classes and other oppressed nations in a united front in order to struggle against imperialism.

We disagree with post-modernist thinking which tells us that we can live a culturally correct existence while imperialism remains intact. We know putting some Raza in government positions or making more money does not lead to Chican@ self-determination. Self-determination requires first liberating the oppressed nations from imperialism. Even then, the revolutionary nationalist vanguards in control of the new state cannot stop our assault on imperialism or the capitalist class solely because the state apparatus is now in our hands. Instead we must unleash the power of the masses and organize our people for the redevelopment of the nation by revolutionizing the economic substructure to meet the basic needs of the people. This focus on people first and not culture allows for the nation to gain not only independence in the economic field, but in the political one as well. This translates into the people finally holding power and this is what revolutionary nationalists are ultimately aiming for.

It's important to note that although revolutionary nationalism is a positive step forward for oppressed nations in the United $tates, nationalism of any sort coming from the oppressor nation is a negative thing. Regardless if the Euro-Amerikan claims to be a revolutionary or even communist, nationalism practiced by them would only be upholding the centuries-long oppressive system that is Amerika's legacy. Thus Euro-Amerikans should work to combat all forms of white nationalism. True Euro-Amerikan radicals, progressives, revolutionaries or communists will see revolutionary nationalists of Chican@ or other oppressed nations as progressive and work to support or help build these movements as it will benefit the struggle more broadly for a better world free of oppression.

The first step in bringing revolutionary nationalism to the Chican@ nation is rupturing the colonial mentality that has calcified in the minds of many. This slave mentality has Raza blaming themselves for their circumstances. Of course we all must have persynal accountability for our actions (such as choosing to work for liberation or not), but if one believes they themselves are responsible for things that are actually products of imperialism, then one will begin to hate oneself, turning to drugs and escapism. Oppressor Amerika wants us to check out so we don't threaten their global hegemony.

Cell Structure, Barrio Committees, and the need for a Vanguard Party

The Chican@ nation should begin to build off of the socialist advancements of past national liberation movements and educate our people and prepare our barrios for future insurrection. We can apply the cell concept to every block, every barrio, city, county, and state. Let us revolutionize Aztlán and do the work no one else has or will. The future of our nation lies in our determination for freedom, and for New Democracy. Look to what worked to emancipate other nations and learn to modify and apply these lessons to our own circumstances. Theory is not dogma; it is to be built on and developed. If we are serious about revolution we should be developing our political line around Aztlán, and we should be starting study groups to teach others and learn from each other on the revolutionary path forward.

We are beginning to really learn about our gente's history and the long path that has been cut by our many predecessors. We begin to see the way forward to liberating Aztlán, and taking our place in helping push the world's societies to free themselves from oppression. As we develop ourselves and our nations politically, we will come to a point when a political party is necessary and essential to reaching our objective of full emancipation from the vile system of capitalist-imperialism. A party is an organization that is poised to take state power.

At this time in the imperialist countries, our movement is relatively weak, and thus the organization of a centralized party poses significant security risks. To step around these security risks, one form of organizing that is becoming more and more popular in the United $tates is the cell structure. The cell structure is a locality-based (or internet-based) political organization, that operates under democratic centralism. Under democratic centralism there is full discussion and openness of political line and operational disagreements within the group. But to the public, the cell practices centralism, with everyone upholding the democratic decisions of the group even if they don't persynally agree. Debate can continue behind closed doors, and the line/strategy/tactics of the group can change. But these changes should only be made public after internal debate and democratic vote. We know the state wants to destroy our movement; practicing democratic centralism within a cell structure makes it as difficult for them as possible. It protects against COINTELPRO-type attacks where the state exploits ideological divisions amongst the membership of an organization.

We will be most effective when working with brown lumpen if we begin with cell organizing. Although not a political party, the cell can function as a center which exerts influence or even orders to the wider movement. A good contemporary example of this is the dissolution of the Maoist Internationalist Movement into various locality-based cells. MIM was an influential centralized party, and in the mid-2000s faced security attacks. In order to combat these security attacks, MIM dissolved into cells. One such cell is the Maoist Internationalist Ministry of Prisons, or MIM(Prisons) for short. MIM(Prisons) focuses on organizing prisoners in the United $tates, and leads the United Struggle from Within (USW), a mass organization for prisoners and former prisoners. MIM(Prisons) is a semi-underground cell which operates under democratic centralism, and provides ideological leadership for the broader Maoist movement via their newsletter *Under Lock & Key* and website prisoncensorship.info.

Chican@ organizations can take lessons from MIM, MIM(Prisons), and USW in establishing organizations and political influence in the barrios. Until conditions change to require a party to step up to seize state power, Chican@s should organize and educate cadre under the cell structure. The main reason for the Chican@ nation vanguard to organize within the smaller cell structure as opposed to the traditional vanguard party is the security advantages that are afforded to the cadre and wider movement as a whole. As the Maoist Internationalist Movement explained in their resolution "Instructions On Forming Cells" at their 2005 Congress, "We oppose having geographic cells coming into contact with each other face-to-face. Infiltration and spying are rampant when it comes to MIM. The whole strength of having a locality based cell is that it's possible to do all the things traditional to a movement. The security advantages of culling people we know into a cell are lost the moment we slack off on security and start accepting strangers or meeting with strangers face-to-face."

The main purpose of forming cells is strictly for security and it does no good to have cells form for security reasons only to have them exposed to danger by meeting with strangers. Though MIM also specifically stated in their instructions on forming cells that, "people you know well are good material for a locally based cell," it should be stressed that we can never know anyone "well" when carrying out revolutionary work. When deciding with whom to form cells we shouldn't only concern ourselves with how well we know someone; rather the key thing to pay attention to is a persyn's level of commitment and political line. Our cadre cells should double as ideological centers for the Chican@ movement, which should likewise be based on the type and amount of work done. Prisoners can also use a similar guideline as each prison is merely a cinderblock barrio.

Barrio Committees (BCs) should also be organized in each neighborhood. A BC can be thought of as locality-based mass organizations which serves as a medium between the Maoist movement and the gente. BCs are above-ground organizations that lead serve-the-people programs and build institutions of the oppressed, promoting revolutionary culture and activism. The BC should consist of the most politically advanced of each barrio or lumpen organization, who will work in coordination with other committees on humyn rights issues, progressive issues, protests or events. Members of the BC serve as popular representatives of their barrio or group and should not overlap with members of the cadre cell. The BC should educate the barrio, and build independent institutions of the oppressed such as newspapers, websites, schools, and other projects to serve the people and mobilize our communities. Cultural leaders in the BC will organize dances, mural projects, productions of theater, song, rap, and spoken word. BCs will organize educational projects, teaching gente how to read and write, and studying revolutionary theory and political thought. BCs will host free labor days, where the people come together to clean up the barrio's parks and rivers, remodel run down homes, provide landscaping for elders, and other free services.

It is especially important for lumpen to be organized into the BCs, so that the divisions that have been wrought between the lumpen and the other classes in the barrios can begin to heal, and we can start to see each other as one community. Participating in and hosting serve-the-people programs will help build a group mentality and trust amongst the gente. Most importantly the barrio lumpen will begin to transform and become productive members of the Chican@ nation. This type of solidarity educates the people, and getting our people familiar with this type of activity is far more important than the actual act itself.

Eventually we want to have complete control of our barrios, and ultimately all of Aztlán. That day is not today, however, so we want to introduce the idea of an alternative authority on a small scale at this point. Eventually we will reach a point where committees solve problems and disputes between the people. We don't need the pigs to come into the barrios to fake like they're going to help us solve a problem. This is a task we can do ourselves, but it needs to begin with trust. For far too long many in our communities have been oppressed by the state as well as mistreated by some lumpen elements. Serving the people through organizing BCs will help rebuild the barrios physically, and more importantly mentally.

This method of structure and operation can also be likened to the committee system within a revolutionary collective in which the higher levels of the organization (cadre cells), guide and oversee the lower levels of the organization (BCs). However, it's important to note that those within the cells should not openly form or be part of the Barrio Committees as this would surely open them up to attack due to the fact that Barrio Committees will be a public presence.

Another type of cell useful to us within our conditions in the First World, both for its security advantages and its stress on pushing the correct political line via scientific reasoning, is the internet-based cell. Though MIM wondered out loud the extent to which internet cells can challenge people to higher levels of commitment without meeting face-to-face, we suspect that internet-based cells can be successful. MIM's and MIM(Prisons)'s prisoner correspondence courses and USW cells function similar to the internet-based cell and are currently meeting higher levels of political commitment and activism, all without meeting face-to-face.

Through these study groups, many prisoners develop behind bars and begin their political activism, only to be released to a mundane lumpen or petty bourgeois existence. Many hard line prisoners give up political work altogether once they hit the streets. Instead these releasees, like the lumpen on the streets, should be organized into the BCs, thus replenishing their barrio with fresh energy.

All the while that this takes place more cells are developing all over Aztlán which continue to raise consciousness, developing programs for the committees, educating, creating revolutionary Chican@ newspapers, journals, and forms of art. This is all preparing the Raza and our barrios for conditions that will call for an actual vanguard party. This process will have to start slow, maybe even one barrio at a time. One barrio may serve as a model for others to develop on and fan out. Once we have built public opinion in the Chican@ nation, and built a strong base and laid the foundation for people's power, and the majority of the Chican@ nation supports the struggle, only then can a strong vanguard party lead us to emancipate Chican@s from the United $tates, and end oppression of our people. Only then will we experience humyn rights and equality.

We have seen what can happen when an uprising has no vanguard party leading it, as with the Paris Commune or more recently with the Arab Spring. If the Chican@ nation is to truly make that leap to winning national liberation it will only come with the creation of a vanguard party to lead the brown masses. Our goal today is to transform social reality and shape conditions to where a vanguard party can not only survive, but thrive! This will be done through hard work and building public opinion in the brown communities. The rupture with the internal colonial apparatus will only come with the creation of a nucleus of Chican@ professional revolutionaries, called cadre. Nothing short of this will ever be fully successful.

A vanguard party is not simply the most conscious political party. It has very real responsibilities to the people. It is up to the vanguard party to constantly undertake class analysis of society, keeping a finger on the pulse of the people. The vanguard party must fully understand the contradictions it is affecting, who the main enemy is, the primary contradiction in any area, and in this way maintain momentum, guide the movement and properly support and lead all aspects of political work.

Our vanguard party will be allied with other Maoists within the United $tates and around the world, with the ultimate aim of advancing the international communist movement and smashing imperialism in all its forms. This alliance will manifest in a united front with all who oppose imperialism, which will be needed to uproot imperialism and its oppression that has plagued Third World peoples for far too long.

National liberation struggles here in the United $tates will be crucial in determining the transition to socialism in North America. Being situated in territory claimed by the United $tates, it will not be possible to liberate Aztlán until the Amerikans have been weakened by the liberation from U.$. imperialism of nations across the globe.

As revolutionary nationalists we should not only build our nation, but we must also be in solidarity with all national liberation struggles of other internal colonies on these shores. It is with these nations that we will need to work in alliance during the transition to socialism. And we must be in solidarity with national liberation struggles across the Third World, which will create the conditions that allow for the overthrow of imperialism here in the United $tates. This united front will respect the independence of each nation and this unity will also help mobilize and arouse the broader masses in the United $tates and internationally.[7]

As we become more politically conscious, and as we become social scientists and communists, we begin to understand the importance of theory and advancing on the best current political line. More importantly, at some point we will understand that practice is the only way to really validate theory. This practice must be on a large scale or in society at large, not just amongst a single lumpen organization or committee of folks setting out to prove their theory. Just as in a scientific experiment you cannot base your findings on what you or a couple of other scientists have done, it often takes years or hundreds of tests to come to a healthy conclusion. In this way our practice will come out of applying our theory out in society at large. Barrio Committees, cells, and vanguard parties all must learn from the actual results of the actual practice of actual groups of people.

Section 4:
Questions of Organizing

The First Nations and Aztlán

ONE CANNOT ADDRESS THE CHICAN@ nation without also addressing the First Nations. Many different natives continue to live within Aztlán yet the First Nation peoples have suffered heavy losses in their struggles against the oppressor, Amerika. Since 1492 the First Nations have struggled against imperialist occupation and genocide, and they continue to struggle today. Of the 300+ native languages once spoken in North America only about half exist today, and 55 are spoken by only one to six people. Only 20 of these languages are spoken widely by children. Today there are around 50 tribes, bands, nations, or communities of natives in Aztlán. All Chican@s should keep this in mind when grappling with the Chican@ national-colonial question today.

The first inhabitants of what is now the Chican@ homeland entered this area around 50,000 years ago. Although every year new evidence arises that points to different dates and data, it is most probable that these first inhabitants crossed from Asia into North America subsisting using hunter/gatherer methods.

We know from archeology that maize was first cultivated in present-day Mexico about 7000 years ago. Maize ensured that societies could rise and prosper anchored in an agricultural base. Food staples, like culture, were known to travel through the Americas in a network of trade routes.

One of the major developments was of the Anasazi culture of the "Southwest" around 200 AD. The Anasazi reached their peak in development between 1000 AD and 1300 AD. The abandonment of their cultural centers like Chaco Canyon happened around 1300 AD without explanation or record. The Anasazi became commonly known as the "Pueblo Indians" because of the way they built their villages.

The Anasazi domesticated dogs and turkeys. They lived mostly as an agricultural society growing maize, beans and squash, building irrigation systems. They would go on to organize the great Pueblo Revolt of 1580 which drove the Spanish out of New Mexico. Many believe the Anasazis to have been the original Mexica Aztec people who migrated south around this period.

There are many other First Nations in the United $tates today: the Apaches, Utes, Navajo, Comanches, Shoshone, and more. Many First Nations people were sent to reservations where conditions are worse than any barrio or ghetto project. Many reservations still have no electricity, and people live without running water in shacks with dirt floors. A notable example is the Pine Ridge reservation in South Dakota. Unemployment is almost 100% on these reservations yet it is flooded with alcohol. This oppression causes many First Nation people to leave the reservation and sell their labor in urban centers.

Chican@ communists should work to unite with First Nation peoples in a united front in opposition to U.$. imperialism to establish a joint dictatorship of the proletariat of the oppressed nations over Amerika.[1] Only then will we liberate the Chican@ nation and the First Nations. The First Nations will contribute in our struggle against the oppressor nation, against our common oppressor. At the time of liberation the First Nations will finally be free from U.$. imperialism, and the Chican@ nation, along with the First Nations and other liberated oppressed nations, will finally be able to mutually assist each other to build our respective nations.

We cannot discuss the Chican@ nation without the First Nations in mind. True justice will only come with the liberation of the First Nation peoples. Aztlán will have to ensure First Nations' land is respected and liberated for indigenous peoples.

Chicanas: Wimmin Hold up Half the Sky

Among the Chican@ struggle exist fierce wimmin standing side-by-side with men, and struggling harder both for and within the movement exactly because of their double oppression. They've struggled against imperialism as Chicanas, as well as struggled against the patriarchy as it manifests within the movement itself.

Patriarchy developed all over the world at different rates, and in different forms, but it was always tied to the emergence of private property and class divisions. Prior to the emergence of patriarchy, parents did not form monogamous pairs, and familial lines were traced via the mother. The accumulation of surplus eventually allowed for private property to develop, and because of the division of labor at the time, biological men became the owners of private property, which led to their rise to dominance.[2] In this context, patriarchy was used in the Americas as a way to oppress and control the colonized. As the economy quickly transformed, the material basis for these ideas solidified and the peoples of the Americas began to take on patriarchal forms of organization based around the male-dominated monogamous family unit.

In response to this gender oppression, many wimmin supported the wimmin's liberation movement that was resurfacing all over the world in the 1960s and 70s. In the United $tates, however, like the efforts of white nation labor, this movement only served to corral the oppressed under white nation leadership. Under Amerikan leadership, this movement proceeded as if all wimmin were white and petty bourgeois, alienating oppressed nation wimmin from their national struggle (which was male-dominated and often misogynistic).

Struggles are many-faceted phenomenons in which two opposing forces battle for supremacy. Within the Chican@ nation this struggle begins in the family unit, which is but a model structure of patriarchal property relations which aim to keep wimmin in a subservient position within the male dominated home. However, Chicanas have proven time and time again that they are not just an equal force within the movement, but have continuously striven and transformed the old stereotype of the super-macho Latino male who expects his wimmin to be confined to the kitchen, barefoot and pregnant.

If we look at today's many protests and struggles, we will see Chicanas in strong presence at many events: in student protests, police brutality marches, everywhere. No longer is the womyn expected to be a homemaker. Strong brown wimmin broke this myth long ago. Chicanas are front and center, leading the nation in all we do. Men and wimmin stand shoulder-to-shoulder fighting, amongst other things, exploitation of wimmin in any form. The Chican@ nation must work to ensure Chicanas are leaders as we liberate Aztlán.

Patriarchy and the sexual exploitation of wimmin is not something that only affects Raza; all people experience this today and it is primarily a result of living in a capitalist society. Capitalism promotes this inequality and oppression. What we see in many sexist behaviors today is really a sickness of being born and raised in a capitalist way of life, a system where everything is for sale and promoted eagerly by the highest levels of power in the United $tates. Pornography and the hyper-sexualization of wimmin, even young children, is a sickness that is encouraged on all levels. We can open up any fashion magazine and see this quite clearly. Television and art are no different. Amerikan culture is saturated in these images and it upholds the ruling class and their ideology. In this way the ruling class shapes the ideas of the population and this influences the general social relations in the United $tates.

While we will look at some contemporary Chicana analysis of gender in our reviews in Part III, Chicana revolutionaries today draw from a long line of revolutionary fighters. We had leaders like Luisa Moreno in the 1920s and 30s, and Elizabeth "Betita" Martinez in the 1950s and 60s. The 1970s saw Dolores Huerta struggling for Raza in the fields, leading strikes and facing beatings and arrest. She continues to support the dignity of Chican@s. The 70s also brought out Olga Talamante who was a fierce Chicana fighter and revolutionary. She went to Argentina and was arrested as a "subversive," for which she was imprisoned and tortured. This ignited mass support in the Chican@ nation, and this activism got her released.

In 1981, the Chican@ nation lost Magdalena Mora to cancer. Mora was a teacher and journalist who led many factory worker strikes and organized Chican@s in many struggles. Mora was a tireless fighter for our nation who was a leader for us all to remember and draw from.

In 1982, we lost another Chicana who led many events and strikes. Victoria Mercado was a Chicana communist who organized oppressed nation workers, and was Angela Davis's bodyguard and housemate. She worked to unite oppressed nations in many struggles. Many believe she was assassinated for her work in the internal colonies. She serves as an example of what it means to dedicate one's life to a better tomorrow and lives on through us all.[3]

Wimmin hold up half the sky!

The Role of Chicanismo

We still need our collective ideology of Chicanismo, although today's Chicanismo must go deeper and further than the Chicanismo of the past. Chicanismo today must have a more revolutionary impulse than of previous generations if we are to truly rupture with any bourgeois residue of yesterday. In this aspect we must apply historical materialism to our understanding of Chicanismo and Aztlán and grasp that even these terms are not static nor exempt from the Marxist laws of materialism. It is counterintuitive for today's Chican@ to narrowly define *Chicanismo* or *Aztlán* as nothing more than grating "mythology" for Chican@s. As social scientists – as all revolutionaries are – we should come to see that *Chicanismo* and *Aztlán* have a connotative meaning that should not be lost in the conversation.

Today's Chicanismo will be stripped of sexism or homophobia of the past because it is communist-led. We still embrace our indigeneity and cultura, but we also know that only a vanguard party will allow us to liberate the land. With today's Chicanismo, patriarchy has been kicked to the curb as an erroneous relic of the past. Only in this way can we take the Chican@ struggle to the next level of development. Chicana feminism today must also be more revolutionary in order to galvanize and strengthen our capacity to push the nation forward. In this aspect we must employ a Maoist approach and mobilize our entire population on a more revolutionary course.

Chican@ Power is not simply about Chican@s being in charge of our own nation. We don't want brown capitalism, nor a Chican@ Kuomintang.[4] Chicano@ Power will be realized when we have self-determination all the way up to secession from the United $tates; when we are free to exercise socio-political and economic power, where socialist relations of production replace capitalism without the influence of U.$. imperialism. Our power can *only* be exercised in this way.

Today's Chicanismo is not on some "hate whitey" trip. We understand our oppression is bound to class contradictions so we guard against this ultra-left deviation. Chicanismo must utilize revolutionary culture and a proletarian morality if we are to be successful in la lucha of today and tomorrow.

Pandillas: Our Red Guards

The discussion has come up more and more about pandillas ("gangs") in the United $tates and of the potential of such groups today. If you look in most dictionaries the definition of gang can be summarized as "a group of criminals." We should understand this is the perspective of imperialists who control not just the capitalist relations of production but also the political ideology of Amerikan society. This control or dictatorship of capital manifests itself in all levels of society with the objective of promoting its program of oppression. This is also expressed in its language which permeates the thoughts and beliefs of the people and shapes their ideas and their material reality.

This label is meant to keep our youth in a constant state of oppression, not only from the state (i.e. the pigs, courts, prisons, etc.), but also to divide the people in the barrio. The state defining our youth as gang members creates a division of the people and cultivates an "us vs. them" mentality. These antagonisms help strengthen the imperialists' agenda by creating a snitch network, or in some cases getting the hatred to build in a village to the point where some physically fight on Amerika's side against their own nation. A people will begin to believe these false labels and not only separate themselves from these labeled people but in some cases help destroy them.

Pandillas as defined in most dictionaries do exist, but we argue it is not the proper word that should be used to define most oppressed nation groups. Those Amerika has labeled as gangs are of the lumpen class in general, specifically of the oppressed nations. Our lumpen youth who happen to hang out together in a barrio park to play ball, cruise around on a Saturday night, or simply stand outside their parents' house with friends, are labeled gang members by police and the state. Barrios can produce lumpen organizations (LOs) as well as loose lumpen social clubs. The lumpen organizations are the more permanent groups in an area which, in many cases, have been there for many years or decades. The looser lumpen social clubs are not as put together, usually without formal hierarchy, and are more temporary (i.e. casual acquaintances, graffiti groups, etc.).

These social developments are not strictly confined to Raza or other oppressed nations. Within white suburban schools or neighborhoods you'll find the stoners, skaters, anarchists, jocks, nerds, skinheads, vegans,

etc., who hang out at school, after school, in specific parks, coffee shops, parking lots, homes, etc. Most imperialists and their agencies are gangs; they are and have always been a group of criminals against the oppressed nations. Police precincts developed as legalized white vigilante groups. More recently, prison guards in California prisons have labeled themselves as gangs acting outside U.$. laws (Green Wall, White Lightening, etc.). The vast majority of oppressor nation LOs are racist and reactionary (i.e. Aryan Brotherhood, Skinheads, etc.). The difference is oppressed nation lumpen are a potential revolutionary force, while Euro-Amerikans have a white privilege, and alliance, that keeps the state from targeting their social groups for repression. Euro-Amerikan youth do have the most potential for radicalization within the oppressor nation. But without committing nation suicide and working against Amerikkka, they do not pose a threat to the status quo.

Amerika labeling our youth as pandillas has more to do with expanding their dictatorship of our people in the mental realm, than actually defining the phenomenon of organized lumpen self-protection. Stalin has written on the topic of linguistics,[5] and Mao described this position on the relationship between language and thought as "the accepted theory of linguistics in the People's Republic of China."[6] Language not only helps revolutionaries advance the consciousness of the people, it can also help support the ruling class and their program. In contrast to the gang label, we refer to organizations of our oppressed nation lumpen as lumpen organizations (LOs). This term encompasses all street organizations, those organizing for revolution or robbery, because we know that imperialism defines the crimes, and then pushes the oppressed nations into committing the crimes.

The best way to deal with how the state has labeled LOs as gangs is to stop calling LOs gangs. This label carries negative connotations and does not serve the lumpen. We need to get our barrios used to the idea of seeing pandillas as LOs, and work to remove this negative portrayal of our youth survival groups. These youth are being hunted by the imperialists' first line of defense, without the ability to find work because of prior arrest history, appearance or lack of experience. These youth often end up hustling and living off the shadow economy. Yet lumpen remain as rebels who despise the state apparatus and challenge the state in many ways.

The lumpen, like the broader Chican@ population and its future expansion, can either help or hinder the movement. They already have nothing to lose, and are well armed. If revolutionized, the lumpen can serve as the fiercest fighters for future revolution. Currently, most lumpen are indoctrinated with the capitalist values of individualism and material wealth. We need to tap into this potential revolutionary reserve, lest they become reactionary forces for the oppressor.

The transformation of lumpen culture can only really be effective if it is transformed from within while aided by revolutionaries. Within the LOs lies a nucleus which most of the LO membership emulate and listen to. Most of these inner cores of LOs reside in U.$. prisons after a life of lumpen activity (which Amerika defines as crime). Thus it is within U.$. prisons where the real key lies in transforming lumpen culture. If revolutionaries ever seek to transform LOs it must be done through prisons, as this is where the most political influence can be found and so it's the fastest path to achieve this change.

Today more and more prisoners are becoming conscious. This was seen in the recent hunger strikes in U.$. prisons in 2011 and 2013, which attracted tens of thousands of prisoners to participate. This new wave of conscious prisoners is due to decades of daily hard work from prisoners to politicize these places from the inside out, along with revolutionary groups and parties flooding prisons with literature and books that give the imprisoned revolutionaries tools to educate the prison population.

We are just now beginning to see the fruit of this decades-long work. And thus the LOs in prisons are slowly beginning to change their culture and this is showing in different ways. Before long this transformation will begin to spread out to the barrios.

The areas where LOs arise are geographically dominated by a specific oppressed nation i.e. barrios are majority Raza, projects are majority New Afrikan. These lumpen areas are naturally interested in single-nation organizing. Nationalism was not only proven to produce the furthest advances in humyn society to date in Mao's China, it also is a practical organizing strategy amongst LOs, who are isolated into barrios and ghettos, and separated along "racial" lines within prisons.

In Mao's China the Red Guards were people's militias who were mostly youth from the cities. These Red Guards supported Mao and the revolution both physically as well as politically. Red Guards went out to the countryside to bring Maoist theory to the peasants and introduce the masses to revolutionary culture. But the Red Guards represent so much more; they represent what happens when youth groups are transformed into people's militias, when all that raw energy is harnessed into supporting liberation and building the new revolutionary society. Lumpen, and more specifically LOs, are our future Red Guards. In the short history of urban lumpen developments in this direction we have seen glimpses of this possibility in the 1960s with the Chican@ Brown Berets, the Black Panthers and the Young Lords. These groups mostly organized amongst the lumpen and LOs and we have seen the fire and the passion of these groups which continue to inspire us all today. This is the power lumpen have when harnessed and unleashed by a cadre.

Let us build on the past, reignite the lumpen and transform the barrios into liberated zones! The first step in this direction is to create a Barrio Committee (BC) in each barrio. This should be our first step in really transforming the pandillas, and really making a leap in what the LOs stand for. The committee is an essential link between the Chican@ revolutionaries and the lumpen; it is the mortar that will help us rebuild our nation and struggle to rehabilitate our communities.

As lumpen we see our survival often coming any way we can and at any expense. But this often results in the destruction of our people, poisoning our youth with drugs that were allowed to cross international borders by the ruling class only to be spread by lumpen hands. We should find new ways to survive while seeing that the oppressor is the culprit who encourages us to "survive" through our day-to-day hustles. This is less like survival and more like a slow extermination in which we are accomplices. We need to come up in a revolutionary way, come up on starting barrio committees, come up on developing new theory, come up on building cadre and a new generation working to transform society. So let us come up on the oppressor and flip the mentality that has been festering in our barrios for decades now. Make it clear to all who care about humynity or a better society that lumpen-on-lumpen crime is contributing to the genocidal program of imperialism; it is helping our oppressor!

Barrios Wrapped in Razor Wire

Our barrios were made similar to colonies initially, in the early 1900s and continuing through today. We work in the fields, growing most of Amerika's food. We live in shacks in labor camps, bathing with a hose or in a creek, often with no running water and dirt floors, forced to live as we did hundreds of years ago. Our neighborhoods are patrolled like a Nazi concentration kamp with all the youth over the age of 10 quickly added to police databases and harassed, threatened, frisked, beaten and shot dead. This terror unleashed on the barrios is meant to control and intimidate Raza. The filling of prisons with Raza until no more fit in the prisons is the repression, the nightmare Chican@s face in the United $tates, but it is not a new thing. As the Chican@ nation grows, the ruling class must install mechanisms to set an example for others in the United $tates who want to rebel.

Chican@s have always had to deal with police repression in our neighborhoods, but Amerika has begun to repackage or reinvent the barrio as we know it. Indeed the classic barrio is slowly being replaced with one of concrete and steel, with gun towers and electric fences. The prison has begun to replace the barrio in the United $tates, and the new barrio is wrapped in razor wire.

Holding 2.4 million people, a greater proportion of the population is locked up in U.$. prisons than any other time or place in world history (with the exception of WWII in the USSR).[7] But what is unique is that a greater proportion of what are called "ethnic minorities" are locked up in the United $tates than anywhere in the world. This points to the internal colonialism that oppressed nations face living in the United

$tates. But this massive criminalization also proves the fallacy of the capitalist system and its society. The questions must be asked: what kind of system creates such an abundance of prisoners? What is the motive behind this prison boom? Some say it is to profit off prison labor. But in relation to how much it costs to house prisoners and operate prisons and how little prison labor as a whole produces, it's safe to say profit itself cannot be the motivating factor overall. Some corporations do profit off cheap prison labor, paying prisoners less than a dollar an hour, in some cases with no breaks, almost no health care, and under armed guard with threats of physical abuse for not working, but these cases are rare. The primary motivation for the dramatic growth of prisons since the 1970s is for control of the oppressed nations.[8]

Raza today are the largest population in the federal prisons and will most likely follow this trend soon in state prisons. Already in California Raza have become the largest prison population, and this is ground zero for Amerika's prison boom. Chicanos are the largest prison population in the state's supermax security housing units (SHUs); 85% of the prisoners in Pelican Bay State Prison's (Crescent City, CA) long-term isolation cells are Raza.[9] The SHU is a prison within a prison where the lumpen are experiencing extreme repression; it has many names throughout the prison system, but they are all control units. In control units, most prisoners are housed in solitary confinement 22 to 24 hours per day, which is widely seen as torture. This isolation is done on a mass scale with over 14,000 people held in control units in California alone. This torture has been proven to cause trauma of all sorts, including insanity and suicide. Prisoners are sent to control units for being jailhouse lawyers, prison leaders, the most radical and revolutionary, and those resisting the state in many ways. Just by the sheer nature of being Chican@, we fit these categories in overwhelming numbers.

This targeting of Chican@s for imprisonment and isolation is evidence that Chican@s are becoming more and more conscious and revolutionary, so much so that the state is forced to resort to torture with no other options to stop this forward progression. This shows the historical development in the Chican@ nation and hints to future possibilities. Mao spoke of this type of repression by the enemy:

> *"I hold that it is bad as far as we are concerned if a person, a political party, an army or a school is not attacked by the enemy for in that case*

it would definitely mean that we have sunk to the level of the enemy. It is
good if we are attacked by the enemy, since it proves that we have drawn
a clear line of demarcation between the enemy and ourselves. It is still
better if the enemy attacks us widely and paints us as utterly black and
without a single virtue, it demonstrates that we have not only drawn a
clear line of demarcation between the enemy and ourselves but achieved
a great deal in our work."[10]

Just as the state is using the label of "gang" to inflict a psychological suffering on the lumpen as well as the broader community, this also occurs within its penal system. And prison itself becomes a psychological weapon, a tool for social control meant to further shackle the mind of those it swallows. Many prisoners will begin to lose their fighting spirit once imprisoned. Prison is designed to mentally declaw our young jaguars and sometimes it is effective in its aim. But we need to see prisons as our new barrios. Many Raza are doing decades or life, and so rather than get stuck on what you can't do anymore, you must begin to think of what you can do now. Prisoners have one advantage that people out in society do not have, and that is time. People out in society, especially in the barrios, do not have the luxury to read a lot of books and study as much as prisoners. Most people out in public society have one or two jobs to pay rent, bills, electricity, babysitters, clothes, food, and spend their time commuting, walking here and there, etc. There is just so much distraction that spare time becomes priceless. Prisoners have time for not just advancing oneself, but also to begin uplifting other prisoners' consciousness as well. Prisons can become cadre schools in the United $tates where lumpen enter these dungeons engaging in social parasitism and leave as educated cadre. Those with life sentences can become political instructors themselves teaching lumpen political science, strengthening and helping to transform prisons into revolutionary schools. The only thing that is stopping this from taking place is prisoners not making it happen. We need to use prisons against the oppressor and use these conditions to our advantage. If Chican@s are going to be the largest prisoner population in Aztlán we will be the largest politically conscious population in these dungeons. If the state seeks to place the most politically conscious in SHUs and other control units then these places will be our cadre universities.

Think of the impact it would have on our barrios out in society, should U.$. prisoners really begin to revolutionize. Barrios would be transformed, the lumpen culture tossed out and a revolutionary culture injected. The flame would be lit from barrio to barrio empowering the Chican@ struggle with a momentum it has not yet seen. So we should not just think of serving the people out in society but serving the people here in prison as well. Some will go back out to society and others will help raise the consciousness from within the cinderblock barrios.

There is a profound amount of urgency and necessity in beginning this project as we have waited for too long. We must develop prisoner cadre to the point where they help the imprisoned masses rather than further dehumynize us. Our social reality as prisoners is such that the state has buried us alive. Only we can dig ourselves out and breathe again. Marx showed how to analyze the world as scientists using dialectical and historical materialism to identify phenomenon and the contradictions within them. Within U.$. prisons there are many contradictions. Our job should be to understand these contradictions and use them to propel the people forward, which in turn propels the broader movement forward, for Aztlán, other oppressed nations in the United $tates, and on a world scale.

So many rebellious elements are caught in the web of the injustice system and stuffed like sardines in these concrete colonies in an attempt to smother the burning embers of resistance. We want power and refuse to be smothered politically! Chican@ power would bring equality to our people, denying the exploiters from ever harming our nation again, and healing the Chican@ nation from the wounds which have totally consumed our way of life since our nation's conception. We need to learn new ways to exercise people's power on small scales to prepare our barrios for larger projects of community control and people's power in the future. In this way the prisoner remains in active service of the revolution and continues to add to advancing political theory.

Part II:
Further Research on Aztlán

Section I:
Obscured for Centuries, the Nation is Bigger Than Ever

by MIM(Prisons)

TODAY IT IS NOT UNUSUAL to hear that revolutionary nationalism is an ideology of another period, and that the idea of semi-colonies in the United $tates is outdated because we live in a globalized world. These propositions are found in the academic trends of post-modernism and multiculturalism. The justifications for such ideas come in a couple forms. One is the traditional Trotskyist line that we must organize the "workers" of the imperialist nations in order to successfully end capitalist exploitation and oppression. This line has been proven wrong in practice by millions of people before us, and summed up by MIM decades ago. The other argument is that civil rights have been granted to the formerly oppressed people in the imperialist countries, and on a global scale that colonialism has been overthrown or died out. But we know that neocolonialism replacing colonialism only indicates a further and higher development of the imperialist system that we live under today. Imperialism is defined by the principal contradiction of the oppressor nations vs. the oppressed nations. From Palestine to India, from Iraq to Nigeria, from Colombia to Mali, this conflict is just as strong today as it was 60 years ago.

But the question of the level of assimilation of the internal semi-colonies into the oppressor Amerikan nation is one that is not so easily dismissed. In fact, we have often addressed this assimilation in our discussions of the class analysis of the whole population within United $tates borders. Material conditions have qualitatively changed over the last 60 years within the internal semi-colonies of the United $tates. Integration into the exploiter classes has become a reality for large sectors of the oppressed nations within U.$. borders. It is for this very reason that migrants continue to risk their lives to come to the United $tates to work. At the same time, this influx of proletarian migrants from exploited countries shifts the class make up of the Chican@ nation closer to the majority of the world, challenging the integrationist trend.

Overall, our analysis recognizes the class bribery that has affected the Chican@ nation, as well as New Afrika, Boricua and First Nations. Yet, as nation remains the principal contradiction within imperialism, including between Amerika and the various oppressed internal semi-colonies in the United $tates, this bribery is not enough to make revolutionary proletarian nationalism totally irrelevant. National oppression in the forms of segregation, police brutality, imprisonment, poor schools and a culture that promotes psychological inferiority, keep the national divisions alive and well. It is U.$. imperialism's dependence on Amerikans as a social base that keeps white nationalism as a potent force and continues to limit the oppressed nations' participation in aspects of Amerikan society. That is the national contradiction in action.

In the previous section we established the historical basis for the Chican@ nation, and then looked at today's conditions where the role of prisons and the lumpen class have become new important features. Here we will look more closely at the national question as it applies to the Chican@ nation in our contemporary conditions to answer our own questions about the role of integrationism. First we will present some demographic research to show the Chican@ nation is a growing social force that remains distinct from, and in contradiction with, Amerika. Then in the following essays that make up Part II we will look at the political implications of how this contradiction is handled today.

A Rising, Vibrant Nation

There are more Mexican nationals in the United $tates today than the total migrant population in any other country.[1] In a world where people are becoming more and more mobile, we expect the national landscape to be transformed. If so, Mexican migrants are one of the prominent groups to study to assess such transformation.[2] The graph below shows the steep growth in migration to the United $tates in recent decades and the important role that Mexican migrants have played in that growth.[3]

Figure 2.1.1 Foreign-Born Population of the United $tates, by Region of Birth, 1960-2005

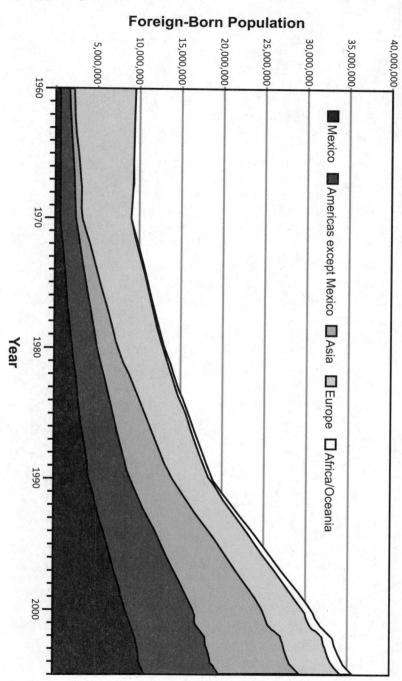

Figure 2.1.2 Reference map of present United $tates boundaries

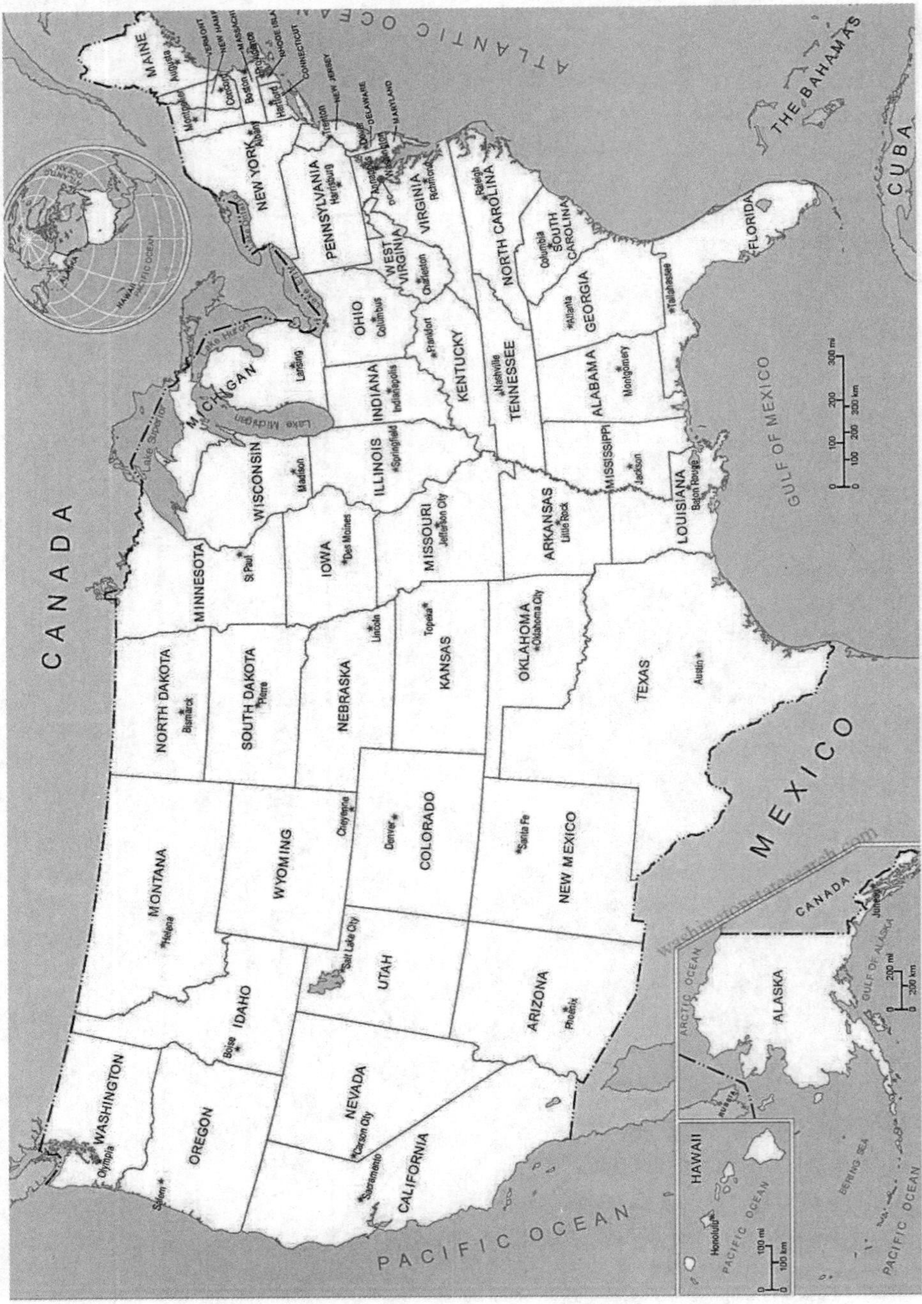

Figure 2.1.1 illustrates that Mexico has the largest influx to the United $tates from another country in history. While the first half of the 20th century was dominated by immigration from Europe at rates similar to today, immigrants accounted for a much smaller portion of the population after WWII. It was around 1970 that a new surge to the United $tates began and this time it was dominated by the Americas, followed by Asia and led to a drop in the percentage of the foreign-born population who have U.$. citizenship by about 20%. The trend in *Figure 2.1.1* continued into 2009, when the foreign-born population had increased to 38,517,234 and the Mexican-born population had reached 11,478,413.[3] However, by 2011 the Mexican-born population in the United $tates had ceased to grow, while the overall immigrant population continued to expand.[4] The decline in Mexican nationals in the United $tates is explained by the economic down turn that began in 2008, President Obama's unprecedented crackdown on migrants and, perhaps most importantly, changing demographic conditions within Mexico. Despite this decline, the last four decades have left more Mexicans in the United $tates than the total immigrant population in any other country in the world. The implications of such a large population movement are still playing out and are to be determined by the path chosen by the Chican@ and Mexican@ nationals.

While not the fastest growing nationality of Raza in the United $tates, from 2000 to 2010 those of Mexican descent accounted for about 75% of the population increase of Raza and 42% of the overall population increase in the country. The overall increase in "Hispanic" population in that period accounted for 56% of the population growth in the United $tates.[5] While these recent migrants most likely belong to a national minority when entering the United $tates, they, and especially their children and their children's children, will likely integrate into the Chican@ nation. As generations pass, others will either remain part of their national minority group, join another Raza-based nation, or even integrate into the Amerikan nation.

The population of Mexican descent in the United $tates was 63% of "Hispanics" in 2010. Boricuas (Puerto Ricans) and Cubans follow with 9.2% and 3.5% respectively. All Central American nationalities made up 7.9% of "Hispanics," and South Americans made up 5.5%. Salvadorans are only 3.3% of Raza, making them the 4th largest group after Cubans.

A look at the geography of the population gives us insight into the continued connection that the Chican@ people have to the territory of

Figure 2.1.3 Percent of Foreign-Born Population
from Mexico and Other Central America: 1960-2010

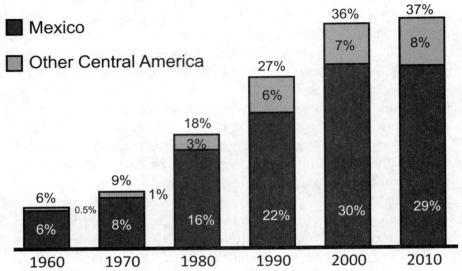

Source: U.S. Censur Bureau, Census of Population, 1960 to 2000 and the American Community Survey, 2010.

Aztlán. The maps in *Figure 2.1.5* show this pretty clearly, with over half of Raza living within the former boundaries of northern Mexico: California, Arizona, New Mexico, Texas, Utah and Nevada plus Colorado is around 56% of Raza in the United $tates. The vast majority of territory that is occupied by 25% or higher Raza population is within Aztlán (see *Figure 1.2.2*). However, if we break down the data a little further, and control for the Caribbean populations dominant on the East coast we see the correlation is overwhelmingly strong. In 2011, over three quarters of people of Mexican descent (24,608,617) lived in those seven states.[6]

In other words, the Raza population in Aztlán is disproportionately of Mexican descent, while Boricuas, Cubans and Dominicans are dominant in other high concentrations of Raza people in New York, Florida, New Jersey, Pennsylvania and Massachusetts.[7]

Let's take a closer look at these states so that we can better understand the landscape of highly concentrated populations of Raza across the United $tates. We have Florida, where the "Hispanic" population is dominated by Cubans. This is a unique situation where the "Hispanic" population is largely of European origin who fled Cuba because of the economic system, which restricted the accumulation of private property.

This phenomenon is also demonstrated in Cubans having one of the highest rates of assimilation compared to all other foreign nationals in the United $tates.[8] While Florida has a large "Hispanic" population due to its proximity to the Caribbean islands, there are also large Central American populations there who came to work as migrant laborers. The Raza populations in New York and New Jersey are dominated by Boricuas, with large Dominican and Cuban populations. The northeast states also have significant Central American populations, which have arrived more recently (see *Figure 2.1.5* on next page).

Figure 2.1.4 Raza as % of Population in 2010[7]	
United $tates	16.3
New Mexico	46.3
California	37.6
Texas	37.5
Arizona	29.6
Nevada	26.5
Florida	22.5
Colorado	20.7
New Jersey	17.7
New York	17.6
Illinois	15.8

Compared to other oppressed nations who migrate to the United $tates, Boricuas benefit from a special relationship to Puerto Rico that allows them to legally move here and enjoy U.$. wealth. While they continue to live as a relatively oppressed minority in New York and New Jersey, Boricuas in the United $tates enjoy better conditions than they do in their homeland and better conditions than the Third World overall. On the other hand, Boricuas also tend to have more African ancestry that seems to influence where they live and their economic success. As a result geographic segregation of Boricuas in the United $tates parallels that of New Afrikans, and is more severe than other Raza. Illinois is just slightly under the average in terms of "Hispanic" population, and was

Figure 2.1.5 Distribution of Largest Raza Populations Across the Continental United $tates

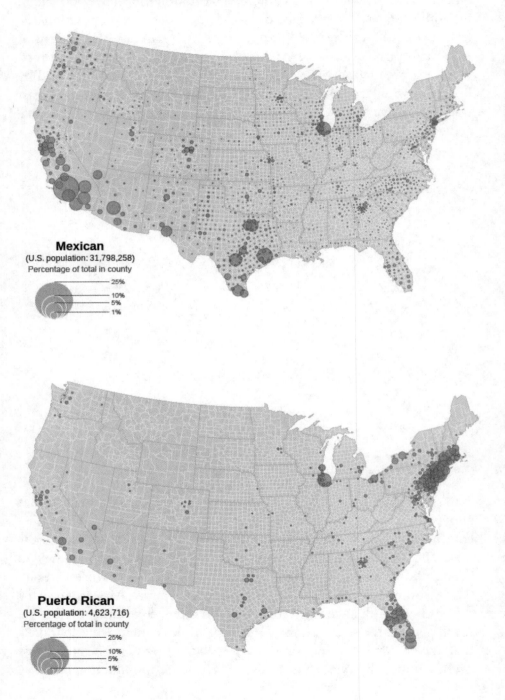

Mexican
(U.S. population: 31,798,258)
Percentage of total in county

25%
10%
5%
1%

Puerto Rican
(U.S. population: 4,623,716)
Percentage of total in county

25%
10%
5%
1%

FIGURE 2.1.5 Census data from 2010 (www.census.gov/dataviz/visualizations/072/). Data is displayed by county, with all counties that have more than 1,000 people in given group. Puerto Rico is excluded from the percentages. Alaska and Hawaii were included, but are not shown here. Shown below are the four largest groups in the U.S. Census "Hispanic/Latino" category.

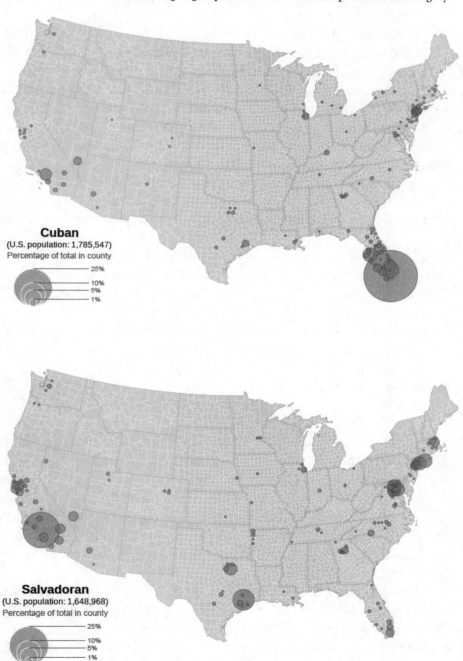

Cuban
(U.S. population: 1,785,547)
Percentage of total in county

25%
10%
5%
1%

Salvadoran
(U.S. population: 1,648,968)
Percentage of total in county

25%
10%
5%
1%

an historically important place for migrant Chican@s as well as Boricuas to work as industrial proletarians in the mid-1900s. The remaining six states with above-average Raza populations, which includes all five states over 25%, are part of Aztlán.

We do see a concentration of people from Central America in specific cities and states in the United $tates. Salvadorans are more likely living in Los Angeles, Houston, San Francisco, New York, and Washington, D.C.; Guatemalans in California and Texas; Nicaraguans in Miami; and Hondurans in Florida and Texas.[9] Most of these places are part of Aztlán, but the data on where people concentrate shows that Central American immigrants are still identifying with their specific home country and not necessarily integrating into the Chican@ nation.

Economic status in one's home country is a strong indicator of ability to economically assimilate in the United $tates. As David Gutiérrez notes in his essay on Latino migration and demographic transformation:

> "Ongoing economic restructuring in South America has led to a situation in which highly educated and highly skilled individuals from countries including Argentina, Chile, Columbia, Peru, Ecuador, and others have emigrated to the U.S. seeking economic opportunities not available to them in their places of origin. For example, according to a recent analysis of 2000 U.S. Census data, whereas only 2.3 percent of all Mexican migrants arriving in the U.S. in the 1980s had bachelor's degrees, 30 percent of those arriving from Peru and Chile, 33 percent of Argentine immigrants, and 40 percent of all Venezuelan immigrants had at least a bachelor's degree."[10]

Further, in 2011, a smaller percentage of South American migrants (14%) lived in households with an annual income below the official federal poverty line than migrants overall (20%). To put this in further perspective, about 15% of U.$. citizens were below the poverty line in 2011. So we see South American migrants doing pretty well overall on the economic integration scale. There were small differences between origin countries with Ecuador leading the group for economic difficulty among migrants.

One analysis that calculates an economic assimilation index based on Census data gives us another basis for comparing people coming from different countries south of the Rio Bravo. A score of 100 in *Figure 2.1.7* means that their economic status is the same as the U.$. population overall.

Overall it appears that people coming to the United $tates from Mexico and most of Central America are more likely to become part of the Chican@ nation than to integrate into Amerika. Ecuador appears to be an outlier in South America, and likely is contributing a larger percentage of immigrants to the Chican@ nation than other South American countries. And there is a big difference between legal and illegal migrants from all of these countries. Legal status means a much greater chance of assimilation in a number of areas, making it possible that migrants don't end up in regions with other migrants and are not exposed to Chican@ culture, language and economics. We know, for example, that people who come to the United $tates legally from Argentina, with enough money and education to join a wealthy suburban community, would easily bypass any association with the Chican@ nation.

Figure 2.1.6 % Living Below Federal Poverty Line by Country of Origin[10]	
Argentina	11
Chile	11
Uruguay	12
Venezuela	16
Paraguay	16
Ecuador	17

"Hispanics" and the Erasing of First Nations

The above data on national origin represents a step forward in the quality of data collected by the U.$. Census, even though they still differentiate Hispanic as an "ethnicity." The history of the U.$. Census reflects a history of erasing the indigenous people of the Chican@ nation, in particular those who were forced to migrate from the south as part of the reshaping of the region to serve the new capitalist economy.

According to the U.$. Census, "'Hispanic or Latino' refers to a person of Cuban, Mexican, Puerto Rican, South or Central American, or other Spanish culture of origin regardless of race." Race is seen as

Figure 2.1.7 Economic Assimilation Indexes[11]	
Argentina	100
Bolivia	100
Chile	100
Colombia	100
Guyana	100
Panama	100
Peru	100
Venezuela	100
Belize	96
Brazil	95
Nicaragua	94
Costa Rica	93
Ecuador	88
Uruguay	89
El Salvador	71
Honduras	70
Mexico	66
Guatemala	63
Paraguay	no data

something separate by the U.$. government. The mythical races that define Amerikan thinking are white, Black, Asian, Indian (native to the Americas) and Pacific Islander. For historical and political reasons this has resulted in the virtual invisibility of Chican@s, Mexican@s and other Raza in Census data. Meanwhile indigenous people are seen as an almost insignificant portion of the population. While the Chican@ nation has a history distinct from First Nations within U.$. borders, the idea that Chican@s are recent additions to Aztlán territory is largely based in the interference by and aspirations of the white oppressor.

The 1930 Census was the first and only time that "Mexican" was included in the list of races.[12] Otherwise Mexicans have been considered part of the "white" race by the Census, in stark contrast to how they have been treated by white Amerikans. This legacy continues, leading us to have to sort out "Hispanic" from "non-Hispanic" when parsing Census data.

The basis for not considering Latinos to be a race is that Raza are most frequently considered of "mixed race," or, in South and Central America, Mestizo. Historically, the ideology that believes that there are separate races of humyns has not questioned the integrity of European nations, which also formed by the merging of many peoples, but it does jump on the opportunity to do so for the colonized nations who have been denied self-determination by European oppression. Here we will quote at length from Jack Forbes, an author who has researched this question in more detail.

> "To place this discussion in proper perspective, let us contrast the situations in Mexico and Spain. North American social scientists and intellectuals and the ruling elite of Mexico seem to agree that Mexico is a mestizo nation, that not only are most of its people racially mixed but that its dominant culture is also mestizo. North American Anglo-Saxon scholars, in particular, delight in using the mestizo and Indo-Hispano concept when discussing Mexico and Chicanos (persons of Mexican background in the United States). It is very clear that Anglo scholars (and the Mexicans and Chicanos influenced by them) regard the very essence of the Mexican-Chicano people as mestizo (except for the perhaps ten percent of the Mexican people who are regarded as indio).

> "Now, is this mestization of the Mexican-Chicano people a concrete social reality or is it primarily the Europeans' imposition of alien descriptive categories upon the Mexican-Chicano masses? Let us look at the situation of Spain and Mexico with this question in mind. Spain is, clearly, far more of a mestizo nation (if that term is ever properly to be used) than is Mexico.

> 1. The Spanish people speak a totally borrowed language, a dialect or branch of Italo-Latin mixed with many thousands of Arabic words. Very few words of the indigenous Hispano-Iberic language remain in use.
> 2. The culture of Spain is a complex mixture of Latin-Italic, North African, Middle Eastern, Greek, Gitano (Gypsy), and other characteristics, with very few indigenous (pre-Roman) traits remaining, except among the Basques and Gallegos.

3. *Racially, the modern Spaniard probably carries relatively few indigenous genes, the latter having been greatly overwhelmed by Carthaginian, Celtic, Latin-Roman, Germanic, Arab, Moorish, Berber, Jewish, black African, and Gitano intermixture.*

"*In both a racial and culture sense, then, the Spaniard is profoundly a mestizo. In fact, it is safe to say that (except among the Basques) the Spanish culture of modern times is almost wholly non-Spanish in origin (in terms, at least, of specific traits) and is thoroughly mixed. Surprisingly, however, one never finds Anglo-Saxon social scientists categorizing the Spaniards as a mestizo. One never finds scholars describing a Spanish subgroup as part Gitano or as a North African physical type. One never finds social scientists attempting to dissect the Spanish people and then to tell them who they are!*

"*Why is this so? We know that during the fifteenth century, for example, there were many subgroups (such as maranos, mozarabes, moriscos, and so on) among the population. We know also that even today regional variations can probably be identified in Spain.*

"*Why is the Castillian-speaking Spaniard allowed to have dignity and security of being simply a Spaniard, of possessing an ethnic identity, a nationality, while the Mexican and the Chicano are even now dissected and categorized, first, as mestizos and only second as Mexicans or Chicanos?*"[13]

In the excerpt below Forbes uses the term *Anishinabe* to refer to people native to the Americas. In this essay Forbes writes,

"*Furthermore modern Mexican and Chicano people possess far greater connection with their ancient Mexican past than many European groups do with their respective past.*

"*For example:*
1. *The Mexicans and Chicanos of today are perhaps eighty percent native Anishinabe descent, while only twenty percent of their ancestry is of European-North African, African, and Asian descent. In contrast, it is likely that Spaniards possess relatively little pre-Roman ancestry (native Iberian), certainly less than eighty percent.*

2. *The Mexican and Chicano peoples' modern language, Spanish, possesses several thousand native Mexican words, while the Spanish is wholly non-Iberian in origin.* [14]

3. *The native religions of Spain have almost, if not completely, disappeared. In Mexico, however, the native religion has survived in many regions and has modified Christianity. Furthermore, Christianity is as foreign to Spain as it is to Mexico.*

4. *The modern culture of Spain is almost entirely non-Iberian in origin. In contrast, the culture of Mexico, even among Spanish-speaking people, is, to a significant degree, of native Mexican origin.*

"In short, the Mexicans and Chicanos possess far greater continuity with their native past than do the Spaniards, and yet the Spanish are categorized as 'unified' people (in spite of great regional variations), while the Mexicans and Chicanos must perpetually carry the burden of genuflecting before the idol of mestisaje." [13]

The baselessness of the racial ideology is further exposed by Forbes via the historical process by which indigenous people throughout the Americas have been transformed into various Mestizo nationalities via economic changes in their position in society. In other words, as the indigenous population becomes more integrated into the nation, economically and culturally, their identity changes without having to have any genetic integration. This phenomenon can be explained via the national model as integration and the formation of nationhood. However, since mixing of genes was not a precursor to this transformation, the racial model falls flat in the face of such realities. Whether by Amerikans or the Spanish, using racial concepts based on appearance and genetic purity or mixing has a long legacy as a tool to divide and conquer in the Americas and many other parts of the world.

The unifying effect of Spanish colonialism, culture and language on the people of South and Central America is undeniable, and is the basis for the umbrella terms *Raza* and *Latino*. However, the influence of Spanish colonialism does not erase the existence of separate nations of Raza, which remain more different than they are the same. Like all things, nations change and evolve with time. Some day nations will no longer exist. However, to deny the existence of nationhood in the age of imperialism is to deny a people their right to self-determination.

Measuring Assimilation

One of the major ways that nations are transformed is through assimilation. The very formation of the large nations that exist today was the process of assimilation of many tribes and smaller pre-capitalist nations. We have shown population numbers and geographic distribution that demonstrate the importance of the Chican@ nation in the United $tates today. While Forbes knocks down some questions of culture and "race" used to dismiss the Chican@ nation historically, in our view there is still a major question of assimilation of the internal semi-colonies into Amerika, powered by the great economic wealth of the leading imperialist country. So to define the Chican@ nation today, it is important for us to look at the question of assimilation.

One analysis out of Duke University utilizing U.$. Census data helps support the existence of a Chican@ nation separate from Amerika.[15] In their analysis the small Nepalese immigrant population was the only nationality that had a lower assimilation index in the United $tates than Mexican nationals. Those from Honduras, Guatemala and El Salvador hovered around the bottom with Mexicans, indicating the similar destinies of people from that region.[15] However, Panama was very distinct in having one of the higher assimilation rates, so we might be amiss to generalize about all of Central America.

The study looked at historical data and found that assimilation has accelerated in the last quarter century, yet the level of assimilation is lower now than at any point in the twentieth century.[17] This means that while people are assimilating faster once they get into the United $tates, they are migrating at even higher rates to lower the overall assimilation level. Both phenomena are consistent with the globalizing nature of imperialism.

The indexes in the Duke University study show Mexicans being slow to assimilate in terms of economics and civics, but not culture. This would correspond to them coming here without legal status (civics) and working low-paid, insecure jobs (economics), both of which amount to forms of oppression as non-citizens. Another form of oppression they face is seen in the 80% higher rate of imprisonment faced by adolescent Mexican migrants compared to migrant adolescents generally.[18] If anything, this imprisonment tends to accelerate their assimilation into the oppressed Chican@ nation, rather than Amerika.

Of course, U.$. imperialism plays a large role in the movement of populations, not just in how it structures the world economically, but in its military involvement. The paper notes the connection between U.$. military involvement in the countries with highest degrees of civic assimilation. This can be explained by the fact that people coming from those countries are coming for political asylum of some sort from governments or conflicts that are opposed to U.$. imperialism. The example highlighted in the study is Vietnam, where many pro-capitalist, pro-United $tates people fled Vietnam when the Amerikans were kicked out by anti-imperialist forces.

Interestingly, the study looks closer at Mexicans and Vietnamese today and compares them to Italians in the early 1900s. They conclude that if Italians were an example of successful integration, then the Vietnamese seem to be following in their footsteps, while Mexicans are not. The Vietnamese have assimilated at faster rates than either Italians 100 years ago or Mexicans today. This is despite the fact that Vietnam as a nation is much poorer than Mexico. Clearly the difference has more to do with

Figure 2.1.8 Percentage of the Foreign-Born Population Who Are Naturalized U.S. Citizens by Country of Birth: 2010

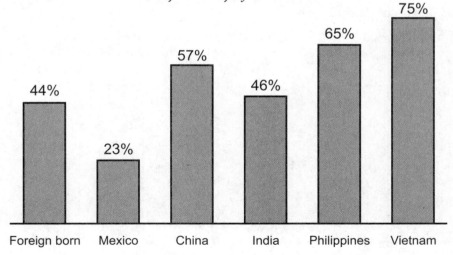

FIGURE 2.1.8 Not having citizenship limits a population's ability to participate in civics. Note the drastic difference in citizenship status between Mexicans who must risk their lives to travel a few hundred miles and Vietnamese who cross the Pacific Ocean as part of the United $tate's ongoing anti-communist political campaign in Asia. Source: U.S. Census Bureau, American Community Survey, 2010

which sectors of society are coming from each country, and why they are coming, than the overall wealth of the nation they come from.

From 1900 to 1920 the calculations show Italians going from assimilation rates similar to Mexicans today to much higher rates, though still at a slower rate than today's Vietnamese immigrants. This change in rate was very fast considering that mass migration of Italians had peaked in this period. At the beginning of the 1900s, Italians and other Southern and Eastern European immigrants were not considered white and were forced into the most difficult and dangerous jobs.[19] However, by the early 1920s, as U.$. imperialism emerged as the dominant economic force in the world, these new immigrants had found that in the "Southwest" "they could move up from worker or tenant to owner and employer through the use of Mexican migrants."[20]

Of course it should be recognized that the Chican@ nation pre-dated these new European immigrant groups in the United $tates, and yet the Chican@s were quickly surpassed by them economically. Despite

Figure 2.1.9 Percentage of Foreign-Born Population by Language Spoken at Home and English-Speaking Ability by Country of Birth: 2010

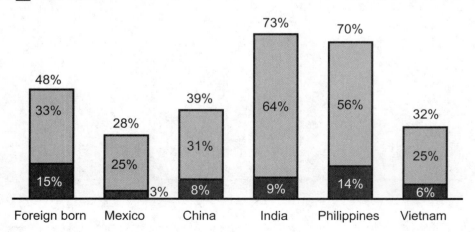

FIGURE 2.1.9 Not speaking English is another barrier to assimilation into Amerika. However, note that the Duke study found Vietnamese to assimilate much more easily than Mexicans despite having similar disadvantages in regards to language. Source: U.S. Census Bureau, American Community Survey, 2010

Figure 2.1.10 % of Population with a Bachelor's Degree or Higher Education by Nativity Status and Country of Birth: 2010

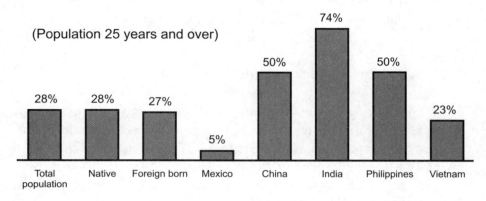

FIGURE 2.1.10 Income and education are the two best indicators to predict class at the group level in the United $tates. Compared to the average Amerikan, and even to other national minority populations, Mexicans are in a clearly disadvantaged position. Source: U.S. Census Bureau, American Community Servey, 2010.

Figure 2.1.11 Median Earnings in the Past 12 Months by Nativity Status and Country of Birth: 2010

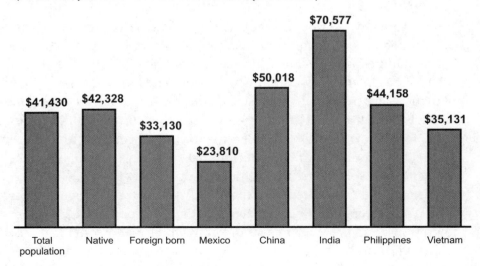

Source: U.S. Census Bureau, American Community Survey, 2010.

the confusing categorizing of Mexicans as white throughout most of U.$. history, this was clearly not the reality on the ground. And the experience of Chican@s in the United $tates is more akin to New Afrikans than it is to the Italians who immigrated here a hundred years ago.

Class Nature of the Internal Semi-Colonies

While our definition of nation lists language, culture and economy as necessary defining factors, we have already established that determining whether a separate nation exists or not is not a matter of the nation having all of these completely distinct from any other nation. Going back to the thesis of Forbes who exposed the oppressive ideology of racism and so-called Mestizo and "mixed-bloods":

> "Both assimilation and proletarianization would demand that the native Anishinabe (or African) cultures and tribes be destroyed. Both would demand that the conquered groups learn new skills, learn European language, and become part of the cash economy. But there the similarity ends. An assimilation policy would require the liquidation of racism, color consciousness, and resistance to intermarriage. Clearly, the white ruling groups of the Americas (even in the so-called relaxed Latin countries) have had no intention of doing that."[21]

Historically, we would agree that proletarianization of the internal semi-colonies, coupled with genocide, was the main strategy of Amerika's conquest and expansion. For Chican@s today, there is still a significant proletarian element. However, the majority of the internal semi-colony populations are no longer sources of wealth for Amerikans. Joining the labor aristocracy and petty bourgeois classes, they have become a competitor for the distribution of stolen wealth in this country. This is the material basis for a fear of competition that reinforces national distinctions within U.$. borders. In addition, the Chican@ people, as well as various national minorities from the Third World, are still identified as Third World people in the racialized thinking of Amerikans. Therefore integration of some Mexicans, and some Chinese and some Indians, while continuing to oppress and exploit those nations poses a difficult contradiction.

This is why we use the term *semi-colony* to describe the distinct oppressed nations within the United $tates. The internal semi-colonies are still colonized by Euro-Amerikans – their land is occupied, their culture suppressed, their self-determination denied. However, for the most part, these nations no longer serve as the source of value that they have historically, so we cannot treat them the same as the neo-colonies of the Third World.

Despite the class transformations that have led to New Afrikans, Chican@s, Boricuas and at least some First Nations being bought off over the last few decades, the national question is still pronounced. Integration is occurring at the margins, but that is almost unavoidable. In the most favorable conditions, it would still take many generations to see the disappearance of the national identities of the oppressed nations within U.$. borders. And the contemporary struggles of the Chican@ people against repression explored elsewhere in this book speak to the potential of the national contradiction becoming stronger, not weaker, in this country.

Battling in the Realm of Ideas

If we can agree that the internal semi-colonies exist, and that they exist in contradiction to the oppressor Amerikan nation, then we have much work to do to propagate that idea in the minds of the masses once again. While the economic integration mentioned above is perhaps the strongest force of integration, it is in the realm of ideas where we determine whether or not there is still a nationalism to fight for.

When one uses the term *racism* to describe an ideology or action it is immediately thought of as reactionary and discriminatory. And it is. But the multiculturalists use identity politics to play the other side of racist ideology while attempting to sound progressive. When people say that national liberation struggles are a thing of the past, we need to ask who would benefit from such a belief? The oppressor nations of course. And this is why, in the oppressor nation universities, you will find post-modernists and multiculturalists pushing identity politics instead of national identities. These ideologies depend on the racialization of individuals.

Identity politics opens one's analysis up to all kinds of subjectivity and made-up categories by throwing out Stalin's scientific definition of a nation. While often believing in the idea of race, these people would have race eliminated, or at least become less of an issue, via intermixing between groups (most often assimilating oppressed nation people into white cultural and educational institutions). In doing so, they hope to erase the national consciousness of the oppressed by dividing them with a slew of different identities based on small differences in class, culture, region, sexuality, etc. For the Liberal white persyn, racism is morally problematic, and multiculturalism serves as a means for them to push the problems of racism under the rug. Meanwhile, oppression and exploitation continue uninterrupted.

While 47% of Raza say they are "typical Americans," another 47% say they are very different. For those born in the United $tates, a full 66% say they are no different than Amerikans.[22] While self-identification is not how we define nationality, it can give us good insight into the question of cultural assimilation. Someone may identify with Amerikan culture because of their desire to assimilate economically, even if they are not assimilated. Those of Mexican descent are slightly less likely to identify as Amerikan than other Raza, but the length of time your family has been in the United $tates, the language you speak and education level were all better indicators of how people identified than country of origin.[23]

As communists, ending oppression and exploitation is our number one concern, not avoiding ideas that make us feel uncomfortable. The twentieth century demonstrated the power of national liberation struggles to combat imperialism and to build more just societies. The right to self-determination of oppressed nations that Lenin and Stalin stressed as an ideological principle for communists to uphold has proven itself in the laboratory of social struggle to be a powerful tool for progressive change.

The Chican@ nation not only existed historically, but it is growing today, as are many contradictions between Amerika and Aztlán. We must expose the racist ideologies of those who try to deny the existence of the nation as part of an overall program of developing Chican@ revolutionary nationalism.

Section 2:
Real Lessons of the Chicano Moratorium and the High Treason Against Maoism

[Originally published by the Maoist Internationalist Movement in 2006 on their etext.org website, following the mass demonstrations of migrants across the United $tates in 2006.]

THERE HAVE BEEN SOME PROFOUND attempts to bury the struggle of the Chicano Moratorium of August 29, 1970. The whitewashed Wikipedia entry refers to the Chicano Moratorium struggle as "Mexican-American" and even for "civil rights."[1] It is possible that there is no battle more important to have right now in North America than over this question. There is nothing more internationalist than the Chicano Moratorium struggle and nothing more objectively chauvinist than the idea of integrating everyone into one working class in the United $tates.

In actuality, the Chicano Moratorium was a group of people organized against the Vietnam War on a nationalist basis – an objectively revolutionary nationalist basis whatever its organizers might have thought. While followers of ex-Maoist Progressive Labor Party (PLP) were complaining that "all nationalism is reactionary," the nationalists were trying to deprive the U.$. army of a portion of recruits. Thus the nationalists proved yet again that Mao was right about "applied internationalism." Even in spite of potential national chauvinism, there is a paradox that nationalism in opposition to imperialism is inherently internationalism amongst the oppressed nations.

Chicanos realized that they were only 6% of the population inside U.$ borders, but over 20% of all Vietnam casualties.[2] This created a basis for even the coconuts to realize that there was some kind of discrimination

In response to 30,000 Chican@s rallying in East Los Angeles to say that they will no longer serve U.$. imperialism in Vietnam the police rioted, instigating street fighting that ended with stores burning and 4 dead. The dead included revered Chican@ journalist Ruben Salazar who was shot by police with a tear gas canister.

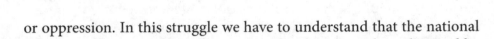

or oppression. In this struggle we have to understand that the national struggle is the root and backbone, not the class struggle as depicted by the multiracial or multinational class struggle advocates. For this we must absolutely learn the difference between Malcolm X and Martin Luther King – a question of theory.

If the class struggle is decisive in this context it must be interpreted correctly. The class struggle AGAINST super-profits is decisive, not for increased super-profits or increased super-profit sharing.

Today the U.S. army is much more careful about creating an impression of discriminatory combat fatality patterns. The Pentagon is not going to let as big a gap develop today as it did in the 1970s, unless of course it absolutely has to under future pressure. Nonetheless, the Pentagon is still disproportionately a drain on oppressed nationalities, simply because Euro-Amerikans have a declining portion of recruitable-age youth. Whites are a disproportionately high share of the elderly and a disproportionately low share of the people who can go to the front lines. In just four years, between 2000 and 2004, Latinos went from 10.4% of new military recruits to 13.0%.[3]

The "civil rights" approach will settle for having Chicano youth being treated the same way as white youth. The "civil rights" advocates are going to give up the anti-militarist struggle.

In fact, the "civil rights" approach improves Uncle $am's recruiting ability. The "civil rights" approach is the same as the "multiracial" or "multinational" working-class approach to class struggle, one that fantasizes a commonality between the white petty bourgeoisie and migrant workers for instance. The integrationists want Third World people to think of themselves as Amerikans and identify with white people. It should be a no-brainer that that is going to contribute to Uncle $am's global wars of oppression.

In contrast, the nationalist approach is what keeps the international proletariat in this game of power struggle against the imperialists. At first it seems like the international proletariat can't offer much that compares with super-profit sharing in the form of U.$. citizenship in return for war. Then we look at what nationalism is based on and we realize that the international proletariat is still in this power struggle. It is not a hopeless loser. People are still bound by culture, territory and economics to a Third World that has no interest in Uncle $am's wars.

It is not an accident that the leading proponents of fake Maoism called the Revolutionary Internationalist Movement are for a "multinational approach" and favor defeat of the Iranian government by U.$. imperialists. If these people are going to be for a U.$. occupation thousands of miles away in Iran, there is no point in being surprised when they favor the white settlers taking over Aztlán too.

No matter what they say or what they think, oppressed nations people and alleged communists fighting for a one working-class or "civil rights" view are fighting to boost Uncle $am's military recruitment. That is why the "anti-racist" struggle is not the key. The key is the struggle of the oppressed nations, and not just to join a multinational entity with the whites.

Today the Chicano share of the military gets higher and higher. We must boost the nationalism of the Chicano people both to prevent recruitment and to influence people who are already in the military. Aztlán's nationalism may be the most important internationalism there is right now, because Aztlán is adding the greatest increases in new troops to Uncle $am's occupation forces. Most of the troops are still rural whites, but the growth is from Aztlán and other oppressed nationalities. In a prior article, MIM has already proved that national liberation is more than eight times more effective in denying Uncle $am troops than the integrationist approach.[4]

The battle between revolution and counterrevolution is being fought in Aztlán and Iran. The fates of the two are linked together. The nationalists do not want Aztlán's people to serve Uncle $am in Iraq, Iran, Afghanistan etc. They want Aztlán's people to serve Aztlán. The proletarian camp in the Aztlán struggle wants a socialist republic of Aztlán, not an integration into imperialism.

Three Views in Politics

The two main views in U.$. politics are the right wing of white nationalism and the left wing of white nationalism. Patrick Buchanan is the leader of the right wing of white nationalism. He wants to preserve Western culture. Yet as aggressive as he is, he knows he needs a left hook, so he appeals to unions about closing borders to preserve jobs. He also admits that the United $tates is overly burdened with international military obligations, just as Hitler did in his early career. Buchanan correctly understands where things are going: if he does not succeed in cutting back U.$. imperialism's overstretch, it is going to admit more and more Third

World people to use as cannon-fodder. As a visceral racist, Buchanan and a large chunk of Amerikkka cannot stomach the result.

The left wing of white nationalism, including everyone from George W. Bu$h to Progressive Labor Party (PLP), says that the United $tates does have to push integrationism. Around the world, offers are going out to make U.$. citizens out of people who serve the United $tates in Iraq – just as happened centuries ago in Roman times. In response to the attack on the World Trade Center in 2001, over 24,745 people were allowed to become U.$. citizens since 2002 by serving in the U.$. military for just one day. Prior to this Executive Order by Bush, non-citizens had to serve for at least three years before being allowed to apply for citizenship.[5,6] So, we need to understand these are 24,745 people Bush admitted to the United $tates. As racist and chauvinist as he is, Bush is not taking the Buchanan line, even though they competed for the same white votes in the presidential election in 2000. The idea underlying the politics from Bush to PLP is simple: use super-profit sharing for integration; thereby boost U.$. military recruitment. Exploit the rest of the world hard; pay the best salaries inside U.$. borders and occupy any country daring to get out of line.

This is important for the scientific communists to understand. Yes, right now, rural whites are the basis of the U.$. military, but each year the trend is downward. Buchanan and Bush both understand this. They are also fighting at the margin and not relying on their stalwart rural whites. Left to themselves, the white oppressor nation would eventually run out of gas, especially once the Chinese working class finally pulls the plug on the U.$. dollar. Bush is actually racing to open the Republican Party to Latinos, the same as he is racing to recruit new citizen material to the military.

There is an important battle of the margin between Bush and Buchanan. There is an even more important battle of the margin between PLP and MIM. It has to be admitted that PLP won the first round of the battle back in the day. While the PLP fell off in size, its line proved more influential than the Maoist one, especially once the state smashed the Black Panther Party. The proletarian side was not well-prepared. What can we say? The Amerikkkans of the 1960s had to do a lot of heavy drugs just to get over the 1950s and consider communism. Today, the MIM line is better-read than the PLP line, but the PLP line still has the numbers behind it.

High Treason Against Maoism

It's often said that people are entitled to their opinion. Actually MIM does not agree. People are not entitled to their opinions which deny the survival rights of others. Nonetheless, there are those who have looked at Maoism eyeball-to-eyeball and decided they were not Maoists. Progressive Labor Party (PLP) is a good example. We welcome them to adopt our position and change their minds, but right now they are not Maoists and they admit it.

PLP used to meet with Mao and his comrades regularly. Then PLP realized it opposes the national bourgeoisie and revisionists in a systematic way, so that it can conceive of no united front with them. In other words, it saw some merit to Trotsky's criticisms of Stalin without calling it that.

Next PLP realized it was different than the Black Panther Party (BPP). So not only was PLP opposed to united front, but also it did not share the lumpen-oriented, national liberation approach of the BPP. PLP came up with "all nationalism is reactionary" as their main thrust; even though it said right in Quotations of Chairman Mao that the nationalism of the oppressed nations is applied internationalism.

PLP did the right thing and broke with Maoism and took up the Martin Luther King integrationist approach to fighting racism, and one working class. We say it was the "right thing," because otherwise PLP would only be lying its way through politics. It's much better to realize one's differences and put an accurate label on them.

There were others who also had Trotskyist ideas, however, but they did not really realize what was going on. These were the slowest sectors of the student movement to take up Marx, Lenin and Mao. They were essentially after-effects of the PLP and BPP – copy of a copy type stuff designed for white worker identity politics. Foremost among these are the followers of Bob Avakian, who took all of PLP's main theses and then vacillated on them whenever necessary. These slower-moving sectors failed to notice that all the main battles of line had already been fought out between the PLP on the one side and Mao and the BPP on the other. Typical of this is that Afakean formed an organization in 1975, long after everyone else had decided their stands. It was not till 1993 that Afakeanists called themselves "Maoist."

When we speak of the Chicano Moratorium question, we must also add Jose Maria Sison to the list of people who are involved in sabotaging Maoism from within. During the upsurge on migrant rights, Sison peddled the same Afakean/Revolutionary Internationalist Movement (RIM) line opposed to Aztlán's liberation. There are few questions today with such immediate practical importance of "applied internationalism."

Learn from practice Joma Sison: there was no multinational or multiracial proletariat for migrant rights rallies in the millions this spring. There were oppressed nations marching.

Learn from practice Joma Sison: There is no successful integrationist one-working-class struggle defeating U.$. military recruiting, of course not, and you of all people should know it. PLP is the leading recruiter for Uncle $am and Revolutionary Communist Party, U$A (RCP=CIA) is the leading organization confusing the ranks of the proletarian struggle.

Joma Sison ought to know that he is under organizational pressure from super-profits. It is what makes some of his people seek separate U.$-based organizations. They rally like nothing else for "immigrant" rights – to heck with the Philippines. Sison sees this, but he does not grab hold of the struggle at the margin. Indeed, he has gone over to the other side completely with his echoing of RIM on Iran.

Here is what even the "Justice 4 Immigrants Filipino Coalition" said back on 14 April 2006 in a message spread by email:

> "New York – More than 100 Filipinos and immigrant allies joined at least 250,000 more in a New York City immigrant rights rally as part of the April 10th national day of action across several U.S. cities, calling for comprehensive immigration reforms amidst the ongoing immigration debate in Capitol Hill. The Justice 4 Immigrants Filipino Coalition (J4I), a broad formation comprised of Filipino organizations and individuals from New York and New Jersey, raised their banners and flags high in a sea of multi-national representation in front of Manhattan's City Hall. The Justice 4 Immigrants Filipino Coalition is an active member of the Steering Committee of the April 10 Coalition.

> "We are the third largest immigrant group, and second largest Asian population in the U.S. Over 60,000 Filipinos migrate to the U.S. every year. We migrate not because we have dreams or illusions of luxury."

From the very name of the organization, the struggle has been abandoned. Justice for immigrants implies a bourgeois integrationist strategy. This sort of thing does nothing but promote the Martin Luther King line and aid the Pentagon in recruiting.

Even worse was Sison's own statement of April 3. Here we were hoping for a scientific communist approach. Instead we got more Martin Luther King reformism:

ILPS Extends Its Solidarity with the People of the U.S. Against the Criminalization of Immigrants and Intensification of the U.S. War of Terror

By Prof. Jose Maria Sison
Chairperson, International Coordinating Committee
International League of Peoples' Struggle
3 April 2006

The International League of Peoples' Struggles (ILPS) extends its firm solidarity with the people of the U.S., especially the millions of immigrants and their supporters who have taken to the streets in order to oppose the Border Protection, Homeland Security, and Illegal Immigration Act, also known as HR4437. We salute and congratulate you for your resounding success in mobilizing yourselves and standing up for human rights against the criminalization of immigrants and the intensification of the U.S. war of terror against the oppressed nationalities of the Americas and in other parts of the world.

The massive rallies that surged up in the last few weeks in various U.S. cities signals the waking of the sleeping giant that is the immigrant communities and oppressed nationalities within the belly of the imperialist beast. It is a just cause to defend and fight for the human dignity and democratic rights of twelve million immigrants and their supporters against imperialist oppression, racism and the looming monster of fascism. Such a just cause enjoys abundant support throughout the world.

House Resolution 4437, or the Sensenbrener Act, named after U.S. Congressperson F. James Sensenbrenner, would have made routine immigration violations "aggravated felonies" and having routine contact with an undocumented person a felony. The measure would have criminalized whole immigrant communities, as well as individuals or organizations that provide basic social services to the millions of undocumented individuals residing and working in the United States. Immigrant advocates, lawyers, priests, service providers and employers would be subject to heavy fines and prison time if they refused or otherwise failed to report their client to the authorities.

While these provisions would have been totally unworkable given the millions of people it would criminalize, it would have no doubt led to intensifying immigrant scapegoating, racial profiling, and providing the license or legal device for the Federal Bureau of Investigation (FBI) to go after critics, political opponents, and advocates of immigrant and civil rights. Congressman Sensenbrener, the author of this bill which passed the House of Representative in December 2005, is the same person who, in June 2005, shut down the House Judiciary meeting on the Patriot Act when his congressional colleagues began to raise tough questions about the curtailment of civil rights in the United States and the Bush administration policy on the use of torture.

Besides the egregious attacks against immigrants, the bill also includes billions of dollars for the construction of a wall between the United States and Mexico border and billions more just to study the feasibility of building a wall on the border of the United States and Canada. These provisions surely were pushed by U.S. corporate interests that stand to benefit through billions of dollars worth of government contracts. These proposed walls promise to further isolate Americans from the rest of the world, and will burden generations of American taxpayers. Surely, this boondoggle will misdirect public funds away from the basic services that the American working people need.

The unprecedented mobilizations of the immigrants and their supporters during the last few weeks have definitely jolted members of the House Judiciary Committee into putting out a version of the bill with a few of the most punitive sections left out. The bill is still replete with provisions that are obnoxiously punitive, biased and discriminatory. Moreover, the bill being considered by the Senate is still fatally packed with extreme provisions that would effectively bar millions of people from the chance to earn legalization, take away the right to a fair hearing, legalize the indefinite detention of non-citizens, and allow domestic military bases to be used for immigration detention.

Since the major mobilizations in Chicago, Milwaukee, Phoenix, and the million-person Gran Marcha in Los Angeles, there has been continuous mobilization of communities – from high school walk-outs to hunger strikes, and now the call for a 40-city national mobilization on April 10. These are promising signs for the further development of a sustained movement for democratic rights against imperialism, fascism and racism. While some are calling this the new civil rights movement, ILPS hopes that the rising consciousness, broad mobilization, and alliance building are revitalizers of a much-needed anti-imperialist movement in the heartland of the number one imperialist nation in the world.

This latest attack against immigrants in the United States is an intensification of the U.S. War of Terror on all oppressed nationalities. Your struggle is one with the struggle of people around the world against U.S. imperialist aggression and outright disregard for human rights. We fully support you in refusing to be scapegoated and labeled as terrorists and criminals. The real terrorists in the world are the imperialists and their local reactionary accomplices that oppress and exploit the people and force an increasing number of them to emigrate, especially to the United States, which has aggrandized itself with resource-grabbing and superprofits under the auspices of neoliberal globalization and the U.S. permanent war of terror against the people of the world.

The International League of Peoples' Struggle looks forward to your ever greater success in organizing and mobilizing more millions of people on April 10 and in subsequent actions to further condemn and isolate the crisis-ridden and increasingly repressive U.S. imperialism, particularly under the aggressive and rapacious Bush regime. We call on the ILPS participating organizations in the United States to join in the forthcoming mass actions, as they have done since last month. We also call on the ILPS participating organizations all over the world to make manifest their fervent solidarity with and militant support for all the oppressed nationalities in the United States and the millions of immigrants who have risen up to oppose the ever hateful anti-people policies of the U.S. monopoly bourgeoisie.

While we expect the masses to have some confusion about the integrationist versus nationalist roads, it's not acceptable in our international leaders. If the communists are not firm against U.$. military recruiting, no one is. Sison's whole piece mentions "oppressed nationalities," but it does not favor liberation of Aztlán. We fail to see how he could not mention that given the context he himself decided to comment on.

Yes, there it was. "Oppressed nationalities" he says. "Anti-imperialism," not "civil rights" he says. Yet then he slides back into a "multinational" one-working-class approach by talking about "immigrants" from the very title of the article. We cannot speak of the migrant movement in the United $tates without Aztlán. If we want "anti-imperialism," we need to name nations instead of talking only about the U.S. Congress. If Filipinos do not want to claim a piece of North American territory, then the least they can do is side with Aztlán. In fact, Sison has already surrendered the question inevitably, because he cannot come out and say that super-profits are generating a massive petty bourgeoisie including Filipino aspiring petty bourgeoisie willing to dump the anti-imperialist struggle for the "civil rights" struggle. He ends with the target of the "monopoly bourgeoisie," while leaving out the role of the integrationist petty bourgeoisie in recruiting for the monopoly bourgeoisie's military. In case he did not notice, monopoly capitalist Bush actually was taking a more moderately chauvinist line than the majority of U.$. public (a.k.a. labor aristocracy) opinion. This same Sison refuses to condemn the fake Maoist RIM's call for Iran's government to be defeated by U.$. imperialism. The treason against Maoism goes together in one piece of conciliation with U.$. imperialism.

This Section modified slightly from http://www.prisoncensorship.info/archive/etext/countries/aztlan/chicano092506.html

Section 3:
Why Revolutionary Proletarian Nationalism?

by MIM(Prisons)

HERE WE UPDATE AND EXPAND on what MIM wrote about the Chicano Moratorium in the previous essay, and address some other major political questions surrounding the Chican@ nation in present times.

Over the last decade we have seen the resurgence of migrants, the majority of whom are from Mexico, as a force of social change within the United $tates.[1] The dominant view of this struggle, due to its translation through Amerikan terms, continues to be one of civil rights and anti-racism. As the last essay demonstrated, framing the migrant struggle in this way serves to support U.$. imperialism and its oppression of people around the world.

Amerika is an exploiter nation. Amerikans built their nation on land grab, genocide and slavery of other nations; not only subjecting Mexican@s and the emerging Chican@ nation, but the many First Nations, the African slaves that they imported, the Chinese migrant workers, etc. This legacy has reached the point where today there is hardly a place you can go where U.$. imperialism has not killed people, destroyed ecosystems and taken by force whatever they wanted. To justify and carry out these acts, racism became an integral part of Amerikan thinking. With U.$. global dominance, racism is now an ideology known to all.

In the late 1960s, the contradiction between the oppressed nations, in particular the New Afrikan nation, and the Amerikan nation came to a head. To weaken this contradiction, the U.$. imperialists supported civil rights for New Afrikans, just as it had 100 years prior. In 1876, Reconstruction ended as the Republican government pulled troops out of the South, where they were stationed to defend New Afrikans from white

Amerikans. In the 1960s there was a similar backlash of white Amerikans against the struggle for civil rights for New Afrikans, but this time the emerging tide of social forces were against the white Amerikans and they lost. This victory for New Afrikan civil rights officially marked the end of any remaining New Afrikan proletariat, who were either integrated into the petty bourgeois majority or left to stagnate as a lumpen population in the ghettos that were once vibrant communities, with many young men being shipped off to concentration camps under close state supervision.

What distinguishes the class structure of the Chican@ nation as a U.$. internal semi-colony is that it is fed by the proletariat of Mexico and Central (and to a lesser extent South) America (as discussed in the beginning of Part II). The populations feeding the Chican@ nation migrate to the United $tates largely to earn higher wages, but often continue to face exploitation here. In contrast, those with the legal right to work in the United $tates benefit from high wages above the value of labor. As a result of civil rights gains, the majority of New Afrikans and Chican@s have now joined the ranks of the labor aristocracy that has long character-ized the Euro-Amerikan nation. The labor aristocracy benefits materially from imperialism.[2]

In our research on the lumpen class in the United $tates, the lumpen population is about 15-20% of New Afrikans based on income. Meanwhile, among Raza, about 10-15% have incomes below legal full-time employment levels, but a majority of them are actually working, just at proletarian or semi-proletarian wages.[3]

While the influx of proletarians from south of the Rio Bravo has an overall positive effect on the political views in the Chican@ nation in terms of opposing imperialism, the majority exploiter country has a negative effect on these migrants who are faced with the temptation of becoming an exploiter too. This is a big deal because the labor aris-tocracy lackeys to imperialism generally do more to support militarism than neo-colonial lackeys. The neo-colonial government in Mexico has not provided troops to imperialism to invade other countries to allow for continued extraction of superprofits to the United $tates. Yet, the Chican@ internal semi-colony has provided six figures worth of troops to the imperialists. In other words, it is harder for the president of Mexico, a U.$. puppet, to provide occupying troops than it is for Chican@s. And this is why anti-racism and civil rights in the United $tates help feed militarism, via integration.

While the most up-to-date statistics show "Hispanics" underrepresented in the U.$. military at only 11.3% of all U.$. military personnel [4], enlistment of Raza has steadily risen in recent decades. This has come from a huge marketing effort by the U.$. military in Spanish-language media and hands-on recruiting in Latino schools. With promises of Amerikan citizenship, and opportunities to study in bourgeois-dominated U.$. schools, Chican@s find strong temptation to risk their lives and kill others for the Amerikan dream.

Figure 2.3.1 Hispanic Ethnicity of U.$. Military

year	Active		Reserves	
	#	%	#	%
1985	N/A	<4	N/A	N/A
1994	N/A	<6	N/A	N/A
2004FY	N/A	9.8	N/A	7.4
2004	127,231	9.0	72,489	8.4
2007	141,419	10.4	74,752	8.9
2008	146.813	10.6	77,437	9.1
2009*	149.845	10.7	78,872	9.2
2010	153,555	10.8	81,181	9.5
2011	158,251	11.2	83,700	9.8
2012	157,206	11.3	85,687	10.1

FIGURE 2.3.1 See citations 4, 5, 6, 7.   * Prior to 2009, "Hispanic" was categorized as a "racial" designation, parallel to Black, white, Asian, American Indian or Alaska Native, Native Hawaiian or Other Pacific Islander. In 2009, Hispanic started being analyzed as a separate ethnic group, layered on top of, rather than distinct from, Black, white, etc.

Why are the imperialists working so hard to expand Raza recruits to the military? One reason, as MIM explained in the previous section, is because Amerikans are aging out.[8] Another reason is that Amerikan youth have other methods to go to college and live with a comfortable exploiter-level income. They don't need to risk their lives to seize this opportunity. For whites that do enter the U.$. military, they are more likely to follow a well-established family legacy, and enter into safe officer positions. This effect was seen during the Vietnam War when Chican@s protested their over-representation in the death counts from the war.

In recent years there has been much discussion about the DREAM Act within the Chican@ nation. There were versions proposed by U.$. politicians that would require military service for migrants to earn citizen status. In those versions, the relationship between U.$. imperialism and migrants is made clear. The standard version that was pushed by the left wing of white nationalism offered citizenship for those who successfully attended college. Both preserve the elite status of Amerikan citizenship, which the oppressed must earn in order to take part in the spoils of imperialist conquest.

Similarly, so-called "immigration reform" has been a hot topic in Amerikan politics for years now as the influx of Mexican migrants reached new heights. The popular rhetoric is that the current system is "broken." For most Amerikans this means we need to tighten up the border, yet many Chican@s echo this terminology to argue for less repression at the border. The status quo has remained a steadily increased militarization of the border. Like many laws focused on oppression of the internal semi-colonies, the Illegal Immigration Reform and Immigrant Responsibility Act was passed by Bill Clinton in 1996. Since then the number of people deported has steadily risen from 70,000 in 1995 to almost 420,000 in 2012.[9] That law also brought increased legal penalties for migrants, leading to migrant prison camps accounting for the greatest increase in the U.$. prison population in recent years.[10]

While immigration from other Third World countries is often driven by U.$. militarism (as we saw with Vietnam in Part II Section 1), the majority of migrants are coming here for economic reasons. Therefore it would be fair to say the problem is one of wealth distribution. To get a sense of the scope of that problem, let's look at some numbers. The settler countries of North America, the United $tates and Kkkanada, own about 30% of the world's wealth, while having only 5% of the world's population. (see *Figure 2.3.2* on the next page) This concentration of wealth is only possible by controlling the flow of humyn beings at the borders of these countries.

Let's imagine that suddenly the imperialists decided that the world would be a better place if wealth was distributed equally, but because wealth is so tied up in local infrastructure, rather than moving wealth around the world, people had to be moved to where the wealth is. This would require an increase in the population of North America by six

Figure 2.3.2 World Distribution of Household Wealth, GDP, and Population in the year 2000

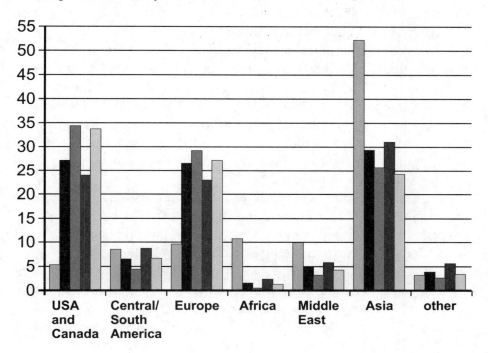

percent of world population

percent of world net worth (PPP)

percent of world net worth (exchange rates)

percent of world GDP (PPP)

percent of world GDP (exchange rates)

source: https://en.wikipedia.org/wiki/World_distribution_of_wealth#/media/
File:World_distributionofwealth_GDP_and_population_by_region.gif

times. That's a migration of over 1.5 billion people. Since Klanada's GDP is not much lower than that of the United $tates, that would translate into about 870 million people moving into the United $tates. Compare that to the currently 38.4 million foreign-born people in the United $tates. Those new immigrants alone would be more than double the existing population of the entire United $tates.

The current number of Mexican migrants who are in the United $tates against U.$. laws has begun to decrease after peaking around 7 million in 2007. The rate of migration from Mexico has decreased from 770,000 per year in 2000 to 140,000 in 2010.[11] Therefore, a generous estimate of the number of people who will be affected by "immigration reform" would be around 770,000, which is less than 0.1% of the 870 million that need to move to the United $tates to achieve an equal distribution of wealth globally.

If each year Amerikan reformists were able to pass a law to improve the conditions of 0.1% of the people whose wealth has been stolen, and countries underdeveloped by the United $tates, it would take them 1,000 years to address global wealth disparity. It only took the Communist Party of China 25 years to overthrow capitalism in their country, and another 15 years to build a booming socialist economy, while eliminating social ills such as hunger, homelessness, concubinism, foot binding, and drug addiction. This is the kind of comparison we make when we say we look at history to find what has worked best to create a better society.

Any "immigration reform" that comes out of the Amerikan political system will not be significant progress for the international proletariat. Reforms may save individual lives and keep some individual families together, but these reforms will still retain the fundamental capitalist system of borders to keep the wealth in and the poor out. Further, such reforms are of concern for the life-blood this could pump into the oppressor nation's military forces' killing of the proletariat, as discussed previously.

The only truly progressive demand in this conversation would be complete demilitarization of the border. But more than asking Amerikans to demilitarize the border, Chican@s must organize around the border. Serve the People Programs that focus on survival pending revolution are needed. There already exist programs that provide some water, shelter and medical aid to migrants along the border. And there are many services for migrants once they reach urban centers in the United $tates. But unless such services are organized under Maoist political leadership with a strong emphasis on political education, then they only serve as band-aids to the current system. Organizing must translate into resistance to the repression seen at the border; resistance that will actually force Amerikans to change their ways.

While we do advocate the end to all borders, we saw in our thought experiment above that it is not a practical rallying point for reform at this time. When we build our socialist state, we will be able to open the borders and redistribute wealth, which will need to happen on a global scale. Of course, the imperialists will never freely redistribute wealth on a global scale anyway, and socialism will be built in the periphery first where conditions under imperialism are worst. Therefore wealth redistribution will be well under way before the imperialist borders are torn down.

Perhaps a more likely scenario of wealth redistribution in our current conditions would be through the institution of a global minimum wage, in particular from multinational corporations. Of course we don't see people rallying for a global minimum wage on the White House steps because it would mean a reduction in Amerikans' own access to this wealth. The Liberalism of the white-nationalist left justifies selling out the majority of the world's people in order to allow a tiny proportion of migrants to get more access to the privileges they themselves have. This is a clear example of the left wing of white nationalism trying to provide some relief to the irreconcilable contradictions faced by imperialism.

In conclusion, any efforts to reduce militarization, oppression and violence on the border are progressive. But increased economic opportunities do nothing to help the international proletariat unless they are universal, such as a global minimum wage. In this sense, there is not likely to be any "immigration reforms" in the U.$. Congress worth supporting. But there continues to be a strong resistance to the border itself that should be a focus of our work.

Section 4:
Democratic Convention Highlights Chicano Assimilationist

by cipactli, 2012

ON 4 SEPTEMBER 2012 THE Democratic National Convention was held in Charlotte, North Carolina. It was broadcast on almost every TV in this facility. Like the Republican National Convention, the Democrats had speakers come out to make a short speech on why you should vote for their candidate. These conventions are a classic "good cop, bad cop" game meant to hoodwink the oppressed.

This year's democratic keynote speaker at the convention was Julian Castro the mayor of San Antonio, Texas. Castro is running for Congress and is seen as an up-and-coming Democrat. Although he merely adds to the rest of the numerous defenders of imperialism, what is different (and thus dangerous) about Castro is that he is a Chicano bourgeois politician. He is now being propped up to fool the brown masses, just as Obama was used against the New Afrikan masses.

Castro's background is similar to many Chican@s today. His grandmother migrated to the United $tates in 1920 in the first wave of migration after the Mexican Revolution. His mother was born in Texas and was actively a part of the Chican@ movement of the 1960s and 70s. As a first-generation college student she joined the Raza Unida Party (RUP) and became one of its leaders.

As mentioned in Part I, RUP came about from the leadership of Crusade for Justice, another important Chican@ organization of that time.

RUP meant to uplift la Raza's consciousness, take community control of social services in the barrios, and take control of schools and development (building homes, parks, etc.). This all seems "progressive." But without completely breaking with the oppressor's politics, these efforts were simply like trying to ride a bike with no chain; you can turn the pedals all you want but the bike stays in the same spot.

RUP naively thought Amerika would stand by and allow an historically oppressed people, an internal semi-colony at that, to build a political party in the barrios, even though it attempted to do so within Amerika's political system. The state would not allow this, as organizing the oppressed for any progressive political activity poses a real potential threat to Amerika's hegemony. Once organized and educated, this force can easily make a leap from working within the current system to working against the system. This is why people like Martin Luther King and Malcolm X were assassinated even though they were not calling for socialism, and pretty much working within the confines of the Amerikan laws. They still had influence and the potential was too much.

RUP was heavily surveilled by the CIA and all the typical COINTELPRO tactics were used to destroy this party.[1] Fault also lies with the more revolutionary elements within RUP for not steering RUP on a path to seek liberation of the Chican@ nation by building for a socialist revolution on these shores.

So this is where Julian Castro comes from, and thus bourgeois nationalism is what shaped his ideas and led him down the road to brown capitalism. He is an outright defender of imperialism. Castro's assimilationist stance shone forth in his speech with statements like "[we need to] do our part as one community, as one United States of America." This is typical language of a comprador whose job is to bring the other oppressed into the fold of the oppressor. His job is always to smother the burning embers of resistance in a people and keep conditions as they currently are. The slave of old who lived in the massa's house would go out to the slave shacks and talk about how good the massa is, how good the slaves got it, maybe even give them a piece of bacon or the good meat with a promise for more so long as they hang on and be content, or say some prayers. This is the approach Castro took in his speech. His focus – like the rest of the Democrats – was on the "middle class," and at one point his petty bourgeois colors intensified as he yelled: "The middle class, the engine of our economic growth!" The brown bourgeoisie must have soiled themselves in excitement at hearing this parasite babble on.

Castro's interests are stripped of the more progressive aspects of the 1970s political line of his mother, Rosie Castro, which he branded as outdated in an interview on Pacifica Radio. As misguided as RUP may have been in their approach, they never spoke of leaving Raza behind, nor were they reduced to telling Raza to "pull themselves up by their bootstraps." Rather, they sought to include even the poorest Raza living in shacks in their reforms, and fought to better their conditions. On the other hand, Julian Castro has aligned with imperialism. As he stated, "We know in our free market economy some people will prosper more than others." The assumption that there will always be the haves and the have-nots is not something we can accept. But Castro sends the message to the ruling class that he is okay with this and thus is not intending to threaten or challenge this status quo. This buys his seat in the imperialist shuttle of Amerikan politics.

The use of Julian Castro is just the latest attempt to get Chican@s and other Raza to feel as if they are part of Amerika. But many Raza still remember the oppression we have faced; it is still too much for many to side with the enemy. According to the 2010 U.$. Census about 2.3 million businesses are owned by Raza. Yet when it comes to voting in bourgeois elections only 60 percent of adult Raza citizens vote, compared to 70 percent of New Afrikan adults, and 74 percent of whites. At the same time approximately 500,000 Raza youth will turn 18 and join the "Hispanic" voting bloc every year for the next 20 years. Castro is the tip of the iceberg where Amerika will begin courting Raza much more than they ever have in history. They are especially recruiting Raza with family history of activism, such as Julian Castro and his mother. This is an attempt to legitimize them in the eyes of the Chican@ nation. But these brown faces in high places will never be legitimate so long as they support the world's most despicable parasites. Those who we see as legitimate are those working to liberate our nation, those working to neutralize the imperialists.

We see Amerika's open repression reaching fascist proportions in Aztlán, especially in prisons and on the U.$.-fabricated border. Most recently we saw along the Texas/Mexico border the U.$. installation of a "mini navy" where speed boats with high powered weapons are guarding the Rio Bravo.[2] These boats were recently baptized in Mexicano blood when they shot and killed a Mexican citizen on the Mexican side who was barbecuing in a picnic area with his family right on the river. Footage on the Amerikan corporate media this week shows the border patrol speed off while cries from families and children erupt in the park. This open war on Raza comes without a peep from bourgeois politicians like Julian Castro, who, rather than condemn this repression in his speech, instead declares "Amerika will prevail" with a wink to massa.

We must also learn from the lessons of the past. We are not free to create our own political parties that struggle for our nations. Look at what happened to the RUP and Panthers and others. Although parties of the internal semi-colonies are not publicly banned in Amerika, they are certainly banned behind closed doors in Langley, in Washington D.C., and their other hideaways. We know this is true when we learn about COINTELPRO and other operations to infiltrate and disrupt peoples parties or groups. And so we refuse to be fed snake oil from the imperialists or their allies. We work to hasten the day when Aztlán and the other internal semi-colonies can be liberated from attacks by Amerika!

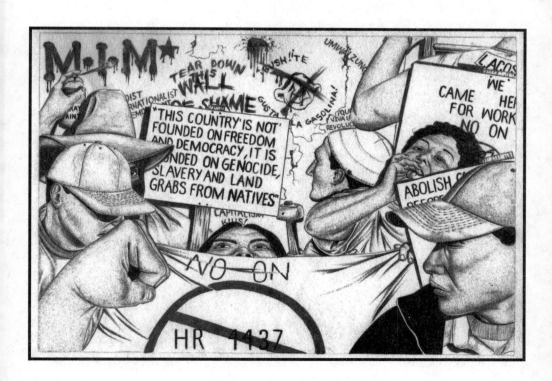

Section 5:
Response to rcp=u$a's Opposition to Aztlán

by a MIM(Prisons) Study Group

THE SOCIETY THAT U.$. PRISONERS dream of is one that turns the pyramid of power upside down, where those on the bottom of today's totem pole are the ones who have a say in running a society. This concept was actualized in the stage of New Democracy in Mao's China where landless peasants were freed from the chains of oppressive feudalism and colonialism. The prisoner in today's capitalist United $tates understands that such a society will not come easy, and we are reminded of this valuable lesson every day when we attempt to change the oppressive environment behind prison walls.

As we gain more experience with political organizing, we see that campaigns or actions that are not coordinated often prove disastrous. We experience first-hand the need for a vanguard organization in our own work. In a large-scale effort like transforming society, combating the capitalists, and building the revolution, we can see how a vanguard political party would be needed to lead the masses on the right path to liberation on all fronts. Understanding this, we, and many others in prison, seek out political parties and begin the arduous work of studying all the revolutionary groups' theories and their political line, so that we can determine who is the vanguard party, and who has the correct political theory on what it will take to reach liberation here in the belly of the beast.

The Revolutionary Communist Party, U$A (rcp=u$a) claims to be a vanguard political party struggling on behalf of oppressed people. While at first glance rcp=u$a literature may seem "progressive," and a novice revolutionary may even think the rcp=u$a is fighting in the best interests of the masses of oppressed people, a closer look into its political line may surprise many prisoners who are still developing their political stance. Rcp=u$a's stance on the oppressed nations' right to self-determination, in particular the Chican@ nation, will be the focus of our critique.[1]

This essay deals with four separate documents produced by rcp=u$a which speak to the question of internal semi-colonies of the United $tates, with focus on their handling of the Chican@ nation specifically. The four documents are titled *The Chicano Struggle and Proletarian Revolution in the U.S.* (2001)[2], *Constitution for the New Socialist Republic in North America (Draft Proposal)* (2010)[3], "Letter to Participating Parties and Organizations of the Revolutionary Internationalist Movement" (2012)[4], and "Everything You've Been Told About Communism is Wrong: Capitalism Is a Failure, Revolution is the Solution" (2012).[5]

The implication throughout these documents is that the rcp=u$a is going to somehow turn the United $tates into a socialist multinational government and economy, led of course by the "majority" Amerikkkan nation. Once the Amerikkkan-led communists have liberated North America, we can finally start talking about self-determination for the internal semi-colonies.

Though shrouded in apparent "communist" rhetoric, the earliest and most specific document we found on this topic, *The Chicano Struggle and Proletarian Revolution in the U.S.* (2001), is nothing more than lying phrase-mongering, the sort of which Lenin warned against in "The Socialist Revolution and the Right of Nations to Self-Determination."

This "discussion paper" by the rcp=u$a attempts to fool members of the Chican@ nation into giving up the struggle for national liberation and self-determination by stating that: 1) The Chican@ nation is not a nation, but a national minority (revising and jumbling the way these two very specific Marxist terms were historically used and defined by Lenin, Stalin and Mao); and 2) by emphatically insinuating that all nationalism is bourgeois in essence. We will first address the many ways they attempt to discredit the struggle for the Chican@ nation's right to self-determination.

How Many Ways Can They
Deny Our Right To Self-Determination?

RCP talks about "minority nationalities" to imply that they are acknowledging the status of these groups as nations. But then we are handled as if we are simply minorities of the United $tates population, or in this case its "socialist" equivalent, the New Socialist Republic in North America. This is also apparent in their reference to Chican@s as "Mexican-Americans" and New Afrikans as "African-Americans." The whole premise that there is an American people that is defined by the borders of the United $tates is opposed to our own thesis on nations.[6] Yet, at the same time, Chican@s in the United $tates today are seen by the rcp=u$a to be one and the same as Mexican nationals.

While Aztlán as a liberating concept was resuscitated and re-popularized in 1969 during the Chicano Youth Liberation Conference as part of *El Plan Espiritual de Aztlán*, it was by no means ever a myth. But the rcp=u$a, like so many before them, limit Aztlán to be "the mythical homeland of the Chicano people." Important for us to understand however is that this dominant-nation obsession of referring to Aztlán as a "myth" has its own roots in the colonialist mentality of the settler state and their need to erase all past knowledge of life before their arrival.

Furthermore, there is much historical and archaeological evidence of Aztlán having existed and being situated in the "Southwest United $tates," so all this talk of Aztlán being a "myth" needs to stop! A nation as a social-historical-political structure is only ever acknowledged by the bourgeoisie so long as it has an army and a navy. Therefore, without an army and a navy it will continue to be looked on as a "myth." Hence, Mao's famous thesis that political power grows out of the barrel of a gun and that without a People's Army the people have nothing! Aztlán is a powerful symbol of resistance to the Chican@ people and it will remain a focal point of struggle for the Chican@ nation. The concept of nationhood of the oppressed internal semi-colonies and the backlash they receive from the left wing of white nationalism are just more examples of power struggles we must wage in the political realm against our so-called "comrades" who in practice prove themselves to be our enemies.

A huge part of the rcp=u$a's argument against the Chican@ nation building a separate nation-state is based on the enforcement of imperialist borders and the RCP's respect for these borders. Now, maybe the rcp=u$a respects these borders, but we certainly don't!

With classic divide-and-conquer tactics, the rcp=u$a also uses the First Nations' development in the "Southwest United $tates" as an argument against the building of a separate nation-state for Chican@s. They do this while simultaneously denying the First Nations' place in history in other documents, one of many logical inconsistencies in their attempts to delegitimize Chican@ nationalism.

There is a long history of the left wing of white nationalism using calls for socialism and worker unity to manage the struggles of oppressed nations by subordinating them to their own, while dividing the oppressed from each other.[7]

Another argument from *The Chicano Struggle* (2001) as to why Chican@s aren't a nation and have no need for a nation-state is as follows:

> *"As we have seen, when the U.S. seized the Southwest territory from Mexico the Mexican settlements there were not sufficiently developed, and their isolation from each other and from Mexico was too great to give rise to their own development into a nation. With the conquest these settlements were no longer connected to Mexico and the nation-forming process taking place there. And in the Southwest in the period that followed the conquest, the Mexican population living there did not develop as a nation. Mexicans in the Southwest were subjected to brutal oppression that forged them into a distinct oppressed people within the U.S.– but a separate Chicano nation never came into being."[8]*

Ugh, what? Nations are not the sole creations of the political process, but of historical forces, and there is actually plenty of evidence contrary to the RCP's position here. In dealing with the national-colonial question of the Chican@ nation it is important that we conduct a concrete analysis of concrete conditions.

The rcp=u$a continues their attacks:

> *"Modern nations first arose and developed with the rise and development of capitalism. For various reasons, some have become dominant over others and, while not always the case, generally the nations where capitalism has developed more quickly have dominated and oppressed other, less capitalistically-developed nations. And, in fact, this domination often prevented groups of people from developing into a nation at all."[8]*

Excuse us, but no developed country has *ever* developed in a "capitalistic" sense absent national oppression – there is such a thing as primitive accumulation of capital and it is what signaled "the rosy dawn of capitalism."[9] The capitalist development of European nations is inextricably bound to colonialism, without which there could have been no developed modern nations; as the development of one nation in the capitalistic sense always presupposes the underdevelopment of other nations. But the rcp=u$a doesn't acknowledge this fact because they don't believe the oppressed people of the world were ever civilized enough to form themselves into nations unless they met a white man somewhere down the road who had the humyn decency to civilize the native by means of guns, germs and steel.

Here the rcp=u$a once again handles the national question of the oppressed in a very chauvinistic manner. They ignore the objective laws of material development and they willingly blind themselves to these laws that nationalism and the political structures it gives rise to aims

> *"towards making national boundaries conterminous with those of the state. Contrary to modernist theories of nationalism (of which Eurocentric Marxism forms an influential subset), pre-modern nations existed and arose from the centralist state structures of, for example, the tributary systems of ancient Egypt, China, Ireland, and Medieval England [and in the case of Chican@s, the Mexica-Nahuatl - Editor]. Yet whilst nationalism undoubtedly appeared before capitalism and hence, outside Europe, the rise of the bourgeois state gave it more widespread significance."[10]*

According to the rcp=u$a, the historical development of the Chican@ "minority nation" began with Amerika's conquest of northern Mexico by the United $tates in their war on Mexico in the 1840s. In the RCP's *Constitution*, it apparently ends there as well. However, as we showed in previous sections of this book, the economic and territorial development of the Chican@ nation began well before the U.$. annexation of northern Mexico, and it continues to develop as a separate nation distinct from Amerika and Mexico today.

> *"The history of the Chicano people is rooted in the conquest of the Southwest by the U.S. ruling class in the war they waged on Mexico in 1846-48, the domination of U.S. imperialism over Mexico, the maintenance of backward*

conditions in large parts of the Southwest, and the persecution and ex-
ploitation of Mexican immigrants. Dispossessed of their land, treated
as foreigners in territory stolen by the U.S., persecuted if they defend
their right to a culture and language different from that of the European-
American nation..."[11]

In saying that the history of the Chican@ people is rooted in the Amerikkkan annexation of the Southwest by "the U.$. ruling class" they objectively negate the more than 300 years of historical development of the Chican@ people in the "Southwest United $tates." They also negate and exonerate the white-settler state's role in the annexation of the Amerikan Southwest. It is an historical fact that it was the white settlers' immigration from the slave-owning South and into Texas (then a Mexican territory) that preceded the annexation and the war, and certainly not the U.$. ruling classes themselves.

Colonies are not colonies without an occupying force, and the occupying force of Aztlán was the white settler nation. The same nation that provided the slave catchers and overseers that occupied the neighboring New Afrikan colony.

Part 2 of *The Chicano Struggle* (2001) is entitled, "The Source of and Solution to the Oppression of the Chicano People." In this section of their paper, the rcp=u$a seeks to "scientifically investigate" the root cause of national oppression in Aztlán. Their conclusion?

"There are two sources – one historical, and one international – for the
ongoing oppression and discrimination against Chicanos. First is their
historic subjugation as a 'conquered' people, which is woven into the so-
cial fabric of this country as a result of and a justification for the theft
of Mexican land and the brutal oppression of the Mexican people who
remained there following the conquest."[12]

"And this oppression is further reinforced and reproduced by the fact that
the U.S. shares a 2,000 mile border with a country that it keeps locked
into an oppressor/oppressed relationship. The U.S. dominates, subjugates
and superexploits Mexico, and at the same time is deeply dependent on
Mexican immigrant labor as a crucial source of wealth for the U.S. capi-
talists, keeping the overwhelming majority of Mexican immigrants in the
bottom rungs of the working class. To maintain this setup and deal with

the potential threat they see to their own stability, the U.S. rulers have institutionalized discrimination against those of Mexican descent and Latinos in general."[13]

In making this statement here, the rcp=u$a not only glosses over, but totally obliterates the historical and the national-colonial character of Aztlán with regards to its relationship to the United $tates. They also effectively and completely take the national liberation struggle of the Chican@ nation off the agenda, attribute the national oppression of Chican@s to the exploitation of Mexico, and relegate the oppression within United $tates borders to a matter of "social fabric." They do not attribute this national oppression to the imperialists and the white settler nation, but to external factors that are less than secondary! Even imperialist-minded scholars have more sense and a keener grasp of the issue than the so-called "Revolutionary Communist Party, USA." Mario Barrera, in his book *Race and Class in the Southwest: A theory of racial inequality*, recognizes this cause and effect.

"In a long memo sent to Secretary of State Kissinger by Arthur Corwin in June 1975, these worries are laid out. ... In it, Corwin argues that the combination of rapid population growth in Mexico, continued inflow of undocumented workers across the border, and rising nationalist and Third World sentiments among Chicanos and Mexicanos in the Southwest could lead to an 'American Quebec' in that area and a 'reconquest of Aztlán.'"[14]

The rcp=u$a further rails against the formation of an independent Chican@ nation-state with the following paragraph:

"Given that the actual historical development of the Chicano people has not been characterized by their development into a nation, in reality and in the scientific sense, the view that Chicano liberation can only come in the form of establishing a separate Chicano nation-state does not represent the interests of the masses of Chicano people and the masses of oppressed and exploited people overall. In fact, it will actually play into the hands of the imperialist bourgeoisie, making it easier for the imperialists to pit the demands of different sections of the people on both sides of the U.S./ Mexico border against each other and to lead the people's struggle into dead ends."[15]

One might read this and think, oh then the logical solution is to reunite Mexico as a powerful anti-imperialist block against the United $tates. But alas, this is not the conclusion of the rcp=u$a. Just as they use First Nations to deny Chican@s a claim to Aztlán, they raise the spectre of conflict between Chican@s and Mexican@s to deny the right of Chican@ self-determination. Yet they do not call for reunification of Mexico, they stick to their efforts to unite Chican@s with Amerikans in this stage of the struggle

In their more recent *Constitution* (2010), the rcp=u$a is ambivalent on whether the "Southwest United $tates" will be returned to Mexico as part of a future transition to socialism in North America. Similarly, they give lip service to the formation of an independent Chican@ nation-state in Aztlán:

> "[T]he necessary consideration shall be given to the situation in the world as a whole, in determining how to proceed with regard to this region [the southwest region of the former United States of America]. In this overall context, and also taking into account the sentiments and aspirations of the people in the region, in particular those of Mexican origin and descent, the question of whether to return at least parts of this region to Mexico, and/or whether there should be established, within parts of this region, a country that is separate from both Mexico and the New Socialist Republic in North America, shall be taken up by the government of the New Socialist Republic in North America."[16]

Outside of this general allusion to "a country that is separate from both Mexico and the New Socialist Republic" (i.e. secession), a lot more detail is given in the *Constitution* on how to form "autonomous areas" in "cities or other areas within the New Socialist Republic in North America which have significant concentrations of Mexican-Americans."

> "The governments in any autonomous regions that are established shall be structured and chosen in accordance with the basic principles and proce-dures that obtain with regard to the central government and governments in various other areas within the overall New Socialist Republic in North America, while these autonomous region governments will also have the right to create additional institutional structures and procedures that may be necessary for the realization and functioning of autonomy, particularly

as regards the language and culture of the nationalities concerned, so long
as this is in accordance with the Constitution and laws of the New Socialist
Republic in North America."[(16)]

What seems to be lost on the RCP is that the oppressed nations, whether Chican@, First Nations or any other, are not going to put their lives on the line to transform this society only to allow themselves to be ruled by what the RCP feels is best. If oppressed nations see a New Socialist Republic government truly working in the interests of the people, it is then up to them to decide to join this republic. The vast majority of the land within the current U.$. borders belongs to the First Nations, Chican@s, and New Afrikans. For rcp=u$a to state they'll decide on who lives where, and who is allowed to control what territory, and how, is ludicrous. This colonization is incorrect and does not represent a righteous revolutionary line.

Rather than tell the Chican@ masses the truth about Aztlán, that the "Southwest" belongs to us, and has belonged to us for hundreds of years, and if we want to be free of national oppression then we must mount a national liberation struggle under a Maoist flag, the chauvinist RCP tells us that we aren't even a nation, but an ethnicity, deserving not a nation-state but regional autonomy. They say that we can have control over what language we speak in Aztlán, and that we can have control over what type of education our children get. We can even have our own loose form of government (read neo-colonial rule), but we cannot be free to control our destiny, because according to them capitalism didn't forge us into a nation in the Marxist sense. But the rcp=u$a is wrong. Capitalism did forge us into a contemporary nation, and if they were truly dialectical materialists like they claim to be they would know this.

No revolutionary should be satisfied with permission to run cultural and linguistic institutions, and make laws that presumably the New Socialist Republic will be charged to enforce. Stalin extensively critiqued similar proposals from the Austrian social democrats and the Bund in Russia, at one point asking, "Can a Diet for cultural affairs guarantee a nation against nationalist persecution?"[(17)] We need our own army to protect our own national territory.

We condemn the chauvinism of the rcp=u$a that is writing the plans for some utopian white socialist state, while asserting the future of Aztlán is uncertain. If anyone's future is uncertain it is the hundreds

of millions of Amerikans whose nation must be destroyed as part of the anti-imperialist struggle. It is hard for us to imagine how this will happen without the internal semi-colonies of the United $tates already being well on the socialist road. If we're going to be predicting the future, we should be thinking about how the socialist republics of Aztlán, New Afrika and First Nations will determine the form of transition for a large Amerikan population who is generally opposed to the socialist project.[18] In their classic style, rcp=u$a fakes left but actually opposes the liberation of oppressed nations, instead favoring the struggles of the Amerikan white oppressor nation for a bigger piece of unearned imperialist pie.

Nationalism is Bourgeois Anyway

Now let us turn to the rcp=u$a's second main line of attack against the struggle for Chican@ Power, which is found in their more recent documents, that completely reject the Marxist-Leninist-Maoist lines on nationalism.

In the piece titled "Letter to Participating Parties and Organizations of the Revolutionary Internationalist Movement," there is sprinkled throughout cautions against the "erroneous tendencies" of nationalism.[19] This letter clarifies that communism and nationalism are not the same thing, which of course we agree with technically speaking. The rcp=u$a takes it further and says that nationalism is actually opposed to inter-nationalism, and opposed to communism. Rcp=u$a does this in an ef-fort to undermine nationalist struggles, going so far as to advocate that nationalism not be part of our revolutionary organizing platform. This ahistorical plan makes sense coming from an Amerkan-led multinational organization, whose interests are wrapped up in being in charge of the revolutionary movement in this country, for their own benefit.

"Mao had argued during the period of new democratic revolution that, 'thus in wars of national liberation, patriotism is applied internationalism.' In fact, this formulation confounds two different questions: the stage of the revolution in China, which needed to carry out new democratic revolution, and the ideology and orientation of the communists, which could not be 'patriotism'. Mao's formulation 'patriotism is applied internationalism' had a great deal of influence on the newly emerging Maoist movement

in the 1960s and '70s. One reason is that this viewpoint dovetailed with
spontaneous tendencies that existed, especially but not exclusively in the
countries where revolution required going through a stage of new democ-
racy, to confound the ideology of nationalism and anti-imperialism with
the proletarian internationalist world view, to make a kind of 'two into
one' of these two ultimately opposite world views.

"Within [the Revolutionary Internationalist Movement] and the [interna-
tional communist movement] there has been discomfort and disagreement
and little desire to engage and struggle over this important analysis by
Avakian and his drawing of a sharp line of distinction between nationalism
and communism as the orientation of communists, even when necessarily
and correctly waging a struggle for new democracy."[19]

This is where the rcp=u$a really demarcates themselves on matters
of proletarian nationalism as a revolutionary force. The rcp=u$a vehe-
mently claims "internationalism" as being at the root of their ideology
and political line, but the sort of internationalism which they speak of
cannot, nor will it ever bring liberation to the oppressed nations, neither will it bring liberation to the fore. The premise of Mao's theory of
New Democracy is that while democratic struggles during the dawn of
capitalism were led by the bourgeoisie, that this class had become impotent as a force of revolution in the stage of imperialism. Thus the era
of imperialism is the era of New Democracy, where democratic struggle
must be led and waged by the masses of the popular classes in a united
front where the primary goal is national liberation. In other words, the
national struggle had become principal. Mao of course proved this theory
in practice in China. Attempting to maneuver towards or establish a
socialist-dictatorship absent the national liberation stage is complete and
utter utopianism and runs counter to the interest of the oppressed nation
masses as Mao, Stalin and Lenin most surely taught us.

In other words, as the rcp=u$a considers whether Aztlán might
become independent or reunite with Mexico after socialist revolution,
we propose that there will be no socialist revolution on these shores until
one of those things happens. And in direct answer to rcp=u$a's proposal
to consider the independence of Aztlán at a later stage, Lenin wrote,
"Just as mankind can achieve the abolition of classes only by passing
through the transition period of the dictatorship of the oppressed class

so can mankind achieve the inevitable merging of nations only by passing through the transition period of complete liberation of all the oppressed nations, i.e., their freedom to secede."[20]

It would appear that the rcp=u$a is more concerned about the oppressed nations submitting to their rule, than to the actual destruction of the imperialist economic system. Communism and the nationalism of oppressed nations against imperialism are both valid forms of struggle at this time. Rather than throwing out all nationalism as bad, we should do as Stalin did and promote all nationalism against imperialism, but warn against cultural and narrow nationalism.[21]

Funny enough, rcp=u$a claims to be against nationalism, but openly advocates for cultural nationalism in the autonomous zones outlined in their *Constitution*.

In "Everything You've Been Told," Raymond Lotta advocates,

"Let's take the crucial problem of racism and the oppression of Black, Latino, and other minority nationalities in this society...

"The new socialist state would immediately outlaw segregation in housing and the apartheid-like system of education in the U.S. and promote integration throughout society. The new society would foster exchanges of experiences and ideas among different sections of people, like Latinos and Blacks.

"At the same time, the new socialist state would uphold the right of self-determination for African-Americans, that is, the right to form an independent state. The new society would also make possible forms of self-government and autonomy for African-Americans, Chicanos, Native Americans, and other formerly oppressed nationalities, and provide the resources to make this real and vibrant. The educational system and media would be combating racist and white supremacist ideas and hurtful myths."[3]

What Lotta suggests is basically neo-colonialism and flies in the face of Lenin's ideas of self-determination. "Forms of autonomy" for an oppressed nation, especially when partnered with "integration throughout society," is unacceptable. It is simply revisionism and white chauvinism at its finest.

Chican@s don't want resources to be doled out in the form of aid or government funding for Latino projects. We want control of our own territory, with reparations paid directly to our own people's government, with no strings attached! Only when the opportunity to have our own liberated territory is actualized can we vote to be included in a multi-national republic. Ultimately this decision will be made by the Chican@ people, and not by the rcp=u$a.

Section 6:
Murder of Chicano Youth Holds Lessons for Revolutionaries

by cipactli, 21 July 2012

This section was originally written as a news article about the murder of Chican@ youth. Although the news is relatively old, the story is repeated daily within the United $tates. The lessons we can draw from the violence against Chican@s, both on the streets and behind bars, is timeless and very relevant to this section of the book.

THE IMAGES COMING OUT OF the corporate media surrounding the recent killing of the Chican@ youth Manuel Diaz at the hands of the pigs in Anaheim, California on 21 July 2012 are horrifying. The corporate media shows the response to this killing by the Chican@ nation and others as righteous outrage over this offensive of terror in the barrios, with people taking to the streets in anger and directing this outrage toward the pig. We see pigs releasing the dogs on non-violent protesters and bystanders including a baby in a stroller! This is what the oppressor thinks of our youth and our precious babies, as bait for their dogs.

What the corporate media has not shown is the witnesses who have come forward stating Manuel Diaz was shot in the ass as he ran from the predator pig and then was shot in the head.[1] This was an execution of another Chicano youth carried out in the street by the oppressor without judge or jury as has been done for 500 years, a true occupation. Manuel Diaz was unarmed, his crime was having lived his 24 years as a Chican@ in occupied Aztlán. The day after Manuel Diaz was killed another Chican@ youth in Anaheim, Joe Acevedo, was hunted down and killed. He was also shot and killed while running from the oppressor. This was the eighth officer-involved shooting in a year for this particular city, and three of those shot were unarmed.

The outright murder of Chican@s is the bald repression we face in Aztlán, and this repression is about control. The settler state has unleashed horrors on our nation ever since they first stepped foot on this continent. The evidence of the Chican@ nation held as an internal semi-colony is reflected not just in the land theft of our states in 1848 but also in Amerikan prisons, particularly in the states comprising Aztlán, and also in the terror unleashed in the barrios.

We are seeing a more unvarnished repression of Chican@s. This is done in large part because of material conditions in this country, in particular the population rise in Raza which has led to Raza now being the largest "minority group" in the United $tates.[2] With the population in the United $tates being 17% Raza and 14% New Afrikan[3] it is no surprise that we will begin to see the cross hairs trained more on Raza in the coming years. The rise in criminalization of Chican@s is used not just for population control (as prisoners cannot reproduce as frequently as those out in society) but as a control tactic in order to terrorize the Chican@ nation, sending the message of what awaits others who may resist the state. This criminalization is also used as a classic dividing tactic, to instill in the internal semi-colonies the viewpoint that "they are in prison because they broke rules" or "I made it because I worked hard." This Bill Cosby-type thinking is used to divide the Chican@ nation with a propaganda wedge between the brown masses and the prisoners, the Chican@ lumpen and the gente. The brown bourgeoisie support this backward thinking as they work as compradors who act like Tío Tomás to keep their crumbs, while ensuring the settler nation has a table from which to fling the crumbs to the comprador.

Most notably we see the fascist-like laws that are springing up across North America like fast food joints really targeting Raza. The most vile being spewed from Arizona which has become the spearhead for Amerika's legal offensive on the Chican@ nation. The U.S. Supreme Court recently upheld Arizona's most toxic portion of Senate Bill 1070 (SB1070), which allows police to question someone's citizenship when detained. Even Supreme Court justice Sonia Sotomayor agreed that states

are able to set up their own laws. She also said she found government arguments "confusing" when they argued to have SB1070 dismissed. She of all people on "the bench" should know colonization when she sees it.

Arizona is not confined to Governor Jan Brewer's settler views, indeed there is a new sheriff in town – or an old sheriff with new publicity. Sheriff Joe Arpaio has been at it with the jail he has run for the last 20 years. Throughout this time he has been allowed to terrorize Raza in his jail. Only when elections were coming up and Obama needed to attempt to counter the one million plus [now over two million - Editor] people he had deported since being in office, the attorney general filed a lawsuit on Sheriff Arpaio. The federal lawsuit charges discrimination against Latinos in Arizona jails. The "tent city" jail was opened 20 years ago and according to Sheriff Arpaio it reaches up to 141 degrees in that concentration camp. The lawsuit states that the guards regularly refer to Latino prisoners as "wetbacks," "Mexican bitches," "stupid Mexicans," and "fucking Mexicans."[4] The suit also claims that the Spanish speaking prisoners were not given medical treatment if they spoke Spanish. Wimmin prisoners were even denied anything for menstrual cycles. There are even allegations that guards sent emails of a chihuahua dog wearing a bathing suit and in the e-mails they call the dog "a rare photo of a Mexican navy seal."[4]

The writer of an article in *Rolling Stone* magazine sounds like he just climbed out from under a rock when he states: "Thirty percent of the county's residents are Hispanic, and their numbers are soaring – up 47 percent over the past decade. But the money and political power in Maricopa still reside in the largely white and conservative suburbs around Phoenix."[4]

The reality is "the money and political power" resides in the hands of the white nation, not just in Maricopa county, but throughout Amerika. In order to truly find a way to resolve the repression unleashed by "Sheriff Joe" we must approach reality as it is via a historical materialist approach. We must first look to the social relations Chican@s have experienced under the heel of imperialism, how we continue to be an occupied people and how Amerika creates millions of "Sheriff Joes" and it always has.

Sheriff Joe is an ex-DEA agent, and he is a concentrated example of imperialism in living form, but the problem is not Sheriff Joe per se. Sheriff Joe is merely a symptom of the disease (imperialism). If Sheriff Joe had a massive heart attack and expired today there would be an eager replacement as quick as you can say "settler." Sheriff Joe is simply an expression of capitalist imperialism.

The loudest excuse used by the right wing of the white nation is that migrants came to Amerika to commit crimes. Yet according to professor of criminology Charles Katz of Arizona State University, migrants are involved in less crime than "native-born Americans." Studies have also shown that those born in the United $tates are twice as likely to use drugs than migrants who mostly come here to work. So the excuses do not hold up, it's not a matter of preventing crime, it's a matter of continuing crime on the people. It is an occupation that we experience in Aztlán and we are beginning to see bald repression as Amerika becomes more and more desperate in its attempt to uphold its global oppression. But this is really nothing new. Acuña said it best: "state-sponsored brutality had existed since the first day for the colonization of the Southwest."[5] This state-sponsored brutality can be found in any occupied nation anywhere on the planet.

At times this underlying current of repression is reinforced by a broad segment of the settler nation in the form of economic oppression. This occurred in South Africa when "The main function of the 'Afrikaner' masses was no longer to produce and support society, but only to serve as the social base for the occupation garrison that imperialism needed to hold down the colonial peoples."[6] As in South Africa, many in Amerika support or serve "as the social base for the occupation garrison," supporting laws against immigration. Even some Raza were found to vote for laws taking "tough stands against immigration." This also should be seen not just as ignorance or backwards thinking but as direct influence of the state seeking to bribe off a portion of the Raza. We must keep in mind that these Raza will be used to railroad the Chican@ nation as well. This has been done throughout history in many different oppressed nations and national liberation struggles. The words of Nkrumah could have been written today in this respect: "as the nationalist struggle deepens in the colonial territories and independence appears on the horizon, the imperialist powers, fishing in the muddy waters of communalism, tribalism and sectional interests, endeavor to create fissions in the national front, in order to achieve fragmentation."[7] And so in our struggle to liberate our nation we should understand these 'muddy waters' and learn from past efforts in our path to Chican@ independence.

Class oppression exists in the Chican@ nation as well and so we should study to learn our class characteristics.[8] According to Marxist theory, class is defined in terms of exploitation and how surplus labor is appropriated from the proletariat or producers of labor. But Marx also saw slaves as a class even though they did not earn wages themselves. Classes are a product of the social relations under capitalist relations of production. These relations will be much different under socialism, when society will be run by socialist relations of production where the people come first and our industries are geared toward sustaining the people rather than making a profit.

Capitalism is a parasitical system which is now in the stages of decay. The oppressed will grasp the power they hold in their hands and use it to transform society. Mao described this quite well when he said: "All reactionaries are paper tigers. In appearance, the reactionaries are terrifying, but in reality they are not so powerful. From a long-term point of view, it is not the reactionaries but the people who are really powerful."[9]

Ultimately it will be the people who realize their power and put an end once and for all to the oppressor using the barrios as their shooting range in their ongoing campaign against the Chican@ nation. Our time will come and the imperialists will be unable to murder at will and instead will become as extinct as the dinosaurs.

Section 7:
Mexicans Targeted for Censorship

by a Texas prisoner, 2010

I AM CAGED UP IN this racist Texas Department of Criminal Justice where Mexicans and Blacks are treated unfairly. As everyone knows, the Texas justice system is one of the biggest in the country. It is so overcrowded. Texas is in debt so bad that they need to make budget cuts to save money. But they won't even consider releasing people as a way to save money.

The reason I'm writing is to address the issue of racism and censorship. Whenever Mexicans attempt to order books on our culture, especially on revolutionaries, it is denied. Their excuse is that it is "gang-related." The general library here at this facility has a few books, maybe five, on a little Mexican history. But when we take notes for our knowledge and future reference, these notes are confiscated by officers during routine cell searches and labeled as "gang-related." Then the person who was in possession of it is placed on a watch list.

The employees all across Texas prisons do this to us. We are being denied our culture, and denied the ability to study it without fear. Meanwhile, all of their racist propaganda material is readily available and allowed to enter with no problems.

We've also had to deal with officers' racist remarks toward Mexicans and Blacks. The grievance system here is useless. This is a whole network of klansmembers, so they all cover for each other. When we speak up and make it known we won't tolerate any of this, we are retaliated against.

I really appreciate your newsletter, *Under Lock & Key*. It is very informative. I can relate to the revolutionary mindset completely. I educate myself as much as possible and I do my best to get others around me to do the same. I stand up for my rights as much as possible. The staff know I won't be intimidated. They can lock me up but they won't take my pride or will to fight for what is right.

Part III:
Chican@ Literature from a Maoist Perspective

Burning Chican@ Books

by cipactli

THE RECENT ASSAULT RAINING DOWN on Raza in the state of Arizona smacks of the rise of the Third Reich in Nazi Germany when Hitler's Brown Shirts began burning books that contradicted fascist ideology. This was not a phenomenon exclusive to Germany; the occupier always attacks an oppressed nation's culture, history and language in order to sap a people's ability to struggle for liberation.

What better way to prevent a people from wanting to struggle than to take away their history of struggle against oppression, and brainwash them with the oppressor's views and version of history? An act that was outright land theft quickly becomes "an honest purchase," and genocidal acts become an almost spiritual or supernatural concept called "manifest destiny." In this way ideas are shaped and people are pacified.

Chican@ studies as a subject of study in public schools and universities was obtained in the first place by courageous struggle. Many remember when the University of California Los Angeles (UCLA) finally obtained their Chican@ studies courses via a hunger strike in 1993. Students at many schools had to protest and struggle to be able to learn about our history. For too long we had been told a version of history from the oppressor nation's view, twisting real history in an attempt to brainwash our youth.

Arizona's attempt to dismantle the advances of the Chican@ studies movement is a serious attack on the Chican@ nation overall. It comes at a time when an increase in repression has been unleashed on migrants by Immigration and Customs Enforcement (ICE) and other government agencies. When viewed in the context of the criminalization of Raza and the "Southwest" states' use of control units to capture and pacify Chican@s at a higher rate than any other nationality, the banning of Chican@ books is clearly no coincidence. Even law-abiding youth who are attending Amerikan schools, thinking if they commit no crime and get an "education" they will have a good life, are facing attacks from the imperialists.

The banning of books was thought to have been a thing of the past, a fascist way of controlling a people's thoughts, yet we are experiencing it in 2012. *Occupied America: A History of Chicanos* by Dr. Rodolfo F. Acuña is one of the books recently banned in Arizona. This book, along with others, was boxed up in classrooms in front of Chican@ students, as if their history is bad, and as if Chican@s are a forbidden people. It was reported that when this occurred some Chican@ youth were crying in class, not understanding the vile white supremacist monster they are up against belonging to an internal semi-colony in the United $tates.

Occupied America is a book that has been required reading in Chican@ studies courses all over the United $tates for decades. It does not promote violence or speak of revenge or retribution, but merely tells the story of imperialism's activity on this continent over the centuries. It uncovers U.$. imperialism's treatment and oppression of our nation. But as the Chican@ scholar Dr. Carlos Muñoz recently put it in regards to the banning of these books, "They are afraid of the truth. You know, the truth hurts."[1] The truth does hurt these parasites. It hurts to be reminded of how they treated humyn beings.

History shows this recent attack is going to backfire on the oppressor nation and spark political arousal in Aztlán. Thanks to the rekindled repression of Chican@s, Raza are awakening, our youth are once more being politicized, and our barrios are once more being revolutionized. Chican@ revolutionaries are organizing and developing new ideology such as the book you have in your hand. Within prisons we are seeing Chican@s becoming politically conscious and taking action. More youth want to know why they are suffering state oppression and many want to know why *Occupied America* is banned. They are purchasing the book to see what all the fuss is about. I myself have ordered it to share with others behind bars. I encourage all Raza to do the same. Learn why the state is targeting *Occupied America* and support our Chican@ historians who stand in the line of fire of imperialism and its repressive apparatuses. Buy it before it is banned even for purchase!

When we see these developments occur to our gente we should understand that the 2010 U.$. Census shows a dramatic growth in the Raza population. Raza will soon be the majority and this calculation is not being taken lightly by the state. They have think tanks who sit around brainstorming and planning ways to stifle and assimilate Raza, and how to break the Chican@ nation's back, especially via our youth. We must see the seriousness in the banning of Chican@ books as low-intensity warfare on the Chican@ nation. Amerika is using deportations, prisons, three strikes laws and schools to force their program onto our nation. We will use the experience of the Chican@ movement of decades past to make a leap in our struggles and push our nation farther than previous efforts, but we need to educate Raza in the barrios and the pintas before it is too late.

When the Spaniards came to the valley of Mexico they burned the Mexica's books (codices) and destroyed most of their written history along with other traces of their legacy. They filled the void with what they wanted future generations to know. When we read what they have written we do not read of genocide and rape because they conveniently left that out. All oppressors have used this tactic of re-writing history. This madness in Arizona will not be solved by just changing Arizona because it is U.$. imperialism which unleashes these fascist laws on our nation and the rest of the world. So long as imperialism exists, book banning will exist. Today it is the Chican@ nation being attacked via its history books, tomorrow the New Afirkan nation's history books will be banned in schools, and then others. Let us stand in solidarity against this coming fascist storm and prepare the people wherever you may be!

Review:
Occupied America

by cipactli

Occupied America: A History of Chicanos, 7th edition
by Rodolfo F Acuña
Pearson, 2014

A WELL-READ BOOK IN ITS seventh edition, *Occupied America: A History of Chicanos* is an in-depth analysis of Chican@ history. It has been a leading text for Chican@ studies for decades. Its clear, uncut content about Amerika's treatment of Chican@s, along with accurate history of Chican@s rising up in resistance, has Amerika scrambling to censor this work. *Occupied America* is one of the books banned in 2012 in Arizona and has since been a hot item for the librotraficantes (book traffickers) who have been defying Arizona's laws and smuggling this book back into the state and into the hands of Chican@ youth. *Occupied America* explains the myth of the oppressor nation propaganda that consumes the "history books" we read in public schools.

Occupied America was first published in 1972, emerging from a peak in national liberation struggles in the United $tates. In 1981 the second edition was released and the author wrote in the preface:

> "*The first edition of* Occupied America *followed the current of the times, adopting the internal colonial model that was popular during the late 1960s and early 1970s. The works of Frantz Fanon greatly influenced the tone and direction of the book. Since then, just like the Chicano movement itself, I have undergone dramatic changes. I have reevaluated the internal colonial model and set it aside as a useful paradigm relevant to the nineteenth century but not to the twentieth. ... I decided to return to the basics and collect historical data.*"

This quote leads us to believe that we would have more unity with the political line put forth in the first edition. More recent editions likely have more updated information, and would be valuable references for that reason. It seems that the changes between editions two through seven are mostly in factual content, with an attempt to avoid polemics.

So what gets the white supremacists so disturbed about *Occupied America*?

Acuña starts the seventh edition of his book in the pre-Columbian times when civilization first started on this continent 50,000 years ago, progressing through history and naturally coming to the European invaders and the beginnings of the forging of the Mexican and then the Chican@ nation. With the Spanish occupation and genocide that soon followed their arrival in North America, Acuña takes us through the social relations of the natives at the hands of the church.

Acuña takes us into the Mexican Revolution of 1810 when Mexico won its independence from Spain. While a great event, it didn't bring socialism to Mexican@s and so the exploitation soon continued. Acuña explains Amerika's theft of Texas which was spearheaded by the white supremacist Stephen Austin starting in the 1820s. This is where the second edition of the book starts, leaving out the history above found in more recent editions.

The myth of The Alamo is cleared up, the Plan de San Diego is discussed, and we learn more about the Treaty of Guadalupe Hidalgo. The book explains the 1960s and the eruption of a new generation of Chican@s that brought the Chican@ movement on the scene. All the Chican@ groups are discussed: Mexican American Student Association (MASA), El Movimiento Estudiantil Chicano de Aztlán (MEChA), Brown Berets, Black Berets, Mexican American Youth Organization (MAYO), United Mexican American Students (UMAS), Alianza, Crusade for Justice and many more. These fiery groups, along with the many Chican@ publications that are mentioned, show the heightened political consciousness in Aztlán in this period.

Although Acuña provides tons of data and information on the entire history of Chican@s, the colonization process, the early development of Chican@s as a nation, and Chican@ resistance, where Acuña falls short is in this book is in failing to point out a correct path forward on how Chican@s should liberate ourselves. Oddly he only provides a short paragraph on communism, briefly discussing how the state blamed communists for Chican@ activism. And so Acuña leads Chican@s to the edge of a cliff but does not tell us how to fly.

Aztlán will only be liberated in a socialist society. When socialist revolution arrives we will finally taste freedom. Any struggles short of this will only lead to a bourgeois revolution and a continuation of oppression under a new management, as happened to Mexico after the Mexican Revolution.

Occupied America is an excellent resource. It has a wealth of information that will continue to awaken and educate our nation. As an historian, Acuña has helped the Chican@ nation to learn our history. Anyone who wants to learn about the development of Chican@s will also enjoy this book. It is clear why the oppressor nation is so scared of this book – because it's truth!

Review:
Mexico's Revolution Then and Now

by cipactli

Mexico's Revolution Then and Now
by James Cockcroft
Monthly Review Press, 2010

MEXICO'S REVOLUTION THEN AND NOW by James Cockcroft analyzes the Mexican Revolution of 1910 in order to examine today's conditions and the future of Mexico. This book includes an in-depth study of the Magonistas and the Partido Liberal Mexicano (Mexican Liberal Party – PLM) who were the ideological spearheads of the revolution. We used *Mexico's Revolution* as a resource in writing *Chican@ Power*, as the historical information is very useful. This review will focus instead on ideological shortcomings of the book.

Besides Cockcroft placing Trotsky next to Marx and Lenin in this book, more of his erroneous tendencies ooze out when he quotes "Trade Unionist" Dan La Botz: "All Mexican workers, and all workers in Canada and the United States – for we are now part of the same labor movement – owe a debt of gratitude to the Mexican women." (p. 94-95)

This is one example of why there has been no socialist revolution on these shores or in Canada. To say those within the super parasite nations of Amerika and Klanada are a part of the same labor movement as the Mexican proletariat is delusional at best. Of course there are some who fall into this same labor movement but it is only a very tiny minority. Cockcroft explained how not even half the population of Mexico is employed regularly and only about 25% earn the minimum wage. He even says that half the population "including 90 percent of pre-school children, suffers from malnutrition and goes barefoot. They have no plumbing, no safe drinking water, and no electricity." (p. 82) He clearly understands the Mexican proletariat and lumpen-proletariat, yet oddly he attempts to claim Amerikan "workers" are in the same boat.

The labor movement within the United $tates is based in the labor aristocracy, which has a strong material interest in U.$. imperialism. Rather than siding with those who seek to end the exploitation that results in higher wages in the United $tates, for the most part they seek more crumbs for themselves from imperialism's superprofits stolen from the exploited workers of the world. [1]

Ultimately this book compares conditions in 1910 which made the Mexican Revolution possible, with today's conditions in Mexico which are similar, and thus hints to a contemporary revolution for Mexico in the near future. The repression on both sides of the border is increasing, as is resistance in the form of people organizing for change. Despite its challenges I recommend this book to learn some of the activity taking place in today's Mexico which the corporate media attempts to censor.

Review:
The Chicanos: A History of Mexican Americans

by cipactli

The Chicanos: A History of Mexican Americans
by Matt S. Meier and Feliciano Rivera
Hill & Wang Publishers, 1994

ALTHOUGH *THE CHICANOS* WAS WRITTEN in 1971-1972 and most of its information is from the 1960s, it is still informative in areas untouched by most other Chican@ books.

The Chicanos rightly starts off describing the indigenous cultures that preceded European invasion and then takes us into the period of the Mexican Revolution of 1810 and Mexico's declaration of independence from Spain in 1821. But what many Chican@ history books avoid, and what we learn in this book, is that Aztlán began to develop economically distinct from Mexico in the years immediately following Mexico's independence from Spain.

Despite this useful information the book suffers greatly in its analysis. For example the authors seem to bend history by explaining the U.$. War on Mexico of 1848 as:

> "[T]he United States and Mexico were moving toward a war for which neither country was prepared. In Texas domestic conflicts between Anglo-Texans and Tejanos coupled with raids on both sides of the border by both Mexicans and Texans intensified mutual antagonisms." (p. 62)

Whether intentional or not, the authors imply that Mexico played an equally antagonistic role in the U.$. War on Mexico. This is preposterous. What occurred in 1848 was a land grab that was built up from years of

Amerikan aggression toward Mexico. To imply that somehow Mexico was just as at fault is not only Amerikkkan apologism, but is ridiculous. It's like saying Palestinians and Israelis both intensified mutual antagonisms when in reality the Palestinians are like the Raza, in a national liberation struggle against a settler state. In this case Amerika provoked a war on Mexico to steal land, plain and simple.

Similarly, Meier and Rivera describe the resistance groups of 19th century much differently than we would. They call resistance groups Las Gorras Blancas (The White Caps) and La Mano Negra (The Black Hand) "terrorist bands." (p. 105) These were revolutionary groups which formed in response to national oppression, land theft, rape of wimmin and lynching of Raza. These groups arose and launched offensives against Amerikkka, whose colonization represented the real terrorism. To equate them to terrorist bands is lining up with the imperialists and serves to uphold the national oppression of Aztlán.

Throughout the book, Chican@ integration into Amerika is promoted. One benefit of the backwards thinking of the authors is that it allows readers to learn about other parts of our history not usually focused on by revolutionary writers. *The Chicanos* go in-depth into the development of the Order of the Sons of America, which later changed its name to the League of United Latin American Citizens (LULAC). While we have already criticized LULAC in Part 1 of this book, it is reaffirmed that the organization was indeed created by Tio Tacos.

Although *The Chicanos* seeks to steer Chican@s to work within bourgeois politics to create change, which has gotten us nowhere, it does explain much unique history of the Chican@ nation, and even tells us about the prisoner publications in the 1960s. The problem is in their lack of advice on how to liberate ourselves from internal colonialism.

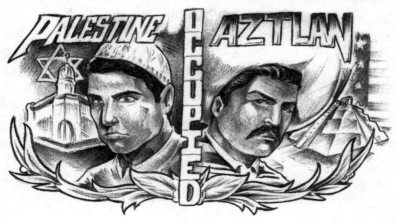

Review:
Youth, Identity, Power

by cipactli

Youth, Identity, Power: The Chicano Movement, 2nd edition
by Carlos Muñoz, Jr.
Verso Books, 1989

IN ADDITION TO BEING ONE of the main organizers of the Chican@ student movement, Carlos Muñoz, Jr. was chair of the first Chican@ studies department ever formed in college in the United $tates. In 1970 he went on to become a leader in founding the Raza Unida Party (RUP) and was RUP's chief organizer in California. So his participation in the Chican@ movement of the 1960s cannot be doubted. Because Muñoz was such a big part of the the political experience and activity during a rich revolutionary period, I wanted to review his book to peel back his thoughts on the Chican@ movement.

At the time of writing *Youth, Identity, Power* Muñoz was Professor Emeritus of Ethnic Studies at University of California Berkeley. The events that have passed since the height of his activism have surely had an effect on his perspective of the movement. This book serves not as a memoir but, as he states, a "critical study" of the Chican@ movement that is meant to help future activists learn from the past.

Youth, Identity, Power begins by rightly pointing out how many books from the Amerikan left, and specifically the "new left scholars," mostly focus on white student activism, omitting brown or Black people's struggles and contributions in the 1960s. Muñoz notes that even a much-praised book by Todd Gitlin, a founder of Students for a Democratic Society (SDS), promotes "[t]he white new left as the 'dynamic center of the decade.'" (p. 14)

This is typical of many from the left wing of the white nation, and even today's "revolutionaries" like RCP-U$A carry vestiges of this white nation chauvinism that compels them to sabotage the idea of Chican@ liberation.

> "Commemorations of the 1960s in the mainstream print media have also followed the same pattern, promoting it as a decade of white political activists. Time *magazine, for example, in its 11 January 1988 issue called 1968 'the year that shaped a generation.' Its headline story and dramatic photos capture many of the events and movement in the news of that year, but the focus is on white liberal and radical political figures and celebrities from Robert F. Kennedy to rock singer Janis Joplin to white student leaders like Mark Rudd. The assassination of Dr. King is mentioned, and the civil rights and Black Power movements receive scant attention. But the Chicano movement is ignored, as are Mexican American political leaders." (pp. 14-15)*

This is common among the Amerikan left today where Chican@s are denied any attention in many of the movement books, papers, or other media. Do your own investigation on the "revolutionary" press in Amerika and see who has even mentioned Chican@s in the years that their publications have been around. Muñoz calls out these Trotskyists and crypto-Trotskyists, but what he leaves out when explaining this is no matter what oppressed nation you come from the people need their own independent institutions – including our own press – in order to raise the banner of liberation for our nation. Many of today's political leaders in Amerika come from an era when Chican@s were excluded from the press and thus many of today's parties continue this rancid tradition. Only true revolutionary organizations today identify the correct line on the Chican@ nation.

At one point Muñoz talks about an event in 1987 held in San Francisco that commemorated the 1960s. This event was called "The Sixties, its Leaders and its Legacy." Once again the featured speakers were "white radical sixties celebrities" including the drug guru Timothy Leary, white feminist writer Betty Friedan, and Abbie Hoffman. Muñoz says when he asked the coordinators of this event if a Chican@ had been invited, he was told that no Chican@s had been invited because they were "probably not involved in the struggles of the sixties." And this response is coming from the so-called leaders representing the white "left"! This is one more example of why we cannot get bamboozled into thinking that

there is no more need for national liberation of the oppressed internal semi-colonies from Amerika. If we don't fight for our own independence, no one will, and our people will be lost to history.

The above cited event was put together by a San Francisco State University history professor, which was ironic since the first major college student strike in the 1960s had indeed occurred at San Francisco State University and was led by New Afrikan and Chican@ students! (p. 15)

Within the swamp of bourgeois nationalism, Muñoz explains that there were revolutionary nationalists whose line collided with the culturalists, and includes one critique given at the University of Riverside in 1973 from a young Chican@:

> *"Cultural nationalism ... points to a form of struggle that does not take into account the inter-connectedness of the world and proclaims as a solution the separatism that the capitalist has developed and perpetuated in order to exploit working people further ... It promotes the concept of a nation without a material basis and solely on a spiritual basis and tends to identify the enemy on a racial basis, ignoring the origin of racism and that it is simply an oppressive tool of capitalism." (p. 113)*

Those who agreed with the above quote and critique of pork chop nationalism – which is a correct position – Muñoz calls "the Marxist faction" of the Chican@ movement. In contrast, the original Brown Berets leaned more toward cultural nationalism, which is where the Brown Berets - Prison Chapter (BB-PC) disagrees with them.(see Appendix 1.a) The BB-PC has undertaken a deep study into the political history of societies in struggle, particularly those who were colonized and who liberated themselves, and advanced society the most. We have found that those societies like Lenin's Russia and Mao's China were not accomplished via cultural nationalism, and neither will Aztlán be liberated in this way. Just as the new prison movement is not being built nor advanced via cultural nationalism, what we are doing is applying the lessons of Marx, Lenin, Mao, Engels and Stalin to our concrete conditions and building our nations from within these dungeons. As a result of this rise in consciousness, or our leap from quantitative to qualitative development, protest and strikes have begun to sweep the prison system like never before. And so Muñoz should have called the principal contradiction within the Chican@ movement revolutionary nationalism vs. pork chop nationalism.

Muñoz neither critiques the contradictions within the Chican@ movement nor tells the reader who was right and who was wrong. He does identify Chican@ intellectuals coming out of the movement who are "most notable" being those applying Marxism to the Chican@ experience, but falls short of stepping over the threshold and letting readers know communist principles will be our only key to real liberation. Many times the author is almost there, but does not break from the pack. He toes the line as if not wanting to offend either side.

Perhaps the greatest contribution Muñoz brings not only to *Youth, Identity, Power* but to the Chican@ Power movement in general is advancing the line of the Chican@ nation as an internal colony. Indeed, Muñoz was the first persyn to reference the Chican@ nation as an internal colony in a paper he delivered to a symposium at the University of California Los Angeles.[1] Muñoz also went on to co-author an article with Mario Barrera and Charles Ornelas titled "The Barrio as an Internal Colony" that delivered theoretical support to this position. Many in the Chican@ movement took up this line and built on it, and this is where we have the most unity with Muñoz.

What Chican@s have in the United $tates is "formal equality." We have equality on paper and in words, but not deeds. Where the oppressor nation feels like allowing us to intermingle, our socio-political and economic existence is repressed by the state. In prison we can't even receive political or historical reading material by mail, much less openly engage in politics that put the people first. In today's society the right to self-determination is denied and our social organization and communities are attacked. A low intensity war or "soft war" in the guise of fighting crime has been unleashed on Aztlán since 1848 when our land was stolen by Amerikkka. This soft war seeks to divide our nation into those who will become vendidos (sellouts) who go along with Amerika, supporting its parasitic capitalist culture, assimilating with U.$. imperialism's exploitation of the Third World, and those on the other side who resist this beast and instead build the Chican@ liberation movement in preparation for socialist revolution.

In the Epilogue, Muñoz lists among other Third World revolutionaries Mao Zedong as contributing to our consciousness in the Chican@ movement, but then goes on to say "multiculturalism" is the way forward and throws out the idea of working for "Latino liberation." Muñoz has obviously questioned and altered his previous beliefs on the Chican@

Power movement. Perhaps what those white nation leftists told him about Chican@s not having participated in the struggles of the 60s hasn't registered. There are some positive points for multinational parties and it's important that we never oppose this dogmatically for all time. At the same time national oppression remains a reality in the United $tates and wishing it away won't change our concrete conditions nor will ignoring it or focusing on other struggles or tactics.

When Chican@s attempted to get the white nation left to struggle with us in the 19th and early 20th century over labor unions, we were not allowed access to white unions and our issues were brushed aside. Thus we formed our own unions. When we relied on the white nation left to struggle with us on pig brutality, land theft, migra terror, etc. we were brushed aside and were compelled to create our own organizations like the August 29th Movement, El Comité Estudiantil del Pueblo (The Student Committee of the People), the Brown Berets and other groups. Of course it's important to support and promote united front efforts in certain struggles that will involve other nations, just like we participate in the United Struggle from Within and the United Front for Peace in Prisons, which involve many different people from different nations.[2,3] And of course our aim is for the long-term goal of communism where there will be no more classes, police, armies or oppression, no matter what nation we're talking about. But this is many, many years in the future when U.$. imperialism and capitalism has been stomped out for good on a global scale. For now in order for an internal semi-colony to build a national liberation movement, it must be done by its respective nation.

What's different about *Youth, Identity, Power* compared to other Chican@ history books is that this book is an analysis of the contradictions within the Chican@ student movement, the Chican@ Power movement as well as the Chican@ leadership during the 1960s and 70s. Additionally, Muñoz uniquely calls out the white nation left on their white nation chauvinism. Muñoz also critiques the Chican@ movement (although selectively) and other leftists in Amerika who neglected gender struggles at that time. Those studying the contradictions that can and do arise within struggles of the oppressed will find interest in this book, particularly those today who are building the liberation of their nation in Amerika at this time. We must learn from the past while we move forward into the future. Free the people! Free the land!

Review:
Chicano Liberation and Socialism

by Ehecatl

Chicano Liberation and Socialism
by Miguel Pendas
Pathfinder Press, 1976

BEING THAT I'M A NEWLY conscious Chican@ revolutionary nationalist, and am attempting to help kick-start the newest round of the Chican@ liberation movement, I've gone in search of the movement's past so that I and others like me can analyze and learn from its history so that we may infer its future. In my attempt to seek out this knowledge, I purchased the pamphlet "Chicano Liberation and Socialism" by Miguel Pendas which is published and distributed by Pathfinder Press. Pathfinder Press is openly a Trotskyist publishing house, and so I wasn't entirely surprised with the political line of this pamphlet. Instead of finding answers on how to push the Chican@ movement forward I found out how to run it into the ground.

The pamphlet begins by asking an honest question. "Is socialism relevant to Chicanos?" It's a good question that needs to be asked, and Pendas answers this question in the affirmative. He starts his pamphlet by making some good points such as:

> *"Marxists think racism can be eliminated because its roots are not in 'human nature' but in particular social system: Capitalism. History and anthropology show that slavery, conquest and oppression of one people by another arose with the division of society into classes, with a privileged few owning the wealth."*

Pendas also correctly frames the origin of racist ideology:

"The theories of inferiority of people of color were developed and promoted to justify the enslavement of Africans, and later the imperialist conquest of Africa, Asia, and Latin America."

Unfortunately for Pendas and his Trotskyist brethren, that is where our unity on everything ends!

Pendas's first mistake is when he states:

"The capitalist system is hooked in racism. It will never give up its fix – the super profits that come from being able to condemn Blacks, Chicanos, Puerto Ricans and other oppressed minorities to the worst jobs, the worst schools and the worst housing."

This pamphlet was first printed in 1976, and the notion that people working legally in the United $tates were being exploited or superexploited (two very precise Marxist terms) by the "big capitalist" class was the common communist rhetoric of the day. So a bit of patience is granted to this Trot for his usage of the term "superprofits." However, revolutionaries with their noses to the ground such as the Black Panther Party for Self-Defense (BPP) had already begun to recognize way back in 1970 that salary- and wage-receiving people within U.$. borders were labor aristocracy or higher unless they were undocumented.[1] Which meant that by 1970 the Maoists Huey Newton and then-politically-sane Eldridge Cleaver had already taken up Lenin and had "written off the economic demands of the middle-classes as imperialist parasitism."[1] The fact that this pamphlet was printed in 1976 is no real excuse for the failure of Pendas to not have conducted a class analysis, not when the possibility for national liberation was still so palpable to the Chican@ people.

Pendas argues that one of the difficulties that real revolutionaries have had with linking the class struggle to the Chican@ liberation movement is:

"Some people who claim to be Marxists have declared their hostility to Chicano nationalism, the concept of Chicano pride, and unity"

and that

> "[T]he most vocal elements of anti-nationalism today are the Maoist groups. These include the October League, the Revolutionary Communist Party (formerly the Revolutionary Union) and supporters of the Guardian newspaper. There are smaller, local Maoist groupings including some Chicano Maoist groups."

Now, Pendas is certainly correct to refer to the rcp=u$a as anti-nationalists, but they are not, nor have they ever been Maoist. This pamphlet was published in the year that Mao died, before Maoism was broadly considered a new stage in the development of scientific communism. Much later the rcp=u$a took up the label of "Maoist," but their ideology has always remained one of crypto-Trotskyism. Pendas himself was a member of the Socialist Workers Party, a neo-Trotskyist organization that publishes *The Militant*. Pendas has an ax to grind with Maoism which I'll get to later, however his main argument with these supposed Maoists is that they put the national struggle on the back burner wherever the class struggle is concerned. He says as much when he makes the statement that Maoists of all shades basically share "the position that struggles of Chicanos as a people are a diversion, or at best, a secondary aspect of 'the class struggle' by which they mean struggles between workers and capitalists."

But if Pendas knew Maoism enough to have authority to criticize it, then he'd know that it was Mao Zedong himself that said in "On Contradiction" in regards to the Chinese civil war and the anti-Japanese national struggle that:

> "[W]hen imperialism launches a war of aggression against a country, all its various classes, except some traitors, can temporarily unite in a national war against imperialism. At such a time, the contradiction between imperialism and the country concerned becomes the principal contradiction, while all the other contradictions among the various classes of the country are temporarily relegated to a secondary or subordinate position."[2]

So what part of Maoism is anti-nationalist or relegates the national struggle to a secondary position with respect to the class struggle, besides the revisionism of a First World revisionist "Maoist" organization? Maoism is revolutionary nationalism and revolutionary nationalism is Maoism. Indeed, all of the revolutionary nationalist struggles when Mao was alive were either outright Maoist movements or were supported by Maoist China. Pendas then goes on to argue:

> *"[S]o-called workers issues, such as demands for higher wages and better conditions on the job are an important part of the class struggle. But wage exploitation is not the only kind of oppression that exists under capitalism. There is also national oppression and the oppression of women as well as special forms of oppression against youth, old people, gay people and others. These are all forms of capitalist oppression, and most of their weight falls on the working class."*

In this quote Pendas starts off with a critique of economism, a milder form of class reductionism, but then goes on to boil everything back down to the class struggle as if all these things will magically disappear of their own accord once a socialist economy is put in place. Of course this is a farce. We know that the oppression of wimmin predates capitalism and is the pillar of patriarchy. For all these forms of oppression to be wiped from this earth, a full attack on bourgeois culture must be waged at all levels of society, from the bottom. This was demonstrated to the world during the Great Proletarian Cultural Revolution in Maoist China (1966-76) in which all the old and reactionary, backward bourgeois ideas that were impeding the progress of communism were dealt with head on by the great masses of Chinese people.

Pendas then goes on to say "Maoists and other sectarians claim that Chicano nationalist demands divide the working class and stand in the way of unity between Chicanos and Anglo workers in struggle against their common oppressors" and "what they're really saying is that Chicanos should lay aside their legitimate grievances in order to not offend racist white workers. But this is hardly the way to achieve unity."

If Pendas really knew what he was talking about with respect to Maoism and the crypto-Trotskyists in the rcp=u$a who are going around masquerading as Maoists, then he'd know that the real Maoists of the time recognized the reactionary character of white Amerika as a whole. This was true of the Black Panther Party (BPP) and the Young Lords Party. The BPP would never have spewed such nonsense! Likewise, the Maoist Internationalist Movement (MIM) took it upon themselves to conduct a class analysis within U.$. borders in order to find out who were our friends and who were our enemies, and lo and behold, what did they find? The same thing that the BPP already knew, or at least had a suspicion of: that the white working class was reactionary and not a friend of the oppressed nation internal semi-colonies. Not, however, because of racism, but because of the stolen superprofits sucked out of the Third World nations. These superprofits are used to give Amerikans the highest living standards the world has ever seen. They not only led to high living standards, but directly to a split in the Amerikan working class the likes of which Engels and Lenin spoke of. This split in the working class produced a stratum of bourgeoisified workers, or the labor aristocracy. And for repeating this truth about the working class in Amerika, MIM was accused of being racist against whites by the Amerikan "left." The Trotskyists and other revisionists complained that the MIM line was hardly any way to achieve unity. And of course they were and continue to be correct in this regard. The catch is those in the MIM camp don't seek unity with parasitic nation and class enemies! We only seek to unite with those who work in favor of the oppressed masses of the Third World, as well as the oppressed layers of the oppressed nation internal semi-colonies.[3]

The section titled "The Two-Party Trap" starts off as a critique of the Republocrats. Pendas criticizes how neither mainstream U.$. political party holds the way out for the Chican@ nation. He talks about how the Republocrats weren't even concerned with the Chican@ vote beyond mere tokenism. Instead he makes the argument for a bourgeois Chican@ party of its own. He points to la Raza Unida Party (RUP) of the 1960s and 70s as the model for how the Chican@ people can effectively begin to come together before they completely break away from the Amerikan bourgeois political structure – an ass backwards form of New Democracy. He claims that RUP was at the forefront of the Chican@ nationalist struggle and that they represented a "break from the capitalist parties."

However, while RUP was at the forefront of reformist and civil rights issues, they were in no way at the forefront of the Chican@ nationalist struggle. Former leading member of RUP and Chicana activist Martha Cotera said that she "wasn't surprised" when the mass of Chican@ activists in Denver "voted not to be liberated" at the 1969 Denver National Conference of RUP.[4]

Pendas is constantly spreading false information in this pamphlet which seriously makes me question his credibility as someone interested in trying to liberate Aztlán. If there's anything good to be taken from this pamphlet it's when he makes the statement that "far from being a middle class ideology, Chicano nationalism has been the ideology of the most militant fighters against the capitalist class. It is to be found in the most oppressed layers of the Chicano community." I would most certainly agree that those who could one day form the most militant fighters against the oppression of the Chican@ nation are to be found in the most oppressed layers of the Chican@ community, except that the most oppressed layers of the Chican@ community are now found in the prisons and jails of Amerika as further elaborated in Part I of this book and elsewhere by Loïc Wacquant.[5]

Likewise, for all the shit Pendas talks about Maoists not supporting the national struggle, you'd think he'd have some better answers as to how to properly uplift the consciousness of Chican@s to actually go about liberating the nation.

All that is nothing compared to the section titled "Leninism and Stalinism." Indeed Pendas really shows his Trotskyist stripes when he proceeds to denigrate both Stalin and Mao. He begins with the statement:

> *"The notion that nationalism of oppressed peoples is contradictory to the class struggle originates with the Stalinists – that is with the followers of the communist parties of Moscow and Peking, the heirs of Joseph Stalin. Their treacherous refusal to support national liberation struggles has nothing in common with the Marxist tradition of Lenin, Trotsky and the Russian Bolsheviks party. Yet because the Stalinists claim to be Marxist-Leininists they have been successful in confusing millions of oppressed people throughout the world as to the true stand of Marxism in regard to national liberation."*

Poor Pendas, there he was right smack in the middle of the Chican@ liberation struggle circa 1976, there was so much he could've done to help uplift the consciousness of Chican@s and instead he took the Trotskyist way out. It was Stalin himself who developed the Marxist theory of nations in "Marxism and the National Question." It was Stalin who analyzed how nationalism of oppressed nations interacts with the nationalism of oppressor nations and other oppressed nations in depth in the collection *Marxism and the National-Colonial Question*. Stalin's development of theory on nationalism proved to be crucial to the Russian Revolution. But Stalin was anti-nationalist according to Pendas, even though Stalin himself was from an oppressed nationality and began his Bolshevik career organizing workers' strikes and revolts in the oppressed nation of Georgia. Stalin was anti-nationalist even though he's stated and elaborated in *The Foundations of Leninism* that the national liberation struggles of Asia, Africa and Latin America were key to the development of the world revolution, because objectively they were leading the fight against imperialism. On the other hand, Trotsky saw very little potential in the national liberation movements of the oppressed nations because they were "uncivilized" and peasant societies. Ho Chi Minh expressed the view of many communists from the colonies in 1924 when he recognized Stalin as the leader of the only party that stood with the national liberation struggles. In fact, Trotskyists around the world are the ones who deride the Chinese revolution not as a national liberation struggle, but as a "guerrilla adventure" of the Stalin-Mao line just as they deride the Chinese revolution itself as a Stalinist bureaucracy.[6]

What about the Spanish Civil War? Was Stalin being anti-nationalist when the Soviet Union, under his watch, was the only country in the world that helped to arm the Spanish popular forces with tanks and planes against the Spanish and German fascists? Stalin was also the only world leader who offered to defend Czechoslovakia against the Nazis. And Stalin persynally supported the development of the Black Belt thesis showing Blacks to be an oppressed nation within the United $tates! Let us also not forget that he was the leader of the world revolution for 30 years; 30 years with a lot of national liberation struggles.

Urben
&
Rural
Struggle

Similar to his criticism of the Maoist line and groups, it seems Pendas does not possess more than a cursory knowledge of Stalin's line either. When making such sweeping accusations as to who follows these ideologies, and what is wrong with them, we should hope that the accuser at least can argue in a principled manner, with facts. It's possible if Pendas actually understood Maoism or Stalinism, he would actually identify with those ideologies. Instead, his criticism just sets back the Chican@ struggle based on misunderstandings and lies.

Finally, Pendas ends his attack on the Stalin-Mao line of national liberation struggles by promoting the Trotskyist multinational approach to party building. There's nothing inherently wrong with multinational party building, if it is led by a true Maoist party. But when led by a Trotskyist party, it essentially means oppressor nation politics in command.

I have to say, I came to this pamphlet with the hope of finding out how Chican@ revolutionaries went about organizing the nation for revolution. And after reading his pamphlet I was left in dismay, not knowing if the Chican@ movement for national liberation would ever again flare back up. The Chican@ movement ultimately failed because of lack of leadership. Leadership skills are slowly developed; but patience is perseverance. If we are to be successful in liberating the nation then we must make sure we're on the right road: the Maoist road. At this current stage of the struggle, national liberation and indeed the science of revolution behind prison walls is inextricably bound up with Maoism. Comrades working both with and within MIM(Prisons) and USW[7] should not be so impatient to break off and form their own single vanguard parties unless all members of that party or cell are already highly developed. Even so, the international communist movement and the revolutionary forces as a whole are in a low ebb period. We should take advantage of that fact to properly regroup and redevelop so that we'll be sure to smash Amerikan imperialism once and for all.

Labor, Family, Feminism and Revolution

by Ehecatl and Wiawimawo

ULTIMATELY, DEVELOPING A REVOLUTIONARY CHICANA herstory requires building revolutionary organizations that address gender in a way that puts wimmin into roles with equal power in determining the trajectory of the movement. By discussing the essays below we hope to take a step towards promoting the Chicana voice, while touching on some key questions of gender that affect the Chican@ national liberation movement.

Many who have come before us have made the error of class reductionism, as if all oppression is a product of and is resolved via the class struggle. In contrast, MIM Thought recognizes three distinct strands of oppression: class, nation and gender. Of course they all very much influence each other and often overlap. In the age of imperialism we believe that nation is the principal contradiction. We therefore prioritize national unity of the oppressed nations. However, unlike the class and nation reductionists, we do not see gender as something that will be just worked out after the revolution. It is a unique thing that must be understood and addressed in today's context, especially as we move forward in our revolutionary struggle.

As we break down below, gender is a social relation, while sex is a biological category. Amerikan biological females may be considered gendered as men because of their gender privilege. We can also refer to such people as the gender aristocracy because their gender privilege is closer to men than it is to the majority of wimmin, and they are therefore tightly allied with the patriarchy and unlikely to oppose it.

Most of the sources discussed below are from a collection of essays titled *Las Obreras: Chicana Politics of Work and Family*, which belongs to a larger collection titled the "Aztlán Anthology Series."[1] Director of the Chicano Studies Research Center at University of California Los Angeles, Chon Noriega describes *Los Obreras* thusly:

> "Las Obreras: Chicana Politics of Work and Family *is at once a proven resource and a new guide toward an interdisciplinary understanding of the 'memory, voice, and lived experiences' of Chicanas within Aztlán, within the family, within the workplace, and within the nation-state."* (p. ix)

Las Obreras is designed to build upon work published in previous issues of *Aztlán: A Journal of Chican@ Studies*, in order to address specific debates and concern within the field. It is mainly intended for ethnic studies within a college setting, however it would be remiss for it to remain strictly within the confines of academia. This book should be made available to everyone within the Chican@ nation to gain a deeper understanding of what Chicana and Mexicana wimmin have historically gone through, and must still go through in their daily lives while living under an imperialist regime. Likewise this book should be made available to all Chican@s and Mexican@s who wish to gain a concrete understanding of the intersections of nation, gender and class oppression in 21st century Aztlán.

Class and Gender

Las Obreras is a compilation of essays, narratives, and interviews which begins with "Claiming Public space at Work, Church, and Neighborhood" in which Vicki Ruiz goes straight to the heart of the matter in explaining how Chicana struggles in the United $tates go well beyond the dominant white-pseudo-feminist war cries of equal pay for equal work. Instead, she shows how racism and patriarchy intersect on the shop floor, in the union hall, and at home. In this essay Ruiz proves that gender roles for wimmin in general, but Chicanas in particular, are a socially constructed phenomenon which have been developed to keep wimmin in their place. The Chicana has proven to be ever-versatile and ever-resistant, as Vicki Ruiz makes sure to both emphasize and exemplify. This point is made clear when Ruiz states in the introduction to this book, "We must move beyond a celebration of *la familia* to address questions of power and patriarchy, the gender politics of work and family." We'll expand on this idea later in this essay.

Although Ruiz's essay is intended to throw the spotlight on the plight of the Chicana, it inadvertently shows that the Chican@ nation can never be free without the active participation of Chicanas both in the struggle for liberation and after independence has been achieved. Or in other words: wimmin don't just hold up half the sky, but must conquer it! This demands that the Chicana not only participate, but that she takes up leadership in the revolutionary struggle.

Struggle on the shop floor is put on display in the Chicana work strike at the Farah Manufacturing Paisano Plant of El Paso, Texas in 1972. This was a Chicana work strike not for equal pay, but for humyn dignity. The Farah workers were essentially treated like shit by the white-family-owned Farah Manufacturing company, as well as by the vendido floor bosses (the Chican@ equivalents of the house negroes). Against seemingly insurmountable odds, Chicanas successfully waged a protracted work stoppage campaign from 1969-72. In this struggle they had to contend with both oppression and insult on the shop floor, and insult and racism from the entire white population of the city of El Paso which was in sympathy with Farah. This racism was a manifestation of national oppression and exploitation by white Amerika at the time, showing the dominant role of nation in what was essentially a class struggle.

Also important to note: the Farah strike differed from many other labor reform movements within the sphere of the U.$. empire in that the Farah strike depended on the participation of children. These children were originally only onlookers. The youngsters were quickly put to use as strikers because their mothers had nowhere else to send the children while they participated in the strike themselves. This is a unique phenomenon when compared to other labor reform movements, and is only mirrored in another Chican@ movement for labor reform: the United Farm Workers' Grape Boycott.[2] The fact that children were not just present, but largely participants in these strikes speaks to the truth that within the Chican@ nation the family formed (as Ruiz writes) "the unit of production in agriculture and consequently focused on the involvement of every family member." (p. 19) While an unusual phenomenon in the First World, this act is old hat in the Third World. It speaks to the proletarian character of the Chican@ nation at the time, while showing how class struggle can serve to undermine patriarchal relations within the oppressed nations by pushing wimmin and children to the front lines. Youth, even more so than wimmin, are gender oppressed under the patriarchy.

We should note here that while the involvement of every family member is still largely a prerequisite for the survival and economic prosperity of the Chican@ family unit, the burden of being the unit of production in agriculture has passed almost exclusively to the Mexican@ family, as well as other national minorities without U.$. citizenship.

"Organizing Latina Garment Workers in Los Angeles" is a more contemporary look at Chicana labor. In this essay Maria Angelina Soldatenko exposes how the Los Angeles garment industry and the International Lady's Garment Workers Union have colluded to use both nationality and gender to oppress and exploit female Raza. Soldatenko also writes about how the arrival of the garment industry in Los Angeles was triggered by the desire for cheap, non-unionized labor and how this became the historic reason for keeping them in "the lowest-paying and most onerous of occupations in the labor market," placing them in "ethnic niches." (p. 141)

Part Two of *Las Obreras* focuses on the domestic front and how Chicanas refused to be pigeon-holed as homemakers, and have gone in search of an identity outside the home. It begins with "Work Gave Me a Lot of Confianza" by Beatriz M. Pesquera, speaking to how participating in social labor promotes gender equality. Indeed, this section is all about gender oppression. More importantly however, this section tackles the fact that Chicana and Mexicana wimmin's need to work stems from the familial economy need of survival in which all economically viable members of the household contribute to the economic needs of the home. Pesquera deems this a "family wage economy." (p. 176) This "family wage economy" seems like a re-phrasing of the family unit of production mentioned earlier, except that the concept of the family wage economy is more accountable to the Chican@ nation as a whole, and not just the agricultural section of the past century.

White Wimmin's Pseudo-Feminism

In the essay "Ambivalence or Continuity?" Denise A. Segura identifies an "ideology of motherhood" which dictates a womyn's role in society as that of solely a mother. She challenges this ideology as nothing more than a social construct that is essentially "a culturally informed role whose meaning can vary and is subject to change." She also speaks to the images of motherhood, the family and the economic sphere. Many say these are mutually exclusive spheres which are never to cross. However, this "mutually exclusive sphere" is nothing more than the epitome of patriarchal-bourgeois relations in which a distinct pluralism is emphasized and practiced, not just for the further oppression of wimmin, but for the privilege of patriarchy. Therefore, they cannot under any circumstance be considered mutually exclusive, but instead are interconnected phenomena that can only be done away with via the proletarian-feminist road. What's more, the conceptualization of wimmin as wives and mothers in the 21st century is steeped in oppressor nation ideology, is reactionary in character, as well as illustrative of Amerika's decadence in that people of all national backgrounds with any proximity to the white oppressor nation now have the wealth to sustain a nuclear family on a single income. This oppressor-nation ideology is irrelevant in practice to many Mexicana and Chicana wimmin who must bear a heavier burden within the family and economic sphere due to the absence of the male as resultant of imperialism's woes. Thus, when this concept of Chicanas solely as wives and mothers has been picked up by Chicanas themselves this is due first and foremost to their privileged positions as U.$. citizens, and secondly as associative with their oppressors in the form of a colonial consciousness.

Where we really disagree with Segura is in her assertion that

> "The social construction of motherhood serves the interests of capital by providing essential childbearing, child care, and housework at a minimal cost to the state and sustains women as a potential reservoir of labor power, or a 'reserve army of labor.'" (p. 184)

Per the Marxist definition, a reserve army of labor can only really be found on the margins of society, whereas wimmin in the First World are an integral part of this society itself. Where Chicana and Mexicana wimmin differ from the white wimmin Segura attempts to identify them with, is that Chicanas and Mexicanas living in the United $tates are a part of the oppressed nations and are often found within the lumpen and semi-proletariat and can thus be considered marginalized; but this is because of their nation and class positions. Gender here is not the determining factor.

The patriarchal nuclear family is still an important building block for the capitalist economy, particularly in the reproduction of the ex-ploited classes. For the petty-bourgeoisie the family takes on a less cru-cial economic role and becomes a mere cultural expression of gender privilege and consumerism. For the sectors of the oppressed nations who are excluded from the economy, we see the weakening of the patriarchy because the lumpen lacks the male provider who serves as the center of the traditional patriarchal household. While this has many negative consequences for all involved, even in our capitalist economy it does provide opportunities for new ways of structuring gender roles that are limited under patriarchal dominance.

In his book *Catching Hell in the City of Angels*, Costa Vargas docu-ments the transformation of a community of New Afrikan lumpen wim-min, who share child care, economic resources and other support into atomized family units, as Raza migrant families move into a housing complex in Los Angeles.[3] These semi-proletariat, patriarchal families displaced the more communal living situation that had existed there. And as we discussed in Part I Section 1, class differences between New Afrikans and Chican@s translates into differences in how gender was handled by revolutionaries in the past as well.

The essay titled "She Has Served in more Intimate Ways" by Emma Perez cites Catherine MacKinnon and Michelle Barrett, arguing:

"In analysis of oppression, a class analysis often subsumes gender precisely because of the social relations that create and are created by gender ideol-ogy. Socialization, then, constructs gender identity (MacKinnon, 1982, p. 531). Gender ideology decodes how a society keeps women in their place and how they, too, keep themselves in their place and sustain a patriarchal, capitalist society that oppresses them.(Barrett 1980)" (p. 44)

This posits the inevitable question that has been asked of white Amerikan wimmin during times of strife: reform or revolution? While in the United $tates this question has always been answered by white wimmin choosing the former, the wimmin of the Third World have continuously hammered and sickled home the answer with the latter. This was true in the Soviet Union, Albania, China, Peru and today in South Asia.

Perez also deals with how domestic service exploits both intimacy and boundaries between servant and family, quoting historian Gerda Lerner who argued that "the practice of using slave women as servants and sex objects has become the standard for class dominance over women in all historical periods" (p. 45), as was exemplified in Mexico both after the Spanish conquest, and after the bourgeois democratic revolution. This abuse is still largely vested more upon the Mexicanas living in the United $tates than on the more Amerikanized Chicana citizen who has legal rights and knows how to have them enforced.

At first read this topic might not seem too relevant to today's Chicana. The underlying and pervasive social-sexual gender oppression makes its weight felt when migrant wimmin attempt to have their rights respected only to have their own supposed promiscuity become the issue of the day – a good example of how the racist patriarchy protects its privilege. Ultimately, Perez shows us that there is still gender oppression as well as national oppression of migrant wimmin in the United $tates, Raza in particular, despite all the Amerikan talk of liberal progression and wimmin's rights. Obviously Raza are excluded from modern wimmin's rights by the biased, piggish practices of the Amerikan patriarchy. MIM Thought recognizes an important distinction between the gender oppression of females of oppressed and oppressor nations. Amerikan biological females have joined the oppressor gender (men) while the Mexicana remains in the role of womyn as seen by her subjection and objectification.[4]

Reproductive Rights

"Women Sterilized as they Give Birth: forced sterilization and Chicana resistance in the 1970s" by Virginia Espino talks about the outright genocidal practices of Amerika on the oppressed nation internal semi-colonies in the form of nonconsensual and forced sterilization of Chicana and Mexicana wimmin during the 1970s, and of the clearly demarcated line between the needs of white and Chicana females. Espino shows us how Amerika's priorities were not "freedom and justice for all," but rather, freedom and justice for white Amerika, and extermination for the oppressed nations. When Amerika chose to fund 90% of the cost of sterilizations through Medicaid, while offering no financial support for abortions, this was made clear. Espino also shows how Chicana wimmin were subsumed within the Chican@ movement itself due to the patriarchy, as well as further subsumed within the wimmin's movement, a movement for and by whites. Espino shows how Chicanas organized and built public opinion to put a stop to eugenic sterilizations. She also makes note of how the average Chicano activist "did not view reproductive rights as an issue worthy of organizational time" (p. 71) but rather thought of wimmin's concerns only in relation to their own machismo. Espino cites the an- thropological studies of Carlos Vélez-Ibáñez and concludes that because of forced sterilization, both Chicana and Mexicana wimmin "'had gone through a process of social disengagement' in every aspect of their lives: as mothers, daughters, sisters, wives and friends." (p. 76) This analysis makes sense when we consider that child-bearing and child-rearing is a highly valued social/cultural function within Mexican life.

Fighting sterilization, as a form of eugenics, has been a struggle fought by all of the internal semi-colonies of the United $tates. As men- tioned in Part I Section 1 the Young Lords Party were exemplary for their work around reproductive rights, including the struggle against forced sterilization. Just recently, in September 2014, California passed a bill banning tubal ligations in prisons. This came after a report of upwards of a 100 forced sterilizations by tubal ligation in California prisons between 2006 and 2013.[5]

Patriarchy in Revolutionary Organizations

Marisela R. Chavez's essay in *Las Obreras*, "We Lived and Breathed and Worked the Movement," discusses revolutionary party building with- in the Chican@ nation and the rightful place of Chicanas within all this struggle. It focuses on El Centro de Acción Social Autonoma (The Center of Action and Social Autonomy – CASA). This essay is useful for its rich historical data with respect to the Chican@ liberation movement, espe- cially in comparing CASA with the Black Panther Party for Self-Defense. The experiences of the BPP and CASA speak to the different conditions of different internal semi-colonies, validating the need for separate vanguard parties within each nation. We got into this history in Part I Section 1.

Distinctive National Culture

In a similar vein, one of the unique issues that we face trying to unite the Chican@ nation is cultural differences between Chican@s and recently arrived Mexican@s. "Creating Community: Mexican American Women in Eastside Los Angeles" by Mary Pardo describes how socially constructed prejudice present within Aztlán due to the Amerikanization process creates difficulties in bridging the community between the newly arrived Mexican@s and the Chican@ people within the barrio. These dogmas and biases are reflective of the prejudices which the newly arrived Mexican@ migrant is subjected to by most Amerikans. Biases such as the false concept that all Mexican@s who migrate to the United $tates come from a rural background, and that their ignorance of Amerikan social mores is owed to such.

Also discussed by Pardo is the fact that both Mexicana and Chicana wimmin are essentially the glue that hold their communities together, whether by establishing neighborhood watch programs, or organizing within the barrio for better schools and parks for their children. Pardo makes an interesting point in discussing neighborhood watch programs: a one-womyn neighborhood watch never called the cops on unruly and destructive children and young men. The organizer, Doña Rosa, threatened to make a citizens arrest when she saw young men racing in their cars up and down the street, though she admitted she'd "never really have the heart to call the cops on them. But I tell them 'really mean,' so they think I am serious!" (p. 110)

Cultural Nationalism

While not primarily related to gender, cultural nationalism is a problem for wimmin as the gender oppressed. Generally cultural nationalists idealize the past and uphold the supposed traditional ways of their people. And unless you're going back to the ways before most documented history, then "traditional" ways will be patriarchal ways. This is the inherent conservatism of the cultural nationalist.

Part Four: Taking Charge starts with "The Synapsis of Struggle: Martha Cotera and Tejana Activism" by Mary Ann Villarreal. This is a compilation of interviews with a founding member of the Texas Raza

Unida Party (RUP), whose initial mission statement was "to implement social change in the barrios and to improve social conditions for La Raza by mobilizing its massive political potential and making its influence felt at the ballot box." (p. 273) According to Villarreal's research, Cotera was a very influential persyn within the Chican@ movement; not because of some supposed elitist pull, but because she simply refused to back down to the patriarchy.

Villarreal and Cotera also explain how the cultural nationalism that is so rampant within Chicanismo is not something that developed within the barrios, as is commonly thought. It is a phenomenon that was formally taught at the universities by the same Anglo-sociologists whom the cultural nationalists so rail against today. Cotera explains that the Chican@ brand of cultural nationalism is also in part a blend of stereotypes presented in the media at that time. Now knowing this, and the fact that cultural nationalism as an ideology tied to a movement has not only done virtually nothing to free the nation, but is actually taught and encouraged as a philosophy within Amerikan universities in the guise of ethnic studies, should give all of us who are working to liberate the nation pause. What does cultural nationalism really propose itself to be? Does it succeed in accomplishing its stated aims? No, it is a farce. Cultural nationalism is to nationalism what revisionism is to revolutionary science: an enemy Trojan horse.

Intersections of Nation, Class and Gender

The last body of work in this book is Gloria J. Romero's "No Se Raje, Chicanita [Don't back down, little Chicana]: Thoughts on Race, Class and Gender in the classroom." Romero states that she chose this title

> "... for a number of reasons: to acknowledge the struggle to revolt in order to survive; to acknowledge the impact of the voice of a working-class woman, a Chicana, on our disciplines of study; to assert that in the destruction of an old way a new way will emerge; and to persevere with the belief that we shall endure." (p. 305)

In addition to an explanation of the title of "No Se Raje," this is a good summary of Las Obreras as a whole. "No Se Raje" is a combination of the author's life experiences of teaching in the departments of psychology, sociology, Chican@ studies and wimmin's studies and is reflective of her own views on the intersections of nation, class and gender, as well as her realization of such an intersection and the radicalization it produced.

Romero gets into how she sought to profess her views on nation, class and gender within the university setting. Interestingly enough, she also comments on the purpose of cultural nationalism within the same university setting and repeats Mary Pardo's opinions and thoughts on cultural nationalism[6] when she states,

> "[I]n this modern day and age, universities, when they address the topic of culture do so with an aesthetically benign view: University administrators prefer to project culture as quaint. As demographics in the country change rapidly, particularly in California, universities have jumped onto the multicultural bandwagon. They celebrate culture and offer workshops on 'managing' diversity. In these workshops conflict rarely arises. Culture is projected with a positive effect. 'Culture does not offend.'" (p. 307)

What does this mean? It means that ethnic studies, i.e. cultural nationalism or multiculturalist class is provided to the oppressed national as a 'healthy' and well-meaning outlet to imperialism, as well as a drain to the revolutionary movement as a whole – a Trojan Horse.

Romero also discusses culture in the age of imperialism as well as imperialism's influence on the culture of the oppressed. She stresses the need to pull back Amerika's covers and expose the true history of the country to counter the twisted history that is presented within Amerikan classrooms. Many other topics are also discussed here, such as how Amerikan schools uphold Amerikan values and imperialism itself. She also talks about how university textbooks ignore conditions of apartheid, neocolonialism, racism, civil war in the Third World, and occupation. All in all, "Race, Class, and Gender in the Classroom" addresses a wide variety of topics useful to the discussion of imperialism and the superstructure. These are topics we must gain a tight hold of if we are to liberate the Chican@ nation.

Las Obreras: Chicana Politics of Work and Family is a must-read for those of us needing to understand the complexities of the intersections of nation, class and gender contradictions in the Chican@ nation, as well as the effects on Chicanismo.

Review:
We Will Rise – Rebuilding the Mexikah Nation

by Ehecatl

We Will Rise – Rebuilding the Mexikah Nation
by Kurly Tlapoyawa
Trafford Publishing
6 July 2006

"We must question the motives of those in the assimilation movement. As it stands, American society is a cesspool of moral decadence, corruption, violence and greed – and by its own admission things are only getting worse. Why then do groups such as LULAC [League of United Latin American Citizens - Editor] and the American GI Forum insist on becoming a part of it? Do they think that their cherished 'equality' with the American power structure can be achieved by stooping down to their level? What exactly are they hoping to become a part of?

"We shouldn't point to the abuse of our people and repeat useless slogans like 'things need to change, we need to exercise our power by voting more hispanics/latinos into office.' In fact our message should be quite the opposite and far more realistic. We should use the abuse of our people to illustrate how this country was designed to operate. Our people need to wake up to the fact that this nation thrives on our destruction, and we must use public organizing as the wake up call. Our organizing should focus on the understanding that we must destroy this system, not become a working part of it."

You can almost hear the war drums beating as Kurly Tlapoyawa charts the history of the Mexica-Nahuatl from their pilgrimage out of

Aztlán, thru the "Southwest" and into present day Mexico in his work *We Will Rise – Rebuilding the Mexikah Nation*, a well-written historical text with its pulse on agitation. Its main motivational concept is the philosophy of Mexikayotl - La Mexikanidad or "everything which is Mexikan" which, according to the author, is "a social movement which was born in Mexiko as a means of providing us with a means for reclaiming our true history and heritage, provides us with taking back who we are as native people..." (p. 4) Part and parcel to Mexikayotl is armed struggle against the imperialist invaders of Aztlán. This book is special because it grapples with Chican@s to seek not only a cultural identity, but also a national identity, outside of Amerika. At a time when so many vendidos (sellouts) are stressing integration and assimilation into Amerika, Tlapoyawa teaches us that there is nothing good or "exceptional" about the U.$. other than the fact that, in the final analysis, Amerikans will go down in the history books as the scourage of humynity alongside the Nazis and the Zionist nation of Israel.

We Will Rise stresses national liberation and self-determination for the Chican@ people and not integration. Tlapoyawa seeks to organize and provide a united strategy for the Chican@ nation to liberate itself from "cultural imperialism" by convincing Chican@s to recognize their true identities as First Nation people. And insofar as he agitates within the cultural realm, Tlapoyawa deals a serious blow to the indoctrination programs of the United $tates, aka "public education." However, even as Tlapoyawa provides us with a lot of insight from the oppressed national's perspective, he also gets a few things twisted.

The book's main shortcoming is also its most important contribution to the Chican@ movement. While Tlapayowa's main argument is that we are not Amerikan's but "Xicano," he incorrectly asserts that Chican@s are really just Amerikanized Mexicans who have been brainwashed and kept in utter ignorance about our historical roots and connection, not only to Aztlán and the broader "Southwest," but Mexico too. Tlapoyawa incorrectly argues that the Chican@ people have not undergone any social-historical development as a separate nation outside of Mexico and within U.$. borders. Even as Tlapoyawa rails against the Amerikans' white-washing of history and all their criminal acts, he also doesn't undertake a materialist analysis of it.

Tlapoyawa implores Chican@s to take up Mexikayotl so that we may expel the settlers from our native lands (which is a very good thing),

and return to our traditional way of living by adapting pre-Columbian knowledge, philosophy, religion and art to today's conditions. This in itself would not be so bad, as the very concept of communism is based to a certain degree on primitive communalism. On that same note however, we can't discard the countless scientific advances made by humynity over the many mythological, superstitious beliefs and practices contained within Mexikayotl.

The concept of Mexikayotl and it's proponents also fail in their insistence that Chican@s return to the Mexican way of life, from which we as a nation have long since departed. Though we are connected with Mexico thru family, language and other common characteristics, we are also to a large degree separated by different aspects in familial, linguistic and cultural connections. We were not created by the same social and material forces which govern Mexican life, but by the imperialist venture of the annexation of the Amerikan "Southwest." Our existence is therefore not defined by the reality of the border, but by the social and material forces that have influenced the way we have developed since before and after its imposition. As such, the doctrine of Mexikayotl proves to be metaphysical for its reliance on ethnic genealogy as determinant of our reality and struggle as a people, while simultaneously ignoring the material forces that have given rise to the nation via the common links of language, territory, economic way of life and a shared psychological make-up manifested in a common culture.

Another mistake on Tlapoyawa's part is his reasoning as to why the ideology of Marxism isn't right for Chican@s, which comes more from a cursory and flawed understanding of the Marxist ideology, as well as his persynal experience with a member of the rcp=u$a. It's unfortunate that Tlapoyawa's one encounter with a "communist" happened to be with someone belonging to a First Worldist, Euro-centric, revisionist organization. One gets the feeling that had Tlapoyawa gained a better understanding of Marxism-Leninism-Maoism he might have taken the path of revolutionary nationalism instead of Mexikayotl which seems to be a special kind of cultural nationalism which advocates eventual armed struggle.

Besides its militant stance against integration, this book is valuable for its proposition of Aztlán's development in the Amerikan "Southwest" since pre-Columbian times. This is an issue which many bourgeois and settler scholars and archaeologists continue to deny today in spite of much historical evidence to the contrary.

Also included in *We Will Rise* is a concise history of the Chican@ struggle, from U.$. annexation to contemporary times. Interesting as well is Tlapoyawa's analysis of the Chican@ Power movement which is similar to our own. Tlapoyawa explains;

> *"During the Xicano Power period (1960-1975) the movement was a pow-
> erful but undirected force. Different political views filled the movement
> and a clear common agenda regarding national liberation was never
> formed. Some believed that liberation would only come by forming our
> own political parties and working within the system, while others believed
> that urban guerrilla-style warfare would lead us to victory. This lack of
> clear perspective, along with infighting, police infiltration, and government
> assassinations of Xicano leaders caused the movement to falter."* (p. 65)

As government repression stepped up, and more importantly without the clear perspective Tlapoyawa mentions, the Chican@ Power movement failed. This is true of all the national liberation movements inside the United $tates to date. While one section of the Chican@ movement used their own political parties to gain wider acceptance into Amerikan society, the other section of the population was tossed out of the economic relations of production altogether and into the prisons – these are the people we call the lumpen.

This book includes some correct and incorrect critiques of terms like "Hispanic" and "Latino," as well as some incorrect criticisms of the Asia-America land bridge theory of the Bering Strait, which postulates that humyns from Asia were the first to inhabit the Americas. Instead, Tlapoyawa states that the birth of civilization and indeed of the humyn species happened between the North and South American continents from where people then spread to the rest of the world. This is due however to his own subjectivist and dogmatic adherence to Mexikayotl and any theory that supports it. Tlapoyawa also pushes an anti-brown-capitalist line, as well as a strong anti-imperialist line as he expresses his solidarity with anti-imperialist struggles from Cuba to China and beyond.

Interesting as well is Tlapoyawa's position concerning what we in the Chican@ struggle today call Aztlán. Tlapoyawa himself believes that Aztlán's ancient location is confined to a specific region in Utah near the Great Salt Lake. When discussing the contemporary concept of Aztlán

Tlapoyawa states:

> "It should be noted that during the Xicano movement, the name Aztlán took on a political assertive meaning. Those in the movement used the concept of Aztlán to identify the entire southwestern 'United States.' In this social political context, Aztlán represents the land which was invaded, occupied and stolen from the Mexikan nation in 1848. This includes the modern states of Utah, Colorado, New Mexiko, California, Arizona and Texas.

> "While I certainly acknowledge the impact this broad concept of Aztlán has had in helping to form the cultural identity of many Xicano-Mexikanos, I do not take this view myself. The southwest is home to many non-Mexikan Indigenous nations, each with the universal right to govern over themselves and exist as a sovereign and autonomous people. Outside the small area in Utah which we recognize as being the traditional Aztlán, I feel we can claim no birthright to the entire southwest. To do so would be to play the european game of cultural imperialism of which we would want no part."
> (p. 118)

In making this statement Tlapoyawa makes us aware of an often overlooked component in the revolutionary struggle for Aztlán. Certainly this is a concern for Chican@ revolutionaries, one which requires a more in-depth analysis, and should help us demarcate between narrow nationalism and revolutionary nationalism. In Part I Section 4 we went more into our current analysis on the question regarding First Nation peoples, but clearly as our liberation struggle develops we will need to deepen our position accordingly.

We Will Rise – Rebuilding the Mexikah Nation advocates not only national liberation and self-determination for the Chican@ people, but strongly emphasizes building independent public and cultural institutions that are geared toward the revolutionary development of the nation of Aztlán. Kurly Tlapoyawa blazes the trail for Chican@s in the spirit of Fanon, and for this we recommend this book. *We Will Rise* also features an interesting bibliography which includes Mao, Lenin, Che, Fanon, Marx and many more. With that said, Down With Imperialism! Que Viva Aztlán!

Appendix

Organizations that made this book possible

1.a Brown Berets – Prison Chapter   221
1.b United Struggle from Within   226
1.c Maoist Internationalist Ministry of Prisons   229

Peace in Prisons

2.a Agreement to End Hostilities   233
2.b United Front for Peace in Prisons   236

Class

3.a Class overview   238
3.b Labor aristocracy   243
3.c First World lumpen   255
3.d Fascism and its class nature: A brief introduction   257

Migrant Farm Workers

4.a Why we use the word "migrant" and not "immigrant"   259
4.b On Cesar Chavez and the Correct and Incorrect Handling of
Contradictions Among the People   260

Organizational Structures

5.a Cell Structure, Vanguard Parties and Mass Organizations   262
5.b United Front   268
5.c New Democracy and the Joint Dictatorship
of the Proletariat of the Oppressed Nations   273

I.a Brown Berets – Prison Chapter

FOR THE PAST FEW DECADES California has been increasingly using control units in the form of security housing units (SHUs) as a method of control. These deprivation chambers are a major part of the state's war on the Chicano nation. Where prisons are used to enforce a slow genocide on La Raza, to disrupt the family unit and implement an internment camp by "legal" means, within prisons also lies the SHU which is equivalent to the chopping block where rebellious slaves who resisted or escaped would get limbs amputated as 1) punishment for resisting the oppressor nation, 2) preventing the slave from making future attempts, and 3) to inflict a psychological blow terrorizing the larger population to what will happen to them should they choose the same path of resistance. So too are the SHUs used in this manner on revolutionary or rebellious prisoners who resist the state. For this opposition to the state we are met with SHU which restricts our ability to resist and punishes us for our refusal to obey our oppressor thus instilling a grave warning to the prison masses of what will happen to them should they take the path of resistance.

This oppression has gone on for decades and has grown to horrific proportions in recent years. Just in Pelican Bay SHU, over a thousand are tortured with solitary confinement. The living conditions here have gone past punishment to the most vile cruelty depriving us of the most basic human rights, it is a place where sunlight is denied and health care is often used to extort incriminating information from those being tortured in this house of horrors. It is a place where prisoners have faced the most horrendous abuses like being boiled in tubs of scalding water to being stripped down in underwear and locked in an iron cage outside in the freezing raining winter morning. These stories would be unbelievable had they not been documented in court transcripts for all to see.

Chicanos are overwhelmingly the majority of those sent to SHU. It is the identification of this war on Aztlán, this silent offensive that you

won't read about in the bourgeois press or see on the corporate news outlets but which we see, live and have analyzed for all to understand.

These developments led to the formation of the Chicano Prisoners Revolutionary Committee (CPRC) in late 2011 here in Pelican Bay SHU. The CPRC was created initially for the efforts taking place surrounding the hunger strikes that swept U.$. prisons in 2011. It was within this effort to analyze and lend a revolutionary perspective to the developments surrounding human rights in prisons that CPRC gave birth to the Brown Berets – Prison Chapter (BB-PC) on 1 June 2012.

The BB-PC was inspired by the original Brown Berets that arose in the 1960s and led the Chicano movement in harnessing the people in the barrios with their many independent institutions from free health clinics, child care, free food programs, schools, newspapers, etc. We draw from this legacy of serving the people and dig deeper in the theoretical realm.

We do not answer to any other chapter nor does any other existing chapter answer to us. We are an autonomous chapter which, due to the extreme repression in Amerikkka's history, operates underground within U.$. prisons. We are the first prison chapter in the United $tates but we expect many more chapters to develop in many other prisons and states as Chican@s develop politically. We do not publish the names of the BB-PC cadre; our chapter resides in Pelican Bay State Prison.

The BB-PC is the Chicano cadre in U.$. prisons that works to transform these pintas and our nation from our vantage point. We are taking the concepts of community organizing and applying them to the pinta, thus these concrete conditions we experience are very different than they are for a chapter out in society. And although our efforts are mostly prison-based and revolve around contradictions prisoners face on a daily basis, our main thrust of course lies in the Aztlán liberation movement. Our ten point program guides us in that direction and allows us to remain in active service of Chicano independence.

We welcome all imprisoned Latinos to partake in the Chicano struggle as a liberated Aztlán will be a place where all Latinos are welcome to be free from oppression.

The following is the BB-PC Ten Point Program:

1. **We are Maoists**: We believe as Mao taught that class struggle continues even under socialism, as a new bourgeoisie develops, as happened in the USSR after the death of Stalin in 1953 and after Mao's death in 1976. Mao advanced communism the furthest thus far in world history and it will be through a Maoist program that we liberate Aztlán.

2. **We are an autonomous chapter.** We are a self-governing chapter that practices democratic centralism. We understand that because of state repression we are more efficient as an autonomous chapter and that as new chapters arise in other prisons across Amerika that they too will be autonomous in each individual prison.

3. **We want to build public opinion in prisons.** At this stage the only struggle in Amerika is in the realm of ideas. We seek to politicize the imprisoned Chicano nation through educating our gente on all aspects of la lucha.

4. **We want Raza unity.** As the largest Raza population in Amerikan prisons the Chicano nation understands its responsibility to maintain Pan-Latino unity and to educate all Raza on the current repression we face. In the prisons within Aztlán, Raza endure institutional

oppression where Raza are overwhelmingly held in SHUs and control units far more than any other of the oppressed. This offensive is meant to neutralize us physically but particularly mentally. We will stand with imprisoned Latinos and resist the oppressor nation as we have done for 500 years and support the Boricuas in their march toward independence free from neocolonialism.

5. **We stand in solidarity with all oppressed and Third World prisoners.** Today's prisons are meant to dehumanize the people and break our will to resist. The internal semi-colonies that are captured and held in these concentration camps face much of the same repression from the state, we understand that to better our living conditions as prisoners it will depend on a united front of oppressed prisoners for legal battles and other efforts to obtain human rights in prisons and we will cultivate this collaboration.

6. **We are revolutionary nationalists.** We understand that true internationalism is only possible when each nation is fully liberated. We identify oppression in Amerika revolving around nation, class and gender which enables imperialism to uphold power and we combat these forms of oppression in our long march to national liberation.

7. **Close the control units.** The SHUs and similar models are designed to unleash population regroupment on the imprisoned Chicano nation. It is well known that the most revolutionary elements of the Chicano prison population are plucked from general population prisons and sent to the SHU or other control units in an effort to isolate the revolutionary vanguard from the prison masses. This isolation is then used to torture Chicanos en masse through solitary confinement and other psychological methods for years and decades.

We understand that this is done primarily to prevent the captive Chicano revolutionaries from mobilizing our mass prison base. We see the control units in Amerika as modern day concentration camps as we are sent to those camps not for physical acts but for thought crimes, beliefs or supposed beliefs that oppose the state. We work to overturn the use of control units in every prison in Amerika.

8. Stop prisoner abuse. We are against oppression in all its forms within prisons. This includes prisoners preying on prisoners, abuse from the hands of guards, patriarchy or any abuse physically or psychologically. In Amerika prisons are tools of imperialism used to inflict terror on the internal semi-colonies out in society and stifle any resistance to their war on poor people. Having experienced and identified the full onslaught of this offensive we take it head on to combat all forms of abuse from the state or otherwise and this includes combatting the state propaganda and tactics of pitting prisoner against prisoner by political education so that prisoners understand who the oppressor is.

9. Free all political prisoners. We not only see political prisoners as those who were politically conscious out in society and came to prison for acts of the movement, we go past that in our analysis and also see SHU prisoners as overwhelmingly political prisoners who are systematically tortured for their ideas or alleged thoughts. We also see most prisoners in U.$. prisons as political prisoners because living in imperialist Amerika many of the "crimes" and criminal injustice system that we face is nothing more than national oppression that is exercised in order to uphold the capitalist relations of production and we work toward freeing the people.

10. We want a liberated socialist Aztlán. Our aim is communism but we understand it will take many years for this to become reality. At this stage we are working for Aztlán independence which will only occur after the defeat of imperialism. We work toward a socialist Aztlán where the peoples' needs are met; things like land, bread, education, health care and many more needs will be met and peoples' power will be exercised in order to transform not just society but prisons as well, to a more vibrant and just environment where all will have an opportunity to grasp revolution and promote production. We will transform these prisons ideologically in order to prepare the ground for these developments as we serve the people.

1.b United Struggle from Within

UNITED STRUGGLE FROM WITHIN (USW) is a MIM(Prisons)-led mass organization for current and former U.$. prisoners. USW is explicitly anti-imperialist in leading campaigns on behalf of U.$. prisoners in alliance with national liberation struggles in the United $tates and around the world. USW won't champion struggles which are not in the interests of the international proletariat. USW also will not choose one nation's struggles over other oppressed nations' struggles. USW should work independently, but under the guidance of MIM(Prisons) to build public opinion and independent institutions of the oppressed in order to obtain state power independent of imperialism. Members don't have to agree with MIM(Prisons)'s cardinal points (see page 230-231) but they can't consciously disagree with any of them.

I.c Maoist Internationalist Ministry of Prisons

MIM(Prisons)
PO Box 40799
San Francisco, CA 94140
www.prisoncensorship.info

MIM(PRISONS) IS A CELL OF revolutionaries serving the oppressed masses inside U.$. prisons. We uphold the revolutionary communist ideology of Marxism-Leninism-Maoism and work from the vantage point of the Third World proletariat. Our ideology is based in dialectical materialism, which means we work from objective reality to direct change rather than making decisions based on our subjective feelings about things. Defining our organization as a cell means that we are independent of other organizations, but see ourselves as part of a greater Maoist movement within the United $tates and globally.

Imperialism is the number one enemy of the majority of the world's people; we cannot achieve our goal of ending all oppression without overthrowing imperialism. History has shown that the imperialists will wage war before they will allow an end to oppression. Revolution will become a reality within the United $tates as the military becomes over-extended in the government's attempts to maintain world hegemony.

Since we live within an imperialist country, there is no real proletariat – the class of economically exploited workers. Yet there is a significant class excluded from the economic relations of production under modern imperialism that we call the lumpen. Within the United $tates, a massive prison system has developed to manage large populations, primarily from oppressed nations and many of whom come from the lumpen class.

Within U.$. borders, the principal contradiction is between imperialism and the oppressed nations. Our enemies call us racists for pointing out that the white oppressor nation historically exploited and continues to oppress other nations within the United $tates. But race is a made-up idea to justify oppression through ideas of inferiority. Nation is a concept

229

based in reality that is defined by a group's land, language, economy and culture. Individuals from oppressed nations taking up leadership roles within imperialist Amerika does not negate this analysis. The average conditions of the oppressed nations are still significantly different from the oppressor nation overall. As revolutionary internationalists, we support the self-determination of all nations and peoples. Today, the U.$. prison system is a major part of the imperialist state used to prevent all self-determination of oppressed nations.

It is for this reason that we see prisoners in this country as being at the forefront of any anti-imperialist and revolutionary movement.

MIM(Prisons) is our shorthand for the Maoist Internationalist Ministry of Prisons. Our name stems from the legacy of the Maoist Internationalist Movement (MIM), and their party based in North America that did most of the prisoner support work that is the focus of what we now do. When that party degenerated, the movement turned to a cell-based strategy that we uphold as more correct than a centralized party given our conditions in the United $tates today. Our focus on prisoner support is not a dividing line question for us. In fact, we believe that there is a dire need for Maoists to do organizing and educational work in many areas in the United $tates. We hope some people are inspired by our example around prisons and apply it to their own work to create more Maoist cells and broaden the Maoist movement behind enemy lines.

MIM(Prisons) distinguishes ourselves from other groups on the six points below. We consider other organizations actively upholding these points to be fraternal.

1. **Communism is our goal.** Communism is a society where no group has power over any other group.

2. **Dictatorship of the proletariat is necessary.** In a dictatorship of the proletariat the formerly exploited majority dictates to the minority (who promoted exploitation) how society is to be run. In the case of imperialist nations, a Joint Dictatorship of the Proletariat of the Oppressed Nations (JDPON) must play this role where there is no internal proletariat or significant mass base that favors communism.

3. **We promote a united front with all who oppose imperialism.** The road to the JDPON over the imperialist nations involves uniting all

who can be united against imperialism. We cannot fight imperialism and fight others who are engaged in life and death conflicts with imperialism at the same time. Even imperialist nation classes can be allies in the united front under certain conditions.

4. A parasitic class dominates the First World countries. As Marx, Engels and Lenin formulated and MIM Thought has reiterated through materialist analysis, imperialism extracts super-profits from the Third World and in part uses this wealth to buy off whole populations of so-called workers. These so-called workers bought off by imperialism form a new petty-bourgeoisie called the labor aristocracy; they are not a vehicle for Maoism. Those who work in the economic interests of the First World labor aristocracy form the mass base for imperialism's tightening death-grip on the Third World.

5. New bourgeoisies will form under socialism. Mao led the charge to expose the bourgeoisie that developed within the communist party in the Soviet Union and the campaign to bombard the head-quarters in his own country of China. Those experiences demon-strated the necessity of continuous revolution under the dictatorship of the proletariat. The class struggle does not end until the state has been abolished and communism is reached.

6. The Great Proletarian Cultural Revolution in China was the furthest advancement toward communism in history. We uphold the Soviet Union until the death of Stalin in 1953, followed by the People's Republic of China through 1976 as the best examples of modern socialism in practice. The arrest of the "Gang of Four" in China and the rise of Khrushchev in the Soviet Union marked the restoration of capitalism in those countries. Other experiments in developing socialism in the 20th century failed to surpass the Soviet model (ie. Albania), or worse, stayed within the capitalist mode of production, generally due to a failure to break with the Theory of Productive Forces.

SERVE THE PEOPLE PROGRAMS

Under Lock & Key and Free Political Books to Prisoners

Under Lock & Key is a news service written by and for prisoners with a focus on what is going on behind bars throughout the United States. *Under Lock & Key* is available to U.S. prisoners for free through MIM(Prisons)'s Free Political Literature to Prisoners Program.

Through our Free Political Literature to Prisoners Program, we mail prisoners political theory and history books and magazines in exchange for political work. Prisoners requesting books need to tell us what work you want to do, or just send in the articles, artwork, poetry, report on a study group you formed, etc. For many prisoners, the easiest way to start is by becoming a ULK Field Correspondent and reporting on what's going on in your prison. When requesting books it is best to ask for general topic areas and let us send you whatever we have on hand.

Our Free Political Literature to Prisoners Program relies on donations of books and money. If you have any contacts on the outside who can donate to our program, or who can hook us up with dictionaries, Mao or Lenin, or other political books, please tell them to contact us.

Political Study

The authors of *Chican@ Power and the Struggle for Aztlán* developed their political understanding with the help of MIM(Prisons)'s correspondence study courses. We run low-cost and work-trade study groups on the basics of Maoism and MIM Thought. For those who complete our introductory study course, we run higher level study groups on various topics related to ending oppresion.

MIM(Prisons) also distributes a continuously-expanding variety of study guides for your own political development and for use in your locality-based study group. Topics include: united front; organizational structure; labor aristocracy; culture; fascism; political economy; strategy; and many more.

2.a Agreement to End Hostilities

12 August 2012

TO WHOM IT MAY CONCERN and all California Prisoners:

Greetings from the entire PBSP-SHU Short Corridor Hunger Strike Representatives. We are hereby presenting this mutual agreement on behalf of all racial groups here in the PBSP-SHU Corridor. Wherein, we have arrived at a mutual agreement concerning the following points:

1. If we really want to bring about substantive meaningful changes to the CDCR system in a manner beneficial to all solid individuals who have never been broken by CDCR's torture tactics intended to coerce one to become a state informant via debriefing, that now is the time for us to collectively seize this moment in time and put an end to more than 20-30 years of hostilities between our racial groups.

2. Therefore, beginning on Oct. 10, 2012, all hostilities between our racial groups in SHU, ad-seg, general population and county jails will officially cease. This means that from this date on, all racial group hostilities need to be at an end. And if personal issues arise between individuals, people need to do all they can to exhaust all diplomatic means to settle such disputes; do not allow personal, individual issues to escalate into racial group issues!

3. We also want to warn those in the general population that IGI [Institutional Gang Investigators] will continue to plant undercover Sensitive Needs Yard (SNY) debriefer "inmates" amongst the solid GP prisoners with orders from IGI to be informers, snitches, rats and obstructionists, in order to attempt to disrupt and undermine

our collective groups' mutual understanding on issues intended for our mutual causes (i.e. forcing CDCR to open up all GP main lines and return to a rehabilitative-type system of meaningful programs and privileges, including lifer conjugal visits etc. via peaceful protest activity and noncooperation, e.g., hunger strike, no labor etc.). People need to be aware and vigilant to such tactics and refuse to allow such IGI inmate snitches to create chaos and reignite hostilities amongst our racial groups. We can no longer play into IGI, ISU (Investigative Service Unit), OCS (Office of Correctional Safety) and SSU's (Service Security Unit's) old manipulative divide and conquer tactics!

In conclusion, we must all hold strong to our mutual agreement from this point on and focus our time, attention and energy on mutual causes beneficial to all of us [i.e., prisoners] and our best interests. We can no longer allow CDCR to use us against each other for their benefit!

Because the reality is that collectively, we are an empowered, mighty force that can positively change this entire corrupt system into a system that actually benefits prisoners and thereby the public as a whole. We simply cannot allow CDCR and CCPOA (the prison guards' union), IGI, ISU, OCS and SSU to continue to get away with their constant form of progressive oppression and warehousing of tens of thousands of prisoners, including the 14,000-plus prisoners held in solitary confinement torture chambers (SHU and ad-seg units) for decades!

We send our love and respect to all those of like mind and heart. Onward in struggle and solidarity!

Presented by the PBSP-SHU Short Corridor Collective:

Todd Ashker, C-58191, D1-119
Arturo Castellanos, C-17275, D1-121
Sitawa Nantambu Jamaa (Dewberry), C-35671, D1-117
Antonio Guillen, P-81948, D2-106

And the Representatives Body:

Danny Troxell, B-76578, D1-120
George Franco, D-46556, D4-217
Ronnie Yandell, V-27927, D4-215
Paul Redd, B-72683, D2-117

James Baridi Williamson, D-34288. D4-107
Alfred Sandoval, D-61000, D4-214
Louis Powell, B-59864, D1-104
Alex Yrigollen, H-32421, D2-204
Gabriel Huerta, C-80766, D3-222
Frank Clement, D-07919, D3-116
Raymond Chavo Perez, K-12922, D1-219
James Mario Perez, B-48186, D3-124

Note: All names and the foregoing statement must be shown verbatim when used and posted on any website or other publication.

2.b United Front for Peace in Prisons

Statement of Principles

THE BASIS OF ANY REAL unity comes from an agreement on certain key ideas. This statement does not grant authority to any party over any other party. We are mutually accountable to each other to uphold these points in order to remain active participants in this united front.

1. **PEACE:** WE organize to end the needless conflicts and violence within the U.$. prison environment. The oppressors use divide and conquer strategies so that we fight each other instead of them. We will stand together and defend ourselves from oppression.

2. **UNITY:** WE strive to unite with those facing the same struggles as us for our common interests. To maintain unity we have to keep an open line of networking and communication, and ensure we address any situation with true facts. This is needed because of how the pigs utilize tactics such as rumors, snitches and fake communications to divide and keep division among the oppressed. The pigs see the end of their control within our unity.

3. **GROWTH:** WE recognize the importance of education and freedom to grow in order to build real unity. We support members within our organization who leave and embrace other political organizations and concepts that are within the anti-imperialist struggle. Everyone should get in where they fit in. Similarly, we recognize the right of comrades to leave our organization if we fail to live up to the principles and purpose of the United Front for Peace in Prisons.

4. **INTERNATIONALISM:** WE struggle for the liberation of all oppressed people. While we are often referred to as "minorities"

in this country, and we often find those who are in the same boat as us opposing us, our confidence in achieving our mission comes from our unity with all oppressed nations who represent the vast majority globally. We cannot liberate ourselves when participating in the oppression of other nations.

5. **INDEPENDENCE:** WE build our own institutions and programs independent of the United $tates government and all its branches, right down to the local police, because this system does not serve us. By developing independent power through these institutions we do not need to compromise our goals.

How to join the United Front for Peace in Prisons?

1. Study and uphold the five principles of the united front.

2. Send your organization's name and a statement of unity to MIM(Prisons). Your statement can explain what the united front principles mean to your organization, how they relate to your work, why they are important, etc.

3. Develop peace and unity between factions where you are at on the basis of opposing oppression of all prisoners and oppressed people in general.

4. Send reports on your progress to *Under Lock & Key*. Did you develop a peace treaty or protocol that is working? Send it in for others to study and possibly use. Is your unity based on actions? Send us reports on the organizing you are doing.

5. Keep educating your members. The more educated your members are, the more unity you can develop, and the stronger your organization can become. Unity comes from the inside out. By uniting internally, we can better unite with others as well. Contact MIM(Prisons)'s Free Political Books for Prisoners Program if you need additional materials to educate your members in history, politics and economics.

3.a Class overview

A CLASS IS A GROUP of people with a common relation to the means of production, to the distribution of the means of consumption, and to other classes of people. Means of production are the tools humyns use to transform nature to meet their needs.

The **bourgeoisie** is the exploiter class most characteristic of the capitalist system. Their wealth is obtained from the labor of others, in particular the proletariat.

The term "bourgeoisie" now usually refers to the capitalist class in common usage. The capitalist class is that class of people who own enough property that they would not have to work to make a living. The capitalist class only works if it wants to. Also included in the term are people with very powerful positions in production or government generally. A ruler may or may not have great assets on hand, but if s/he really wanted them, s/he has the power to get them. For example, Ronald Reagan made a speech in Japan with a $1 million fee after he retired from the presidency. If he had been "poor" during the presidency, he still would have been part of the "capitalist class." What he was doing was central enough to the ruling class of capitalism that he had de facto access to the means of production, even if he had gambled away his ranch and other assets in Las Vegas while he was in the White House.

An overly restrictive definition of "capitalist" is someone who owns the means of production – factories, tools and patents for example. What is important is not the literal ownership of means of production but access to those means of production. Such access could be merely the ability to get a loan so large that it is possible to live off the business connected to such a loan. Access to political information in the military, intelligence or executive branch would make it possible to be rich making a speech like Reagan did or by selling secrets to foreigners. People with such access to information also may be bourgeoisie. For example, Reagan could take his $1 million speech fee and convert it into means of production such as ownership of tools and factory buildings. Whether he does that or not, we can say he has "access" to the means of production.

Wealth Flow in the First World

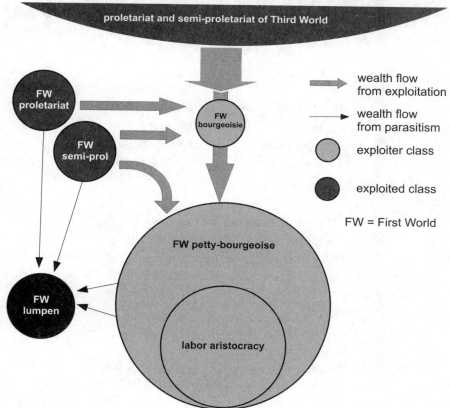

proletariat and semi-proletariat of Third World

wealth flow
from exploitation

wealth flow
from parasitism

exploiter class

exploited class

FW = First World

FW proletariat

FW semi-prol

FW bourgeoisie

FW petty-bourgeoise

labor aristocracy

FW lumpen

In colonized nations, the **comprador bourgeoisie** is a class which acts as junior partners to the imperialists in exploiting the colonized people. It owes its existence to the imperialist capitalists and cannot function on its own as a capitalist class. Their interests are tied closely to those of the imperialists even if they have a national interest in independence. They sell out their nation for persynal benefit.

Generally the **petty bourgeoisie** is the group between the bourgeoisie and the working class, sometimes called the "middle class." They are economically self-supporting or even earning more than they consume for their own support. This class includes those who own their own means of production and work for themselves. They cannot generate sufficient surplus value from exploitation of others to live without working themselves, so they are not primarily exploiters, unlike the bourgeoisie. In imperialist countries, this class has two sub-groups:

1. **Owners of Capital (small businesses, real estate, stocks, etc.):** Owns their own business or has means to or has ability to get loan to start a small business. The pure petty bourgeois class is separated from the labor aristocracy by their ownership of wealth.

2. **Labor Aristocracy:** Unlike the traditional petty bourgeoisie, they do not own their own means of production and so must work for others. But unlike the proletariat and semi-proletariat the labor aristocracy in the First World earn more than the value of their labor and therefore have interests that fall in the bourgeois camp allying with imperialism.

Portions of the **semi-proletariat** are similar to the petty-bourgeoisie in that both groups are gaining material benefit from ownership of some capital. These semi-proletarians are distinguished from the petty-bourgeoisie in that they work for themselves, but earn income similar to exploited workers. In the Third World this includes semi-owner peasants, street vendors, and small handicrafts workers. In the First World we see those self-employed in small businesses in the ghetto, barrio or reservation (i.e. cutting hair in their home).

The semi-proletariat also includes portions of the proletariat who must sell their labor to survive but work outside of the productive sector. These workers are exploited by others, unable to earn the value of their labor. These non-productive workers mostly exist in the Third World as shop assistants, poor peasants on semi-feudal farms, technicians, and civil servants. The non-productive sector in the First World is dominated by petty-bourgeois labor aristocrats, so to distinguish between these two groups we draw the line at the international average value of labor.

Full time minimum wage workers in the United $tates today are above this level and so not part of the semi-proletariat. The international average value of labor has been conservatively estimated around $5 per hour in 2014. People only earning enough to average $5/hour or less in a 40 hour work week, outside of the industrial proletariat, would be representative of those who do not own their own capital, do not work in production, and so would be included in the semi-proletariat.

Unlike the traditional petty bourgeoisie, the **labor aristocracy** does not own its own means of production and so must work for others. But unlike the proletariat and semi-proletariat the labor aristocracy in the

First World earn more than the value of their labor and therefore have interests that fall in the bourgeois camp allying with imperialism.

In Lenin's day the labor aristocracy was the "upper strata of the proletariat." Lenin wrote that he was "obliged to distinguish between the 'upper stratum' of the workers and the 'lower stratum of the proletariat proper.'" (*Imperialism, the Highest Stage of Capitalism*) "The capitalists *can* devote a part (and not a small one, at that!) of these superprofits to bribe *their own* workers, to create something like an alliance (recall the celebrated 'alliances' described by the Webbs of English trade unions and employers) between the workers of the given nation and their capitalists *against* the other countries." (*Imperialism and the Split in Socialism*, Lenin's emphasis).

In the First World today we define this group as the lower segment of the petty-bourgeoisie, working for a wage and earning more than the value of their labor but without the means to get a loan to start a small business themselves. This group benefits from the imperialist world's super-exploitation of the Third World. They are bought off by the imperialists with these super-profits. In the First World this group is not exploited and so not part of the proletariat. On the contrary, their incomes are often higher than those traditionally classified as the petty bourgeoisie in the Third World, further demonstrating their bourgeois character.

The **proletariat** is the group of people who have nothing to sell but their labor power for their subsistence. The proletariat does not draw any profit from any kind of capital because they have none. Proletarians are propertyless and thus have "nothing to lose but their chains." The proletariat is the least conservative element of society. There are several groups that fall within the proletariat:

1. The working proletariat are exploited by others who make a profit off of their labor.

2. The non-working proletariat make up the reserve army of the proletariat. In current times this group is usually temporarily unemployed and seeking employment. The long-term unemployed usually fall into the lumpen-proletariat.

3. The lumpen-proletariat, a group of people who are unable to sell their labor power in the long term and so end up living as parasites

on other proletarians. This group is found in the Third World, and is distinct from the First World lumpen.

The **First World lumpen** is the class of people in the First World who are excluded from the productive process. By virtue of living in the First World this class, on average, receives more material benefits from imperialism than the global proletariat. As such their interests are not the same as the exploited classes and we do not include them in the "lumpen-proletariat." But their conditions in many ways parallel those of the lumpen-proletariat standing in stark contrast to the majority of the First World populations.

Classes outside of the First World

In a world where the vast majority must sell their labor power to survive, the **lumpen-proletariat** are those who are not able to sell theirs due to the limitations of capitalism at providing full employment. This class is rarely employed, often living as parasites on other proletarians. A small portion of the proletariat in Europe when Marx first wrote about them, the lumpen-proletariat has become an important class in itself. With the rise of mega-slums in the Third World following the period of neo-colonialism, this class has surpassed 1 billion people.

The **peasantry** is the class of people who labor on the land and possess their means of production: tools and the land itself. A defining characteristic of the peasantry is that it must pay rent or a tribute to maintain its possession of the land. Members of this class are peasants.

3.b Labor aristocracy

MIM trashes the myth of white exploitation

Raise the Minimum Wage to $2.50

Recommended Reading on the Labor Aristocracy

MIM TRASHES THE MYTH OF WHITE EXPLOITATION
excerpt from a response to Doug Henwood
printed in *MIM Theory 1: A White Proletariat?* (Spring 1992)
by MC5

To understand the position of the white working class, the labor aristocracy, it is necessary to make international comparisons. Because of the issue of superexploitation and the overarching role of imperialism, it is necessary to accept an international standard. Today's world market includes, as a rule, military dictatorships designed to keep the international proletariat down. The labor aristocracy is not only not in line with the Third World proletariat, but it is also not in line with the Third World petty bourgeoisie.

Before bringing out other data, we have to define what we are talking about theoretically.[1] Once we do that, MIM believes most people will find that they have always had more than enough information at hand to make a decision about this theoretical conflict concerning the labor aristocracy. The analysis is key because if the labor aristocracy is exploited, then organizing it will be a progressive thing. If the labor aristocracy is not exploited, then organizing it will only result in white chauvinism and greater strength for imperialism, whatever the intentions of the organizer.

Amerikan leftist political economy vs. Maoist political economy
When Marx first wrote about the market for labor power, there was not the kind of superexploitation we have today. It was just starting compared with the level it has now reached. Yet even in the 1800s, Marx warned that slavery and colonialism were corrupting influences

243

on European working classes.

Marx said that wages were the culturally and historically determined product of a market for labor power. In other words, the wage was what that society deemed necessary to reproduce its workers. In this regard, Henwood is correct. [Doug Henwood is an Amerikan economist - Editor]

In Marx's day, the capitalists appropriated surplus labor from the white workers despite paying wages, so the workers were exploited. In the 1800s, it was possible to look at the dead labor that went into reproducing British labor power and say it was basically British. A loom or hoe used in production by British laborers pretty much came from the dead labor of British laborers.

Since the time of Marx, imperialism has grown many fold. Having expanded after World War I, imperialism continued to expand after World War II. One small indication is U.S. direct investment abroad. In 1950 it was $11.8 billion, but by 1980 it was $200 billion. Moreover, a list of the top 76 manufacturing firms shows that 37% of their assets are abroad (which includes Europe, not just the Third World).[2]

The advent of supertankers, airplanes and faster transportation and communication of all kinds made the plunder of the Third World a much more central fact of economic life. But today, thanks to dead Third World labor, the labor that goes into "reproducing" the white working class is greater than the labor done by the white working class.

Closed borders: separate markets for labor power

Amerikan society and its "leftists" would have us believe that [in 1992 - Editor] an average of $10 an hour and a $44,000 house for whites is necessary for the reproduction of the white working class as workers. That is strictly ideological obfuscation. Why?

If the U.S. imperialists paid $2 an hour and threw open the borders, they would have no problem reproducing the working class. Indeed, the population would grow enormously both from immigration and natural growth. The only reason that does not happen is that the imperialists agreed with the labor aristocracy (and not just its labor bureaucrat lieutenants, judging from the popularity of anti-immigrant laws) to close the borders and establish a minimum wage. The agreement is very similar to the basic agreement in South Africa, but the blatant Jim Crow laws and superexploitation are not as prevalent in Amerika. Whites are a majority here, but not in South Africa.

Henwood pretends that U.S. labor would not reproduce itself if it were not for the Amerikan alliance with the imperialists that generates a $10-an-hour wage. By this he means U.S. labor would die and then the system would also, as Marx said about the British workers and their system of the 1800s.

This is a false assumption. MIM has looked around enough to know that proletarians can reproduce and keep the capitalist system going for a lot less than $10 an hour. There is no need to fantasize about the oppression of First World people, except as required for imperialist nation unity.

The Amerikan leftists want us to accept the standards of the white working class as necessary for its reproduction, so they can go on saying that the labor aristocracy is exploited and go on begging for the cross-class white unity which benefits imperialism.

In contrast, MIM looks at things from the perspective of the Third World proletariat. MIM uses a rough international standard wage necessary for reproduction of workers under late imperialism. MIM could economistically struggle for $1.50 an hour and that would still double what the Pico Products workers made in south Korea in the late 1980s, and south Korean labor is more organized than most and living in closer-to-imperialist conditions than just about any Third World country.

In the "Communist Manifesto," Marx said communists differ from other labor organizers in that communists look at everything from the perspective of the international proletariat, not just any one of its sections. The only reason Euro-Amerikan workers make $10 something an hour is that the borders are closed by force. That is the most significant factor in the market for labor power and it must never be forgotten.

The wage for Amerikan workers should be put on par with an international standard for the proletariat. MIM believes that the white working class' wages are not determined merely by market conditions for labor power; hence, its wages go beyond what is necessary for reproduction of the white working class in the capacity of workers (not the reproduction of the white working class in their role as parasites).

The search for surplus labor

Another definitive answer to the question is from the point of view of the capitalists. Where surplus labor is not appropriated, there are no profits. Of course, without profits, capitalists go out of business. Without profits, even capitalists wouldn't want the capitalist system to exist. Henwood's writings lead one to think that the capitalists have it made, thanks to how little the Amerikan workers make. The reality of profit rates is a little different though.

Even the social democrats who wrote the book *Global Reach* recognized that multinational corporations rely on the Third World for their profits. This is the same reason all the banks are scared of Third World default on loans and asking for the government to bail them out if the time comes. First World banks are in trouble. From 1983 to 1990, First World banks received $325 billion more than they put into Third World countries in terms of loans and loan repayments.[3] That's just one avenue of exploitation that the banks count on in terms of the Third World. What would happen to the First World banks without the Third World?[4]

Without the Third World, U.S. capital would die, because it pays white labor too much to make a profit from those workers alone. Put a British naval embargo around French international commerce in the 1800s and the French capitalists would still expand and survive in that progressive phase of capitalism. Put a Maoist blockade on the commerce of U.S. imperialism in 1992, and the ball game is over. Anyone who doubts this should look at First World profit margins and where they come from. Imperialists do not appropriate surplus labor from white workers right now and could not survive without their source of profits: the Third World. To make profits without the Third World, the First World capitalists would have to cut First World workers' wages drastically.

Henwood's answer shows both ignorance and Amerika-first chauvinism. Taking GNP and dividing by the number of hours worked in the United States, Doug comes up with a figure of $27.85 per worker per hour.

This calculation shows that Henwood did not understand MIM's argument regarding superexploitation of the Third World. The GNP is the monetary value of all the goods and services sold in the United States for a year. The GNP includes the value of the unremunerated dead labor of the Third World. That dead labor is paid for by the time it reaches the sales stage, the point at which the GNP is calculated. However, the people who get paid for that dead labor are not the Third World laborers, but the imperialist exploiters and the labor aristocracy. The income the GNP counts is from the exploiters and the labor aristocracy and the Third World within the borders of the United States. The GNP figures do not say where that income largely comes from – the dead labor of the Third World.

Another problem with comparing wages with GNP figures is that GNP figures include items that go to the labor aristocracy beyond wages such as public service. The only part of the GNP that does not go to salaries or wages (and other incomes) is profits.

Where do the profits go?

The other calculation that Henwood trots out is the added value from manufacturing workers. To the extent that he implies that capitalists take the bulk of added value from manufacturing workers (64% in 1988) and simply keep it as profit, MIM does not agree. To the extent that Henwood points to a relationship between manufacturing workers and other sectors of the labor aristocracy, there is a point. The 64% does not go to the capitalists as profit, but to other labor aristocracy people – clerical and sales people – again mostly white-collar white workers.

A capitalist class raking in trillions in profits every year is convenient for the fantasy of white working-class exploitation. Unfortunately, most Amerikan leftists have a naive view like this. They imagine their critique of capitalism depends on the amazing consumption of the capitalists and the tremendous inequality within the Amerikan nation. But they grossly exaggerate that inequality. The problem is not that capitalists make trillions in profits, but that production is organized in a capitalist fashion – thus creating the wrong goods, overproduction, environmental degradation and world war.

Instead, the bulk of the 64% fluff Henwood refers to is attributable to the fact that over half of Amerikan workers are white-collar, according to the 1980 census. Part of that fluff is collected in the form of taxes, which does not go directly into capitalist pockets. But most of the 64% goes into the labor aristocracy's pockets, especially retirement pensions and workers in the military – with a percentage of profits leftover for the corporations supplying the government.

MIM should thank Henwood for replying and simplifying the chore of proving that the Amerikan left has no sense of proportion. Perhaps in future articles Henwood or someone from MIM could treat the wealth of the capitalist class. Listening to Henwood, one would have thought that the United States created thousands of billionaires every year.

Instead, if people look at the new wealth of the capitalist class created every year, they will find that it is much smaller than the superprofits sucked in from the Third World each year. The reason is that the labor aristocracy produces no surplus labor for the capitalists and instead gets a share of the Third World superprofits. The capitalist class accumulates wealth fast, but not fast enough to suck in both superprofits from the Third World and profits from the labor aristocracy.

The implication of both Henwood's GNP and value added figures – that the capitalists suck in trillions in profits every year – is just a calculation error of the overly excited Amerikan left. Profits have never exceeded even half a trillion dollars a year. In 1990, they were $293.3 billion, or 6.6% of the $4.4 trillion GNP, and that was a good year for profits.[5]

After-tax profits in 1989 (the most recent figures) mounted to $172.6 billion. Out of that the capitalists admit to obtaining $50.9 billion from abroad, which still does not count superexploited labor done in the Third World.[6]

Even in these profits, the labor aristocracy takes a large part in dividends – both in privately owned and pension owned stocks – and in shareholding in banks, especially credit unions. The capitalist class is not raking in $173 billion in new wealth every year. Only a vulgar Marxist view fantasizing about the consumption of the capitalist could imagine anything close to what Henwood is talking about.

Overall, those $173 billion in profits are puny indeed. Any comrade who thinks about what it means that only 3.9% of GNP is profits will realize that it is simply not possible the white working class is exploited. In fact, those profits are so small because of overpayment in dead labor to the labor aristocracy.

Within those puny profits, the capitalist class owns a large share. The top 1% of families owns 51% of the market value of the stocks owned by families (as of figures collected for 1960 and 1971 which are the most recent available). That means that 49% of those stocks privately held are held by people outside the top 1%! That's not to mention the stocks held by institutions, the profits of which go to benefit the labor aristocracy – colleges, pension funds, etc.

The assets of the top 1% are always in the 50% to 60% range. One could dispute the number of capitalists in the United States and say this 1% figure is too low. But if we look at the top 2%, 5% or 20% of the population and call them capitalist, we are talking about a lot of people who are not millionaires. In 1958, it only took $60,000 in assets to make it into the top 1.5%.[7] As of 1970, there were still fewer than 1 million millionaires. That was only about 1% of the population if we assume a household size of 2.5. In fact, according to J. Sakai, citing the top 1% of the population as capitalists overestimates the size of the capitalist class. In 1970, the average wealth of that group was $1.32 million, which means a large portion of that group owns less than $1.32 million since we must account for the billionaires and multi-millionaires. According to Sakai, that 1% is partially petty bourgeoisie.[4]

Considering the distribution of assets and hence profits, it seems possible that only a half or two thirds of each year's $173 billion in profits actually ends up in the hands of capitalists – people who can live off of owning the means of production. (MIM uses this definition so that people who own merely 1 share of stock or even 100 shares of stock are not counted as capitalists.) And that other large share of profits goes to the labor aristocracy, even after the labor aristocracy receives inflated, non-exploitative wages.

Puny profits that actually end up in capitalist hands each year – under $150 billion or 3% of the GNP – are easily explained by the exploitation of national minority workers within U.S. borders. These workers get about 70% of what white workers get, and that's only if they're documented. Let's be generous to the labor aristocracy and assume that the imperialists pay all the documented and undocumented workers an average of 70% of what white workers get (a very liberal estimate). Now look at the portion of GNP accounted for by national minority workers within U.S. borders - 20%. Giving 70% of that amount to minority workers leaves 6% of GNP as the difference in pay between white and national minority workers generated by discrimination, alone. Six percent of GNP is nearly all the profits before taxes! That leaves the labor aristocracy to get paid for all its dead labor while receiving all the superprofits from the Third World outside U.S. borders.(see Glossary for "national minority")

There is no way that the white working class is exploited. The $173 billion does go almost entirely to the top half of Amerika, according to Domhoff. But we've already shown that the profits are just too small not to be accounted for solely by exploitation of the national minorities within U.S. borders.

In Marx's day, the value of the British GNP was pretty much the result of the labor of British workers, especially compared with today's GNP. In 1991, Henwood makes the mistake of keeping Marx's assumptions as they apply to individual First World markets. Henwood makes no effort to account for the exploitation and superexploitation of Third World workers that go into making the U.S. GNP. The reason Henwood does not count the unremunerated Third World labor and simply assumes that all GNP is the product of U.S. workers is simple – Amerika first chauvinism.[8]

MIM does not attempt to organize the white working class as a group because it is not exploited and does not have a material interest in revolution. Working to organize the white working class would make the party a pro-imperialist, reformist party - the history of the Amerikan working class makes this clear.

The mass base for revolution will come from the exploited and superexploited - mostly in the Third World - and MIM seeks to organize all who work in the interests of the truly oppressed.

RAISE THE MINIMUM WAGE TO $2.50
by Wiawimawo of MIM(Prisons)
January 2014

Recently the small town of SeaTac, Washington passed a ballot measure to raise the minimum wage to $15 per hour. Across the United $tates the Service Employees International Union (SEIU) labor union has led an effort to demand $15 per hour for all fast food workers. For a 28 November 2013 strike, organizers said that there were demonstrations in over 100 cities.[1]

In 2014 the minimum wage will be going up in many states. Leading the way are Washington($9.32) and Oregon($9.10), with New York making the biggest jump to $8.00 per hour. New York City was center to the recent fast food strikes. Meanwhile, Democrats in Congress have plans for a bill this year that would raise the federal minimum from $7.25 to $10.10 per hour.[2]

Another place that minimum wage struggles made a lot of noise in 2013 was the garment industry in Bangladesh. As we mentioned in the last issue of *Under Lock & Key No. 35 (November/December 2013)*, those workers had a recent victory in the minimum wage being raised from $38 to $68 per month. In Cambodia, garment workers have been promised a raise in the minimum wage from $80 to $95 per month. Unsatisfied, the workers have joined recent protests against the current regime to demand $160 per month.[3]

With 48-hour work weeks, garment workers are making around $0.35 per hour in Bangladesh, and $0.42 in Cambodia. Believe it or not, these are the privileged workers who have special protections because they are in important export industries. The common Bangladeshi has a minimum wage of $19 per month, which is less than 10 cents an hour.

The proposed $10 per hour minimum in the United $tates would put the lowest paid Amerikans at ONE HUNDRED times the income of the lowest paid workers in Bangladesh. This is why on May Day we called out the chauvinist white worker movement for skirting the issue of a global minimum wage.[4]

Now, the first cry of our chauvinist critics will be "cost of living, you forgot about cost of living." Our proposal for a global minimum wage would tie this wage to a basket of goods. That means the worker in the United $tates and the worker in Bangladesh can afford comparable lifestyles with their pay. Maybe the Amerikan gets wheat where the Bangladeshi gets rice, for example. But the Amerikan does not get a persynal SUV with unlimited gasoline, while the Bangladeshi gets bus fare to and from work. To maintain such inequality the Bangladeshi is subsidizing a higher standard of living for the Amerikan.

It happens that the World Bank has taken a stab at this calculation with their Purchasing Power Parity. Using this calculation, the minimum wage in Bangladesh, which appears to be $0.09 per hour, is really a whopping $0.19 per hour.[5] So, we must apologize to our critics. The proposed minimum wage of $10 per hour would only put the lowest paid Amerikans at fifty times the pay of the lowest paid Bangladeshi if we account for cost of living.

Recently the New Afrikan Black Panther Party (Prison Chapter) accused our movement of dismissing the possibility of revolutionary organizing in the United $tates because we acknowledge the facts above.[6] Just because struggles for higher wages, and other economic demands, are generally pro-imperialist in this country does not mean that we cannot organize here. But revolutionary organizing must not rally the petty bourgeoisie for more money at the expense of the global proletariat. Besides, even in the earliest days of the Russian proletariat Lenin had criticisms of struggles for higher wages.

While we expressed doubts about Chokwe Lumumba's electoral strategy in Jackson, Mississippi, we remain optimistic about the New Afrikan Liberation Movement's efforts to mobilize the masses there. Organizing for cooperative economics and self-sufficiency is a more neutral approach to mobilizing the lower segments of New Afrika than the SEIU clamoring for more wages for unproductive service work.[7] While our concerns rested in their ability to organize in a way that was really independent of the existing system (creating dual power) the SEIU's begging for more spoils from the imperialists does not even offer such a possibility. To really address the inequalities in the world though, we must ultimately come into conflict with the capitalist system that creates and requires those inequalities.

One agitational point of the fast food protests has been that 52% of the families of front-line fast food workers need to rely on public assistance programs.[1] One reason this is true is that most fast food workers do not get to work 48 or even 40 hours a week. Throw children and other dependents in the mix and you have a small, but significant, underclass in the United $tates that struggles with things like food, rent and utility bills. Most are single parents, mostly single mothers. Collective living and economic structures could (and do) serve this class and can offer a means of political mobilization. The Black Panthers' Serve the People programs and Black houses (collective living) are one model for such organizing. But state-sponsored programs and the general increase in wealth since the 1960s makes distinguishing such work from working with imperialism a more daunting task.

The campaign for a global minimum wage has little traction among the lower paid workers in the United $tates, because they do not stand to benefit from this. This is a campaign to be led by the Third World and pushed through international bodies such as the World Trade Organization. We support it for agitational reasons, but don't expect mass support in this country. It allows us to draw a line between those who are true internationalists and those who are not.[8]

Any campaign working for economic interests of people in the imperialist countries is going to be problematic because the best economic deal for them will require teaming up with the imperialists, at least for the forseeable future.

RECOMMENDED READING ON THE LABOR ARISTOCRACY

WE HAVE ATTEMPTED TO GIVE a brief, but thorough, outline of our thesis on the labor aristocracy question above. For those interested in getting deeper into it, we outline some must-read books and magazines on the subject below.

In 2012, MIM(Prisons) added the newly released *Divided World Divided Class* by Zak Cope to the labor aristocracy section of our must-read list. In 2014, Kersplebedeb printed an updated second edition of this book.

Before addressing this new book, let us first put it in the context of our existing must-read materials on the labor aristocracy, which has long been the issue that the Maoist Internationalist Movement differentiated itself on. MIM(Prisons) recently assembled an introductory study pack on this topic, featuring material from *MIM Theory 1: A White Proletariat?* (1992) and *Monkey Smashes Heaven #1* (2011). We recommend this pack as the starting point for most prisoners, as it is both cheaper to acquire and easier to understand than Cope's book and other material on the list.

Settlers: The Mythology of the White Proletariat by J. Sakai is a classic book documenting the history of Amerika as an oppressor nation whose class nature has always been bourgeois. It is for those interested in Amerikan history in more detail, and particularly the history of the national contradiction in the United $tates. While acknowledging Sakai's thesis, Cope actually expands the analysis to a global scale, which leads to a greater focus on Britain in much of the book as the leading imperialist power, later surpassed by Amerika. This complete picture is developed by Cope in a theory-rich analysis, weaving many sources together to present his thesis. H.W. Edwards's *Labor Aristocracy: Mass Base of Social Democracy* is a less cohesive attempt at a similar approach that is almost half a century old. Edwards is wishy-washy on the role of First World "workers," where Cope is not. Edwards provides a number of good statistics and examples of his thesis, but it is presented in a more haphazard way. That said, *Labor Aristocracy* is still on our must-read list and we distribute it with a study guide.

MIM went back to the labor aristocracy question in *MIM Theory 10: The Labor Aristocracy* (1996). This issue built on *MIM Theory 1: A White Proletariat?* (1992) some, but primarily focuses on an in-depth look at the global class analysis under imperialism by the Comintern. The importance of this issue during WWII is often overlooked, and this essay gets deep into the two-line struggle within the communist movement at the time. We have a study pack on this piece as well.

The last work that we include in the canon is *Imperialism and its Class Structure in 1997* by MC5 of the Maoist Internationalist Movement. This book is most similar to Cope's work, with Cope seeming to borrow specific ideas and sources without ever acknowledging MC5's work. Since Cope is very generous in acknowledging ideas he got from others, one suspects that there is a political motivation behind ignoring the number one proponent of the position he is trying to defend in his book. We think MC5 would see Cope's work as a compliment and a step forward for the scientific analysis, particularly since Cope does not bring in anything to oppose the MIM line or to confuse the issue. Cope's book is very well researched and put together as an original work, and we have no interest in defending intellectual property.

The major new contribution in Cope's book is the historical analysis of the labor aristocracy in the context of the global system of imperialism. He also does some original calculations to measure superexploitation. His analysis of class, nation and modern events is all found in contemporary Maoism. Cope seems to be walking a line of upholding MIM Thought, while not dirtying his reputation with the MIM name. This is seen in his discussion of nationalism, which is often a dividing line between MIM Thought and the social democrats of academia. Cope gives a very agreeable definition of nation, and even more importantly, an analysis of its role and importance in the imperialist system related to class divisions. Yet, he fails to cite Stalin in doing so, while Maoists are honest about Stalin's contributions on the national question. So what we have is an excellent book on the labor aristocracy that avoids other issues that are difficult for the left-wing white nationalists to handle. In a way, this sanitized version of what is already a very bitter pill for readers in the First World may be useful to make this theory more available in an academic context. But no serious communist can just ignore important questions around Stalin and even the smaller, yet groundbreaking work of MIM itself.

3.c First World lumpen

by MIM(Prisons)

SOME CLAIMING MARXISM TELL US that those we call lumpen are really part of the proletariat; they are just part of the reserve army of labor that Marx talked about being necessary to keep wages down among the workers who were employed via competition. But as explained in Appendix 3.b, there is no significant proletariat in the United $tates. And while there is a contradiction between employers and employees over wages, this has not been an antagonistic contradiction in post-WWII U.$.A.

To the extent that there is a proletariat in this country, they are migrant workers. And therefore the reserve army of labor is found south of the Rio Grande and elsewhere in the Third World.

The First World lumpen are the remnants of a long history of national oppression. The question that they face is whether the oppressor nation is willing and able to continue to integrate them into the Amerikan petty bourgeoisie, or if racism and economic crisis will lead to an increased lumpenization of the internal semi-colonies as Amerika pushes its problems off on them. Because of this context of national oppression we define the First World lumpen as a distinct class that is only evident in the United $tates within the oppressed nations.

Given the volatility of the people who are still young and are excluded from the system economically and along national lines, the imperialists have no interest in an expanding lumpen class. And the only internal contradiction that would force an expanding lumpen class in the imperialist countries is extreme economic crisis.

The capitalists depend on the consuming classes to keep productive capital circulating, and they depend on the productive classes to keep producing new value. Integrating peoples into the global capitalist system means maximizing their productive labor time and/or maximizing their consumption in leisure time. Both the exploited oppressed people and the privileged oppressor people play many other roles in realizing profits and/or maintaining the stability of the system. The lumpen are neither producers nor big consumers as a class, even in the First World.

Assuming that a large First World lumpen is not vital to maintaining drug sales, the capitalists would avoid a significant growth in idle oppressed people in their own countries. Such an increase would therefore indicate a serious crisis had hit the heart of imperialism.

As a baseline we can say conservatively that around 2010 the lumpen class represented about 20% of New Afrika, 5% of Aztlán and 30% of First Nations. This population represents about 4% of the overall population of the United $tates, and there is no strong evidence of the First World lumpen increasing in a significant way in recent years.

One example MIM had cited in support of the Black Panther Party's theory of an expanding lumpen due to mechanization was the skyrocketing prison population centered around the 1990s, spanning the time between the demise of the Panthers and today. While the numbers are staggering, this is still a tiny proportion of the oppressed nations. And rather than being the product of shifting economic times, we argue that they are primally a product of the open conflict between the white nation and oppressed nations in the United $tates via the white power structure of the state.

The police and prisons were the white nation's stick and the economic opportunities and integration were the carrot presented to the oppressed immediately following the strong liberation movements of the 1960s and 70s. Therefore, if we see oppressed nation prison populations shift into a downward trend, that would support the idea that the carrot is increasing in effectiveness in integrating them into Amerika.

The flip side of that is as long as oppressed nation prisoners keep increasing, we have strong evidence of an antagonistic contradiction along the lines of nation in the United $tates. Of course we have seen the trend level off a bit in recent years, ironically, largely in response to economic crisis. But it is too soon to say what that means.

The above article is an excerpt from MIM(Prisons)'s forthcoming book on the lumpen class.

3.d Fascism and its class nature: A brief introduction

by MIM(Prisons)

AS FASCISM ROSE IN EUROPE, the head of the Comintern, Georgi Dimitroff, wrote that fascism "is medieval barbarity and bestiality, it is unbridled aggression in relation to other nations and countries."[1] This is opposed to the civilized and professional manner in which healthy imperialism exports finance capital and extracts profits from the majority of the world that is proletariat and peasants. We write this both in relative terms and tongue-in-cheek. Of course, imperialism kills millions of people, more than any other political system to date, including fascism because of its length of existence. Yet, the day-to-day operations of healthy imperialism pass as reasonable professional activity. Fascism, in contrast, fools no one.

It is for this reason that the imperialists do not favor fascism under normal conditions, they do not want their brutality and exploitation exposed bare for the world to see. To do so heightens the class struggle.

Some influenced by the writings of J. Sakai et al. today (including our co-publisher Kersplebedeb)[2] repeat the line that fascism is a movement of the petty bourgeoisie, or outside the contradiction of proletariat vs. bourgeoisie, which Dimitroff attacked in his essay quoted above. Sakai goes so far as to put oppressed nation organizations at war with the imperialists in the fascist camp. This is a critical error in this line.

So if fascism is so bad for the imperialists, how can they be behind it? As Stalin said, it is forced upon them. Specifically, the contradiction is found in the declining rate of profit that Marx exposed as an inherent characteristic of capitalism even before imperialism was well developed. While imperialism expanded the means of extracting profits from the laboring classes beyond the simple model explained in the beginning of *Capital* by Marx, the imperialists are still limited by the inherent contradictions in capitalism. These contradictions include the class struggle of the proletariat who seeks to free itself from imperialist exploitation. When profit rates approach zero, production slows to a stop, and imperialism resorts to what Marx called "primitive accumulation." Therefore, we expect fascism to raise its head again, probably doing more damage than in the 1930s and 40s, as the class struggle heightens.

MIM Thought more fully developed the theses of Engels and Lenin that whole nations are bought off by imperialist plunder. These nations' vast majority are allies of imperialism, though not actually part of the imperialist class. This class will feel the crunch of imperialist crisis more acutely than the imperialists themselves, as the imperialists pass the costs along to the majority of the oppressor nations. It is for this reason that the labor aristocracy are on the streets calling for oppression, forced exploitation, occupation and even extermination of oppressed nations, and therefore appear as the initiators of the movement for fascism. But in the fundamental contradiction of capitalism, between the bourgeoisie and the proletariat, the petty bourgeoisie has always been seen by Marxism as an impotent vacillator between the two sides. This has not changed, but the concentration of the petty bourgeoisie as whole nations that are parasitic on the world has increased their visibility as a class. A class that too many dogmatists still wrap up in the proletariat camp.

Fascism is a mass movement in the First World. It is not so in the Third World. The mass support in oppressor nations is indicative of their alliance with imperialism, not their opposition to it.

MIM(Prisons) upholds the MIM line on fascism as defined in their various congress resolutions on the subject. For further study, we distribute a study pack that features these resolutions. Other good resources on the history of fascism include *MIM Theory 6: The Stalin Issue* and *Arms & Empire* by Richard Krooth.

4.a Why we use the word "migrant" and not "immigrant"

by MIM

MIM USES THE WORD "MIGRANT" in preference to the word "immigrant" in reference to U.S. borders, because "immigrant" is often presumptuous in reference to the undocumented workers crossing the Mexican border and other borders.

The word "immigrant" implies that the persyn so named wants to be a U.S. citizen. In actuality, some people believe they are temporary workers who want to return to another country. Others support the idea of the national liberation of Aztlán located in the southwestern region trapped inside U.S. borders. MIM supports the liberation of Aztlán, so we prefer not to use the word "immigrant."

The exceptions in the use of the word "immigrant" occur where we are sure it is correct and refers to intentions and actuality. Another exception is in reference to U.S. Government policies and legislation. House representative Tom Tancredo sponsored a Congressional bill to crack down on migrants in the guise of "immigration reform."

The above article is an excerpt from an article published on etext.org.

4.b On Cesar Chavez and the Correct and Incorrect Handling of Contradictions Among the People

by MIM(Prisons)

CESAR CHAVEZ AND THE UNITED Farm Workers (UFW) are a well-known part of the history of the Chican@ nation. For many the name Cesar Chavez is synonymous with civil and humyn rights struggles. But if the re-emergent Chican@ national liberation struggle is ever to develop with the same power and strength as that of the last Chican@ struggle then a serious examination of Chavez as martyr for oppressed Raza everywhere needs to be taken up by the new generation of Chican@ activists and revolutionaries. The Cesar Chavez question is a general line question in the age of imperialism particular to the Chican@ nation for its embodiment of the very many contradictions that continue to plague us today.

It is undeniable that the actions of the UFW, under the leadership of Cesar Chavez, helped relieve the suffering of the mostly Chican@ and Mexican@ field workers in the United $tates. Initially Chavez rightly challenged agri-business, and through the UFW many field workers were organized. But the mobilization of campesinos for decent wages and safe working conditions faced obstacles created by U.$. imperialism. Corporate agri-business responded to UFW strikes by importing more Mexican@ labor in order to bypass UFW organized labor. This challenge would have been best tackled with an internationalist perspective, looking at how to achieve progress for all oppressed people. But Chavez and the UFW had a narrow focus on improving conditions for documented farmworkers within U.$. borders. Instead of building a cross-border movement, in the early 1970s the UFW actually supported laws and actions that led to deportation of Mexican workers and stricter measures aimed at migrant workers.[1] Lacking a communist or revolutionary nationalist perspective, the UFW sacrificed undocumented workers to their narrow goals. These actions provide us with a teaching moment on the contradictions created by a capitalist society which demands that Chican@s attack Mexican@s, not only to survive but to protect their privilege.

Chavez serves as an example of what can occur when socialist revolution is taken out of the conversation. One may set out to help the people but trip when faced with obstacles. Facing criticism from Chican@ and Mexican@ activists, Chavez and the UFW later reversed their stance, demonstrating the internationalist character of the migrant farmworker movement. It should also be noted that the UFW of today is increasingly pro-migrant and perhaps known better for its stance on immigration reform than for its labor activism. This is reflective of the overall progressive nature of the proletariat and semi-proletariat of Aztlán.

Had Chavez taken on an internationalist approach with a communist ideological perspective he would have not only resisted state repression of migrant labor but he would have also built a labor movement spanning both sides of the Rio Bravo. Had Chavez been a revolutionary Chican@ he could have been the bridge to link the mostly urban Chican@ movement with the Mexican@ proletarian migrants into one movement aimed at fighting the root cause of our oppression: U.$. imperialism.

In the end Chavez was a reformer who was not trying to liberate Aztlán, nor was he attempting to overthrow Amerikkkan imperialism. He set out to better the working conditions of field workers who were mostly Raza, and he succeeded. As revolutionaries, Chican@s should not glorify Chavez, rather we should take an objective look at Chavez and the UFW and learn from their approach so that we find ways to do better and avoid the mistakes that they made. Let us strive to correct the mistakes of the past by developing together and learning from history so that we may move as one and retrain our sights on the world's number one enemy: Amerikan imperialism.

¡Abajo Con El Imperialismo!

5.a Cell Structure, Vanguard Parties and Mass Organizations

Reassessing Cell Structure 5 Years Out

Debating the Need for New Organizations: Cell Structure and United Fronts

REASSESSING CELL STRUCTURE 5 YEARS OUT
by MIM(Prisons), 2010 Congress Resolution

OVERALL, MIM(PRISONS) STANDS BY THE Resolutions on Cell Structure passed at the last MIM Congress in 2005. After 5 years of putting that resolution into practice there is experience to sum up and questions that still need to be answered.

The theoretical basis for the cell structure is that the strength of a centralized party comes into play when vying for state power, whether by elections or otherwise. That is not in the cards for Maoists in the imperialist countries at this time. Maoism is a minority movement in the First World and will continue to be so for the foreseeable future. This makes it even more important that we utilize our strengths and shore up our weaknesses.

One of the main lessons to take from the cell structure resolutions is that

"[w]e oppose having geographic cells come into contact with each other face-to-face. Infiltration and spying are rampant when it comes to MIM. The whole strength of having a locality-based cell is that it is possible to do all the things traditional to a movement. The security advantages of culling

people we know into a cell are lost the moment we slack off on security and start accepting strangers or meeting with strangers face-to-face."

We find it frustrating that critics of what happened at etext.org as MIM faced repression are willing to ignore the lessons of those setbacks.

At the last MIM congress in 2005, they spoke of a "MIM Center" that put out the newspaper, among other tasks. Soon after, there was no *MIM Notes* newspaper, followed by the degeneration of the original MC cell and finally the shutting down of their last institution, the website at etext.org.

One of the challenges of small cells is developing and maintaining line. Much work has been done, and if every new group or every revolutionary had to start from scratch, we would never advance. That is why when etext.org was repressed, MIM(Prisons) posted an archive of the MIM site on our website. While we still do not have a regular newspaper for the movement as a whole, the website is a crucial reference for us all.

Fraternal organizations do not agree on everything; they agree on cardinal principles that are determined by the conditions of the time. The etext.org site is not something Maoists must agree with 100%, but there is no doubt that it is still the most comprehensive starting point for any Maoist organization in the First World.

Democratic centralism is important for security and for political line development. Yet until we are organizing on a countrywide basis, there is no need for democratic centralism at that level, not to mention internationally.

In guerilla warfare, the cell structure has been applied in a way that was hierarchical so that action cells were separate from each other, but each cell could be traced to the top of the organization. This relies on a centralized organization or center. While MIM mentions such a center being based around *MIM Notes* and etext.org in their 2005 resolutions, we do not see the need for this center given the current circumstances. As we have recognized before, certain ideological centers are bound to exist based on the law of uneven development. Yet such centers are not structural, but fluid, based on the type and amount of work done.

All that said, there is an inherent contradiction in the cell strategy. Since organizing strategy and security tactics are not dividing line questions, once the cell strategy is adopted and full decentralization has occurred, it is possible for cells to change their line on this question.

Even the majority could do so and a new centralized party could push remaining cells to the periphery. Since we work to build a movement and not our individual organizations, and our work is already on the periphery, we should not be concerned about the impacts of such a move on our organization. It is, however, worrisome to the extent that we see our comrades opened up to attacks through faulty security.

Part of accepting cell strategy is distinguishing between cadre work and mass work. The self-described anarchist movement is able to mobilize large numbers in mass work while abhorring centralized organization. We should learn from their example, while not succumbing to Liberalism in our security practices or abandoning scientific leadership.

Getting the correct balance of cadre work and mass work will be more challenging with a cell structure. There is no way to impose a balance on the movement as a whole without a center, but we can pay attention to what is going on around us and get in where we fit in. Leading cells should not be shy to point out where the movement needs more investment of resources.

One amendment we would make to the Resolutions on Cell Structure is to cut the suggestion that a one-persyn cell "in many ways... has the least worries security-wise!" Certainly, one-persyn cells should maintain high standards for admitting others. However, the value of criticism/self-criticism on the level of day-to-day work is something that is stressed within Maoism, and we've benefited from in our own practice in MIM(Prisons). We still need democratic centralism with the cell structure to provide crucial discipline and accountability. The criticisms we can give and get from other cells will be limited in nature if our security is correct. And we have seen how one-persyn cells can degrade or disappear quickly.

DEBATING THE NEED FOR NEW ORGANIZATIONS: CELL STRUCTURE AND UNITED FRONTS
by an Oregon prisoner, May 2012

SO OFTEN I HEAR ABOUT all these "new" groups popping up, and I can only laugh. It's 2012, there is nothing "new." The foundation for our political beliefs has already been laid. There is nothing "new" about these stances/agendas and their supposed political beliefs. The only thing that is different is the day and age we live in. The root of our problem remains the same, the haves oppress the have-nots. However, the point of this writing is to address my thoughts, feeling and opinions on all these "new groups" popping up.

There are any number of them, with a wide range, variety and jumbled assortment of colorful names. The names range from political to outright comical in wording/phrasing. Some state just who and what they are. Some are rather ambiguous and then others are as laughable and colorful as a male peacock strutting in full plumage. And as we're aware, no matter how a peacock struts, it hides in the trees the first time a storm threatens.

It's cowardly, and more importantly, embarrassing. For all the strutting and plumage behind the colorful names, the truth is they do nothing, accomplish nothing and solve utterly nothing. If anything they present more of a problem, because of the loud, attention-craving racket, and absolutely no productive political action, they cause the people (the ones we struggle for) to laugh and not take anyone serious. All they see is the "bells and whistles" of colorful names.

All this does is take away from the true, sincere and actual revolutionaries striving to bring about the true and necessary changes and reforms to society, which is needed to overcome the corrupt imperialist swine oppressing us. Remember, that's the goal. To bring communism to the forefront of political power. Not to be dividing into numerous groups with no true moral fortitude to accomplish what's needed. Each time I see or hear about "new" groups claiming to have and hold the same beliefs, views and stances as already well-established, virtuous organizations are already firmly grounded, it presents me with a question: why?

Why are these people so eager to form "new" groups? And why aren't they able to fit in with the already proven, reliable and established organizations? The answer I come up with is disturbing but can only ring true: Because these people lack of true moral fiber, and they possess one or more character flaws that prevent them from being accepted in and part of an already structured, active and producing organization. They are unable to follow the rules and regulations and necessary leadership to steer the group, and society as a whole, towards the ultimate goal: revolutionary change to overcome the oppression from the capitalist/ imperialist swine. It's either that or these individuals who start "new" groups have outrageous delusions of grandeur, so they hop from group to group or create their own groups all in hopes to try and get their fix of feeling "important."

We can all attest to the effect that there is no possible way to trust someone who hops from group to group, from cause to cause, showing absolutely no loyalty to anyone or even to their own proclaimed beliefs.

In either of the above mentioned answers, I only see comical groups of misfits who do more harm than they bring about actual political change.

So, since there are already well-established, grounded and virtuous groups out there being productive, find one! And devote your time, support and efforts to an organization already striving for the ultimate goal we're all struggling for. The entire point of this struggle is to work together, as one, for a common goal. The common goal. And only in uniting will that goal be reached. Continuous divisions amongst ourselves only slow the process of growth.

Instead of dividing attentions, assets, resources and comrades, find a firmly established organization already fighting and struggling for the betterment of the people. And assist them in bringing about that betterment.

It makes me sick when I hear about see or read of some "new" group of misfits breaking away, and who have no firm education in political maneuvering or strategy. And quite frankly it's insulting to see or hear a new colorful name or term like "gangsta this" or "gangsta that."

Are ya serious? That's embarrassing, especially when all those character-flawed people are trying to do is get attention to their no-account group by using a virtuous group to put their group name in print because none of their actions are meritorious enough to be deemed worthy of it any other (and the proper) way. Truly I hope not another group's name is printed. If you're a Maoist, then that's name enough.

In closing, stop dividing and start uniting. As one people, in one struggle, doing one work, to overcome the imperialist pigs who oppress us.

MIM(Prisons) responds: On the one hand, we agree with this comrade on the importance of not forming new groups just for the sake of recognition or self-aggrandizement.[1] Ultimately we need unity behind common Maoist principles for successful revolutionary struggle. However, at this current stage of struggle within imperialist Amerika, there is a practical need for organizing in a cell structure, where regional independence provides security.

As we have demonstrated in our work with even the best of these new organizations which are claiming to uphold Maoism, we hold everyone to a high standard of work and don't just look at the labels and names they choose. This was seen in our work with the New Afrikan Maoist Party (NAMP) with whom we found some significant developing disagreements over line and strategy. We published a self-criticism about our working relationship with that group.[2]

The other important point to make here is that we should not hold everyone to the standard of Maoism to work with them. We need as many strong committed revolutionary comrades as possible. But for those individuals who are not at the level of communist theory, we can unite around anti-imperialist goals in a united front. We don't want these folks blindly signing up for Maoism; we would rather they study and learn through practice about the value and seriousness of communism. And if there is no anti-imperialist cell or organization in their place, we support the creation of such a group. It is in forging this unity that we are building the United Front for Peace in Prisons and this is the basis for the names of groups being printed in *Under Lock & Key* declaring their participation in this united front. We do our best to verify that these groups have an actual progressive practice, but we cannot be everywhere checking out everything, so we rely on our comrades to vet these organizations and look at their work over time for confirmation of their anti-imperialist orientation. In line with this comrade's critique, we have shifted our focus for united front writings in *ULK* to practical reports, rather than statements of unity that were causing more trouble than they were worth.

5.b United Front

How to Build a United Front

MIM Policy on Building a United Front

The Questions of Independence and Initiative Within the United Front

◇◇◇

HOW TO BUILD A UNITED FRONT
by MIM
excerpt from *MIM Theory 14: United Front*, p. 61

MIM, AS A MAOIST PARTY, upholds the strategy of the United Front led by the proletariat. This means that we believe it is possible to unite various classes in the anti-imperialist struggle under the leadership of the proletariat. Of course, some of these classes are not going to be fighting for socialism, but because they will unite with us in the principal battle, the fight against imperialism, it is important for us to make use of their assistance.

Historical lessons from the Chinese revolution in particular can instruct us on how to correctly carry out the united front. Prior to 1949 the communists there allied with many classes in Chinese society including the national bourgeoisie in the struggle against Japanese imperialism. First they made a serious mistake in giving up proletarian leadership in this united front and that led to the massacre of many communists. They learned from this error the importance of proletarian leadership.

At this stage in the struggle we do not expect to unite large numbers in this country. But we do seek to lead as many people as we can in both the smaller legal battles and the larger revolutionary struggles. But we recognize that in order for communists to continue their work within the united front we must retain independence of initiative and ensure proletarian leadership at all times. With these things clear we can unite all who are willing to unite with us.

MIM POLICY ON BUILDING THE UNITED FRONT
by MIM, 1998 Congress Resolution

MIM HAS HAD DIFFICULTIES WITH the united front (UF). Our work should feature the following simplified guidelines.

1. NO LIQUIDATION – maintain the possibility and capability of criticizing our allies, since we represent the proletarian pole.

2. HARD BARGAINS – look for what we are getting from the deal with other classes.

3. NO PIMPING – the most backward masses should be able to see what the difference is between us and our allies, except for fraternal parties on issues that are not the third cardinal.[1]

4. NO NEO-COLONIALISM – always keep the perspective of the international proletariat and do not use the UF as an occasion to cut "a special deal" for one oppressed nationality.

5. NO TROTSKYISM – uphold the national question and alliances with classes that have any interest however temporary against U.$. imperialism.

6. NO TAILING – take initiative in UF activities or don't get involved at all. See also NO PIMPING and NO LIQUIDATION. Either the proletariat leads or we stay out.

THE QUESTIONS OF INDEPENDENCE AND INITIATIVE WITHIN THE UNITED FRONT
by Mao Zedong
November 5, 1938
from *Selected Works of Mao Tse-Tung, Vol. II*, pp. 213-217.

Help and concessions should be positive, not negative

All political parties and groups in the united front must help each other and make mutual concessions for the sake of long-term cooperation, but such help and concessions should be positive, not negative. We must consolidate and expand our own Party and army, and at the same time should assist friendly parties and armies to consolidate and expand; the people want the government to satisfy their political and economic demands, and at the same time give the government every possible help to prosecute the War of Resistance; the factory workers demand better conditions from the owners, and at the same time work hard in the interests of resistance; for the sake of unity against foreign aggression, the landlords should reduce rent and interest, and at the same time the peasants should pay rent and interest. All these principles and policies of mutual assistance are positive, not negative or one-sided. The same should be true of mutual concessions. Each side should refrain from undermining the other and from organizing secret party branches within the other's party, government and army. For our part we organize no secret party branches inside the Kuomintang and its government or army, and so set the Kuomintang's mind at rest, to the advantage of the War of Resistance. The saying, "Refrain from doing some things in order to be able to do other things",[1] exactly meets the case. A national war of resistance would have been impossible without the reorganization of the Red Army, the change in the administrative system in the Red areas, and the abandonment of the policy of armed insurrection. By giving way on the latter we have achieved the former; negative measures have yielded positive results. "To fall back the better to leap forward" – that is Leninism.[2] To regard concessions as something purely negative is contrary to Marxism-Leninism. There are indeed instances of purely negative concessions – the Second International's doctrine of collaboration between labour and capital [3] resulted in the betrayal of a whole class and a whole revolution. In China, Chen Tu-hsiu and then Chang Kuo-tao were both capitulators; capitulationism must be strenuously opposed. When we make concessions, fall back, turn to the defensive or halt our advance in our relations with either allies or enemies, we should always see these actions as part of our whole revolutionary policy, as an indispensable link in the general revolutionary line, as one turn in a zigzag course. In a word, they are positive.

The identity between the national and the class struggle

To sustain a long war by long-term co-operation or, in other words, to subordinate the class struggle to the present national struggle against Japan – such is the fundamental principle of the united front. Subject to this principle, the independent character of the parties and classes and their independence and initiative within the united front should be preserved, and their essential rights should not be sacrificed to co-operation and unity, but on the contrary must be firmly upheld within certain limits. Only thus can co-operation be promoted, indeed only thus can there be any co-operation at all. Otherwise co-operation will turn into amalgamation and the united front will inevitably be sacrificed. In a struggle that is national in character, the class struggle takes the form of national struggle, which demonstrates the identity between the two. On the one hand, for a given historical period the political and economic demands of the various classes must not be such as to disrupt co-operation; on the other hand, the demands of the national struggle (the need to resist Japan) should be the point of departure for all class struggle. Thus there is identity in the united front between unity and independence and between the national struggle and the class struggle.

"Everything through the united front" is wrong

The Kuomintang is the party in power, and so far has not allowed the united front to assume an organizational form. Behind the enemy lines, the idea of "everything through" is impossible, for there we have to act independently and with the initiative in our own hands while keeping to the agreements which the Kuomintang has approved (for instance, the Programme of Armed Resistance and National Reconstruction). Or we may act first and report afterwards, anticipating what the Kuomintang might agree to. For instance, the appointment of administrative commissioners and the dispatch of troops to Shantung Province would never have occurred if we had tried to get these things done "through the united front." It is said that the French Communist Party once put forward a similar slogan, but that was probably because in France, where a joint committee of the parties already existed and the Socialist Party was unwilling to act in accordance with the jointly agreed programme and wanted to have its own way, the Communist Party had to put forward such a slogan in order to restrain the Socialist Party, and certainly it did not do so to shackle itself. In the case of China, the Kuomintang has deprived all other political parties of equal rights and is trying to compel them to take its orders. If this slogan is meant to be a demand that everything done by the Kuomintang must go through us, it is both ridiculous and impossible. If we have to secure the Kuomintang's consent beforehand for everything we do, what if the Kuomintang does not consent? Since the policy of the Kuomintang is to restrict our growth, there is no reason whatever for us to propose such a slogan, which simply binds us hand and foot. At present there are things for which we should secure prior consent from the Kuomintang, such as the expansion of our three divisions into three army corps – this is to report first and act afterwards. There are other things which the Kuomintang can be told after they have become accomplished facts, such as the expansion of our forces to over 200,000 men – this is to act first and report afterwards. There are also things, such as the convening of the Border Region assembly, which we shall do without reporting for the time being, knowing that the Kuomintang will not agree. There are still other things which, for the time being, we shall neither do nor report, for they are likely to jeopardize the whole situation. In short, we must not split the united front, but neither should we allow ourselves to be bound hand and foot, and hence the slogan of "everything through the united front" should not be put forward. If "everything must be submitted to the united front" is interpreted as "everything must be submitted to" Chiang Kai-shek and Yen Hsi-shan, then that slogan, too, is wrong. Our policy is one of independence and initiative within the united front, a policy both of unity and of independence.

5.c New Democracy and the Joint Dictatorship of the Proletariat of the Oppressed Nations

IN SUPPORT OF SELF-DETERMINATION AND NEW DEMOCRACY
by MC5 of the Maoist Internationalist Movement

IT IS PERHAPS MOST APPROPRIATE to start this issue with a quotation from Eldridge Cleaver, when he was still a politically sane leader of the Black Panther Party:

> "Another proposal of the Black Panthers which is winning more and more support in the black colony is the call for a U.N. supervised plebiscite in black communities across the nation. The purpose of the plebiscite is to answer the question, once and for all: just what the masses of black people want. Do the masses of black people consider themselves a nation?"[1]

Later in his book, *Post-Prison Writings and Speeches*, Cleaver said:

> "There have been too many people and too many organizations in the past who claimed to speak for the ultimate destiny of black people. Some call for a new state; some have insisted that black people should go back to Africa. We Black Panthers, on the other hand, don't feel we should speak for all black people. We say that black people deserve an opportunity to record their own national will."[2]

Some have advised MIM to go no further than this quotation. They believe that agitation for the right to self-determination is the complete Marxist-Leninist-Maoist platform on the national question.

But the position put forward by the Panthers and other national liberation organizations around the world is the point of departure and point of return. Like the early Black Panthers and other national liberation groups, MIM agitates for the right to self-determination, and like the Black Panthers and other national liberation groups, it also has an opinion about what the oppressed people should do within North America – liberate their own national territories.

This recognizes that no socialist government will oppress any nation or encroach on the territory any anti-imperialist nation inhabits or has seized from Amerika.

The question is how best to get to the point where oppressed peoples can really have the choice of living in their own liberated territories. If the revolutionary forces accumulate the power to make that a real possibility, then it is appropriate to ask the question, "integration or liberation?" Then there should be a plebiscite or series of plebiscites to decide the question. Asking the question before the oppressed nationality has the power to control territory only proves what the people will say when the imperialists are twisting their arms behind their backs. The people must have a genuine choice, not a choice dictated by the imperialists. Then we can trust an oppressed nation plebiscite – the outcome of the ballot box among the people.

MIM does not support the concept of plebiscites that would allow integration with imperialism as expressive of true self-determination.

The need for the power to hold a fair plebiscite where the oppressor does not force the oppressed nation into choosing between two lesser evils is the reason why the slogans "Black Power," "Red Power," "Yellow Power" and "Brown Power" make sense. And perhaps they should be "Black Power," "First Nation Power," "Aztlán Power" etc. These slogans do not force decisions down the people's throats. They build for the day when the oppressed peoples can make their own decisions and have them implemented.

At this time, we are "creating public opinion to build the independent power of the oppressed." That means we are using legal methods to put forward our view and build independent institutions.

As the people find themselves more organized they often end up in armed struggle with the imperialists who want to keep the people dependent on imperialist institutions. When a Canadian mayor seized some land from the Mohawk nation, there was armed conflict at Oka. Not surprisingly, within the Mohawk territories, the Mohawks are already running their own schools, border police, hospital and fire department.

Hence, after a certain level of success in creating public opinion and building evermore independent institutions, the imperialists crack down and the masses must defend their gains in armed struggle. All around the world, the people find themselves repressed by U.S. imperialism and take up armed struggle to defend their independence and also their right to eat and have shelter and clothing.

New Democracy

After armed struggle, the war between the oppressed nations and oppressor nations reaches a certain stage; then finally we can speak of a new democratic period in North America. In this stage, the Maoist-led forces will have defeated the imperialists and seized state power. The Euro-Amerikan people's government will be put into a receivership of the oppressed nations to prevent the restoration of imperialism.

Meanwhile, the oppressed nations will get on their feet in this stage. This will mean the people exercise dictatorship over their white nation oppressors. In this stage, the national bourgeoisies of the oppressed nations will play some role in organizing their peoples economically and politically.

Under New Democracy the oppressed people will learn what it means to live without imperialist police terror and they will learn to speak their mind without fear of the consequences from the oppressor. Also during this period, the oppressed nations will learn what it means concretely to choose a piece of land and nationhood.

The new democratic period will complete itself in plebiscites on nationhood. The peoples will decide for themselves if they want their own separate nations or some other arrangement.

The completion of the plebiscites will mark the transition to socialism and the end of the new democratic period. The peoples will have found their way of building cooperative economic relations among nations. In the course of organizing plebiscites for national self-determination and/or regional autonomy, the Maoist forces must work to develop the first stage of the new democratic revolution so that it may quickly transform into the second stage – socialism.

In the whole new democratic and socialist periods, the danger of counter revolution exists. Hence, we cannot predict that the Maoist-led forces will win at every step. We only outline our strategic plans and goals. To recapitulate, the major strategic stages as seen in history so far and crystallized in Marxism-Leninism-Maoism (principally Maoism), take the following form in North America:

1. Now: Create public opinion and independent institutions of the people to prepare to seize power.

2. After an accumulation of power in the first stage, the second stage is a qualitative leap characterized by armed struggle for state power.

3. New Democracy is an abbreviated stage relative to that in Third World countries. This stage includes dictatorship of the oppressed nations over the oppressor nation.

4. Individual dictatorships of the proletariat within the oppressed nations; joint dictatorship of the international proletariat over the Euro-Amerikan nation.

Trotskyist groups, including crypto-Trotskyist groups like the Revolutionary Communist Party, U$A and Progressive Labor Party, deny that oppressed nations in North America require a new democratic stage, because they are not preparing the actual conditions necessary for the self-determination of the oppressed nations.

Since there are not many vestiges of feudalism in North America, the new democratic period will have fewer tasks in North America than similar periods in the Third World. At the same time, the political super-structure is not far removed from the days in which superexploitation of oppressed nationality peasants did take place. There remains some question of "civil rights" that would be respected in a radical bourgeois democracy.

Historically, under the dictatorship of the proletariat, the bour-geoisie has lost its civil rights. Select other counterrevolutionaries have also lost those rights. This is a universal truth of the dictatorship of the proletariat.

But in self-determination of nations, the issue is one of entire peoples. Since MIM is sincere about creating the conditions for national plebiscites of the oppressed nations no matter how small, MIM sees that New Democracy is essential. After all, in these plebiscites, the entirety of the oppressed nation, including its labor aristocracy, petit-bourgeoisie and bourgeoisie should be allowed to have a say as to whether or not there will be a separate nation. Hence, we cannot refer to these plebiscites as part of the dictatorship of the proletariat.

The one thing that must guide the whole new democratic stage is the dictatorship of the oppressed nations led by their proletarian parties over the Euro-Amerikan nation, the agents of U.S. imperialism. It is inevitable that this joint dictatorship of the oppressed nations will not be perfect and will not reflect the participation of all oppressed nations instantly. However, the proletarian parties must act toward this goal in order to absolutely assure that there is no restoration of imperialism.

If the proletarian parties do not take a firm hand in the situation, and if the national bourgeoisie comes to dominate in too many oppressed countries, there will be a reversion to neo-colonialism with a new lineup of imperialist powers. The organizations most responsible for organizing the overthrow of U.S. imperialism have the international responsibility of ruling in the interests of the international proletariat and its allied classes and thus ensuring the forward motion of history. Only if the revolutions are led with the ideology in the international proletariat will it be possible to make progress.

The joint dictatorship of the oppressed nations over Euro-Amerika and U.S. imperialism will not be able to instantly cleanse the Euro-Amerikan nation of influence from its parasitism. That is why we advocate that the oppressed nations go forward and build their own nations and institutions while the dictatorship of the oppressed nations over Euro-Amerika and U.S. imperialism prepares the basis for the civilized entry of the Euro-Amerikan people into the community of the human race.

On the other hand, it is possible that the oppressed nations have such great faith in their powers to exercise joint dictatorship over Euro-Amerika and U.S. imperialism that they may feel it is unnecessary to liberate their own national territories. That choice is up to the oppressed nation people in the plebiscites of the new democratic period.

MIM advocates that the oppressed nations liberate their own national territories, but it will respect the decisions of plebiscites. National territory is defined as the land which a nationality inhabits, or seizes.

MIM believes that with the development of the Maoist movement, the correct analysis and strategy leads to national liberation. The only way that people are going to get a real choice between integration and national liberation is by the organization of a national liberation movement. Hence, MIM has pushed into the details of national liberation. All the while it reminds people that the final choice is the peoples'.

This excerpt is from an article originally printed in *MIM Theory 7: Proletarian Feminist Revolutionary Nationalism* (1995). In our present conditions, we would promote the terms "New Afrikan Power" and "Chican@ Power" instead of "Black Power" and "Aztlán Power" respectively.

Notes

ON REBUILDING THE NATION AND REGIONAL DIVISIONS

1. See Appendix 2.a. for the Agreement to End Hostilities

INTRODUCTION

1. MC12, 1995, "The Duality of Nations: Seize the Revolutionary Imperative," *MIM Theory 7: Proletarian Feminist Revolutionary Nationalism*, p. 25.

2. Huey P. Newton, 1974, *Revolutionary Suicide*, New York: Ballantine Books, p. 181.

3. Conference of the National Movimiento Estudiantil Chican@ de Aztlán at Phoenix Community College, 1999, "M.E.Ch.A. Philosophy."

4. Some spell Chican@ with an "X," as Xican@. We do not see this as anything to quarrel about, and choose to use "Ch" because it is more familliar with the masses.

5. Olin Tezcatlipoca, no date, *Mexica Movement, An Indigenous Guide to the 21st Century, the Documents of the Mexica Movement.*

6. Gloria J. Romero, 2000, "No Se Raje Chicanita: Thoughts on Race, Class and Gender in the Classroom," *Las Obreras: Chicana Politics of Work and Family*, Vicki L. Ruiz (editor), University of California Los Angeles.

7. Jane Degras (editor), 1971, "Platform of the Communist International adopted by the First Congress," *The Communist International: 1919-1943 Documents, Volume I 1919-1922*, London: Frank Cass & Co., p. 32.

8. See Appendix 3.b. for an in-depth look at the labor aristocracy

9. See Appendix 3.c. for more on the definition of the lumpen class

10. J.V. Stalin, 1913, "Marxism and the National Question."

11. See *MIM Theory 2/3: Gender and Revolutionary Feminism* for a discussion of the practice of gender-focused organizing in the United $tates and the interaction of gender and national contradictions. Also see Mao Zedong's essay "On Contradiction" for a thorough discussion of analyzing the contradictions within a thing.

PART I SECTION I

1. Rodolfo F. Acuña, 2006, *Occupied America: A History of Chicanos*, 6th edition, Longman Publishers.

2. Matt S. Meier and Feliciano Rivera, 1994, *The Chicanos: A History of Mexican Americans*, Hill & Wang Publishers, p. 5.

3. Acuña 2006, p. 33.

4. Meier 1994, p. 32.

5. Meier 1994.

6. Meier 1994, p. 44.

7. Acuña 2006, p. 41.

8. Reginald Horsman, 1986, *Race and Manifest Destiny: The Origins of American Racial Anglo-Saxonism*, Harvard University Press, p. 241.

9. Alfredo Mirandé, 1987, *Gringo Justice*, University of Notre Dame Press, p. 16.

10. Communist Collective of the Chicano Nation, Spring 1974, "Report to the Communist Collective of the Chicano Nation on the Chicano National Colonial Question," sub-section: "After the Anglo-American Invasion, The Bourgeois Democratic Movement," *Proletariat*, No. 4.

11. Mario Barrera, 1989, *Race and Class in the Southwest: A theory of racial inequality*, University of Notre Dame Press.

12. Armando B. Rendon, 1976, *Chicano Manifesto: The history and aspirations of the second largest minority in America*, New York: Collier Books, pp. 75-78.

13. Meier 1994.

14. William D. Carrigan and Clive Webb, 2013, *Forgotten Dead: Mob Violence against Mexicans in the United States, 1848-1928*, Oxford University Press.

15. J.V. Stalin, 1924, *Foundations of Leninism*, pp. 5-6.

16. Mirandé 1987, pp. 95 and 97.

17. Ward Sloan Albro III, no date, *Magónismo: Precursor to Chicanismo?*, Texas Arts and Industries University at Kingsville.

18. Acuña 2006, p. 41.

19. Benjamin Heber Johnson, 2003, *Revolution in Texas: How a forgotten rebellion and its bloody suppression turned Mexicans into Americans*, Yale University Press, p. 137.

20. James D. Cockcroft, 2010, *Mexico's Revolution Then and Now*, Monthly Review Press, pp. 56-57.

21. J. Sakai, 1989, *Settlers: The Mythology of the White Proletariat*, 3rd edition, Morningstar Press, p. 32.

22. "Race War in Arizona; Death List is Sixteen," *Los Angeles Times*, 20 August 1914.

23. Robert Kern (editor), 1983, *Labor in New Mexico: Unions, Strikes and Social History since 1881*, Albuquerque: University of New Mexico Press.

24. Aviva Chomsky, 2014, *Undocumented: How Immigration Became Illegal*. Beacon Press, p. 53.

25. Johnson 2003, p. 81.

26. Johnson 2003.

27. Johnson 2003, pp. 116 and 120.

28. Meier 1994.

29. Meier 1994, p. 240.

30. Meier 1994, p. 149.

31. Sakai 1989, pp. 82-83.

32. See Appendix 3.d for more on fascism.

33. Douglas S. Massey, Jorge Durand and Nolan J. Malone, 2003, *Beyond Smoke and Mirrors: Mexican immigration in the era of economic integration*, Russell Sage Foundation Publications, p. 36.

34. Massey 2003, p. 39.

35. Meier 1994.

36. Leo Grebler, Joan W. Moore and Ralph C. Guzman, 1970, *Mexican American People: The Nation's Second Minority*, Free Press, pp. 106 and 126.

37. Richard W. Slatta, Fall 1975, "Chicanos in the Pacific Northwest: An Historical Overview of Oregon's Chicanos," *Aztlán: A Journal of Chicano Studies*, Vol. 6, No. 3, p. 335.

38. Robert Coles and Harry Huge, 19 April 1969, "Thorns on the Yellow Rose of Texas," *New Republic*.

39. Acuña 2006.

40. See Appendix 4.b on the United Farm Workers and Cezar Chavez

41. Carlos Muñoz, Jr., 1989, *Youth, Identity, Power: The Chicano Movement*, 2nd Edition, Verso Books, p. 15.

42. Dial Torgerson, 17 March 1968, "Brown Power Unity Seen Behind School Disorders," *Los Angeles Times*, pt. C. p. 1.

43. Muñoz 1989, p. 83.

44. Muñoz 1989.

45. Muñoz 1989, p. 115. Original statement published in *Sin Cadenas*, Vol. 2, No. 1, 1975, pp. 5-6. This publication was the propaganda organ of CASA, which eventually became the organization's newspaper, *Sin Fronteras*. Citation provided, and quotation shortened, by Muñoz 1989.

46. Muñoz 1989, p. 177.

47. Editor Note: The August 29th Movement later joined I Wor Kuen to form the League of Revolutionary Struggle (LRS) in 1978. LRS upheld China under Deng Xiaoping as a socialist country. In the early 1980s the Maoist Internationalist Movement (MIM) emerged from the contemporary student movement of that time. MIM was the first organization to claim to uphold Marxism-Leninism-Maoism in the United \$tates, and one of the earliest in the world. One of their dividing line questions was that China became state capitalist after Mao's death in 1976. MIM struggled with LRS <http://www.prisoncensorship.info/archive/etext/wim/wyl/RCLLRSmerger.txt> over this issue for years to no avail. LRS later joined the Revolutionary Communist League lead by Amiri Baraka.

　　While we do not have information on how ATM progressed from a seemingly righteous Chican@ communist organization to the blind revisionism of the LRS, there are hints in one of their defining pamphlets "A Revolutionary Position on the Chicano National Question." This pamphlet offers up an in-depth argument for the existence (so often denied) of the Chican@ nation and promotes its right to self-determination via the line of Lenin and Stalin. They even quote Lenin extensively, including the line: "That is why the focal point in the Social-Democratic [communist - Editor] programme must be that division of nations into oppressor and oppressed which forms the essence of imperialism, and is deceitfully evaded by the social chauvinists and Kautsky." Yet in analyzing the struggle in the "Southwest" involving Las Gorras Blancas and the mostly-white Knights of Labor, ATM concludes "the movement must clearly see its enemy as imperialism and not Anglo-Americans in general; this is a political struggle for liberation, not a race war." While obviously correct to oppose race war, this does not mean that the Anglo-Amerikan nation as a whole is the ally of the oppressed. Such a line suggests that the analysis here is correct and that ATM's move towards multinational organizing was based in an incorrect analysis of the contradictions within imperialism and not a strategic united front. See Appendix 5.b for more on the united front.

48. Acuña 2006, p. 265.

49. National Chicano Youth Liberation Conference in Denver, Colorado, March 1969, "El Plan Espiritual de Aztlán."

50. Ernesto B. Vigil, 1999, *The Crusade for Justice: Chicano Militancy and the Government's War on Dissent*, University of Wisconsin Press.

51. Acuña 2006.

52. Young Lords Party, 1971, *Palante: Voices and Photographs of the Young Lords, 1969-1971*, Chicago: Haymarket Books, pp. 4-5.

53. Laura Pulido, 2006, *Black, Brown, Yellow, & Left: Radical Activism in Los Angeles*, Berkeley: University of California Press.

PART I SECTION 2

1. J.V. Stalin, 1913, "Marxism and the National Question."

2. Seth Motel, 21 February 2012, "Statistical Portrait of Hispanics in the United States, 2010," Pew Research Center. <http://www.pewhispanic.org/2012/02/21/statistical-portrait-of-hispanics-in-the-united-states-2010/>

3. Stalin 1913.

4. Ana Gonzalez-Barrera and Mark Hugo Lopez, 1 May 2013, "A Demographic Portrait of Mexican-Origin Hispanics in the United States," Pew Research Center. <http://www.pewhispanic.org/2013/05/01/a-demographic-portrait-of-mexican-origin-hispanics-in-the-united-states/>

5. Jack Citrin, Amy Lerman, Michael Murakami, and Kathryn Pearson, March 2007, "Testing Huntington: Is Hispanic Immigration a Threat to American Identity?," *Perspectives on Politics*.

6. Alba Richard, December 2004, "Language Assimilation Today: Bilingualism Persists More than in the Past, but English Still Dominates," New York: Lewis Mumford Center, University of Albany.

7. Andre Gunder Frank, 1972, *Lumpenbourgeoisie: Lumpendevelopment – Dependence, class, and politics in Latin America*, New York: Monthly Review Press.

8. See Maoist Internationalist Movement Position Paper on the Little Dragons, 26 August 1992, <http://www.prisoncensorship.info/archive/etext/countries/korea/fourtigers.html>

9. See Appendix 3.a for class definitions

10. Aviva Chomsky, 2014, *Undocumented: How Immigration Became Illegal*. Beacon Press.

11. CNN, 21 June 2014, "Operation Fast and Furious Fast Facts." <http://edition.cnn.com/2013/08/27/world/americas/operation-fast-and-furious-fast-facts/>

12. Kwame Nkrumah, 1965, *Neo-Colonialism, the Last Stage of Imperialism*, London: Thomas Nelson & Sons Ltd.

13. Mario Barrera, 1989, *Race and Class in the Southwest: A theory of racial inequality*, University of Notre Dame Press, p. 194.

PART I SECTION 3

1. *The Correspondence of Marx and Engels*, International Publishers, p. 247.

2. See Appendix 4.a on the terms "immigrant" and "migrant"

3. Frederich Engels, 1891, *The Origin of the Family, Private Property, and the State*, 4th edition (1942), New York: International Publishers.

4. J. Sakai, 1989, *Settlers: The Mythology of the White Proletariat*, 3rd edition, Morningstar Press, p. 49.

5. MC5, 1995, "In Support of Self-Determination and New Democracy," *MIM Theory 7: Proletarian Feminist Revolutionary Nationalism*, p. 19. (see Appendix 5.b for further excerpts from this article)

6. There are many excellent books about Chinese communism under Mao. Below is a short list of books on this topic which are distributed through MIM Distributors's Free Books for Prisoners Program.

- Jean Daubier, 1974, *A History of the Chinese Cultural Revolution*, Vintage Books.
- William Hinton and Fred Magdoff, 2008, *Fanshen: A Documentary of Revolution in a Chinese Village*, Monthly Review Press.

- Jan Myrdal, 1972, *Report from a Chinese Village,* Vintage Books.
- Allyn and Adele Rickett, 1973, *Prisoners of Liberation: Four Years in a Chinese Communist Prison*, Anchor Press.
- E.L. Wheelwright and Bruce McFarlane, 1973, *The Chinese Road to Socialism*, Penguin Books.

7. See Appendix 5.b for more on the united front

PART I SECTION 4

1. See Appendix 5.c on New Democracy and the Joint Dictatorship of the Proletariat of the Oppressed Nations

2. Frederich Engels, 1891, *The Origin of the Family, Private Property, and the State,* 4th edition (1942), New York: International Publishers.

3. Melba Beals, 23 January 1978, "Still Planning for Revolution, Angela Davis Hasn't Changed her Mind, Just her Haircut," *People*, Vol. 9 No. 3.

4. The Kuomintang was the Chinese Nationalist Party, which was anti-Communist and pro-imperialist in its later years. It began as a revolutionary party struggling against the feudal relationships of the Qing Dynasty. During the patriotic war against Japanese imperialism they wavered between working with the Communist Party of China to combat the Japanese and allying with various imperialist forces against the communists. Ultimately they insisted on battling the Communist Party in a civil war, which led to them being pushed out of the mainland to the island of Taiwan.

5. J.V. Stalin, 1950, *Marxism and the Problem of Linguistics.*

6. Winfred P. Lehmann (editor), 1975, *Languages and linguistics in the People's Republic of China.* Austin: University of Texas Press, p. 128.

7. Marc Mauer, 2006, *Race to Incarcerate*, New York: The New Press, p. 33.

8. MIM(Prisons), April 2009, "MIM(Prisons) on U.S. Prison Economy," <http://www.prisoncensorship.info/news/all/US/420/>

9. Center for Constitutional Rights, December 2012, "List of Issues Submission to International Covenant on Civil and Political Rights." <http://www.ccrjustice. org/files/ICCPR%20List%20of%20Issues%20Submission%20on%20Soliltary%20 Confinement%20-%2012%2017%2012-FINA%20%20%20.pdf>

10. Mao Zedong, 26 May 1939, "On the Third Anniversary of the Founding of the Chinese People's Anti-Japanese Military and Political College."

PART II SECTION I

1. Jeffrey Passel, D'Vera Cohn and Ana Gonzalez-Barrera, 23 April 2013, "Net Migration from Mexico Falls to Zero – and Perhaps Less," Pew Research Center.

2. See Appendix 4.a on the terms "immigrant" and "migrant"

3. U.S. Census Bureau, 2012, "Table 42: Foreign-Born Population by Citizenship Status and Place of Birth: 2009," *Statistical Abstract of the United States: 2012.* <https:// www.census.gov/compendia/statab/2012/tables/12s0041.pdf>

4. Passel 2013.

5. Sharon R. Ennis, Merarys Rios-Vargas, and Nora G. Albert, May 2011, *The Hispanic Population: 2010*, U.S. Census Bureau.

6. U.S. Census Bureau, 2011 American Community Survey, Table S0201. <http://factfinder2.census.gov/faces/tableservices/jsf/pages/productview. xhtml?pid=ACS_11_1YR_S0201&prodType=table>

7. Ennis 2011.

8. Jacob L. Vigdor, May 2008, "Measuring Immigrant Assimilation in the United States, Civic Report No. 53," Manhattan Institute, p. 4.

9. David Gutiérrez, "An Historic Overview of Latino Immigration and the Demographic Transformation of the United States," National Park Service. <http://www.nps.gov/latino/latinothemestudy/immigration.htm>

10. Sierra Stoney, Jeanne Batalova, and Joseph Russell, 2 May 2013, "South American Immigrants in the United States," Migration Policy Institute. <http://www.migrationinformation.org/USfocus/display.cfm?id=949>

11. Vigdor 2008, p. 4.

12. David Hendricks and Amy Patterson, Summer 2002, "Genealogy Notes: The 1930 Census in Perspective," *Prologue*, Vol. 34, No. 2, National Archives and Records Administration. <http://www.1930census.com/us_census_history.php>

13. Jack D. Forbes, 22 January 2013, "The Mestizo Concept: A Product of European Imperialism," *In Xinachtli, In Milpa*. <http://inxinachtliinmilpa.blogspot.cz/2013/01/the-mestizo-concept-product-of-european.html>

14. Editor's note: As we noted in Part I Section 2, we believe the common language of the Chican@ nation to be English today. However, this point by Forbes still stands in terms of arguing why Mexican@s and Chican@s are more connected to the indigineous culture of their territories than the Spanish. Even as English dominates in Aztlán, the Spanish spoken in Mexico, with all its indigenous words, has a great influence on the culture of the Chican@ nation.

15. Vigdor 2008.

16. Vigdor 2008, p. 35.

17. Vigdor 2008, p. 1.

18. Vigdor 2008, p. 54.

19. J. Sakai, 1989, *Settlers: The Mythology of the White Proletariat*, 3rd edition, Morningstar Press, p. 64.

20. Sakai 1983, p. 75.

21. Forbes 2013.

22. Paul Taylor, Mark Hugo Lopez, Jessica Martinez, and Gabriel Velasco, 4 April 2012, "When Labels Don't Fit: Hispanics and Their Views of Identity," Pew Research Center. <http://www.pewhispanic.org/2012/04/04/when-labels-dont-fit-hispanics-and-their-views-of-identity/>

23. Paul Taylor, Mark Hugo Lopez, Jessica Martinez and Gabriel Velasco, 4 April 2012, "When Labels Don't Fit: Hispanics and Their Views of Identity," Pew Research Center. <http://www.pewhispanic.org/2012/04/04/when-labels-dont-fit-hispanics-and-their-views-of-identity/>

PART II SECTION 2

1. <http://www.wikipedia.org>, an online encyclopedia

2. <http://www.0101aztlan.net/moratorium/moratorium.html> (This citation link is no longer active but there is much documentation about the Chicano Moratorium and deaths in Vietnam such as: http://latinopia.com/latino-history/1970-national-chicano-moratorium/)

3. Roberto Lovato, 3 October 2005, "The War for Latinos," *The Nation*. <http://www.thenation.com/doc/20051003/lovato/2>

4. MIM, "When it comes to militarism: Civil rights or national liberation." <http://www.prisoncensorship.info/archive/etext/agitation/milit/mexicantroops.html>

5. *Contra Costa Times.* <http://www.contracostatimes.com/mld/cctimes/14633274.htm> (This citation link is no longer active but there is much documentation on the Bush Executive Order on citizenship post-9/11 such as: http://www.americanbar.org/publications/gp_solo/2013/september_october/hidden_immigration_benefits_military_personnel.html)

6. Molly F. McIntosh, Seema Sayala and David Gregory, November 2011, CNA Analysis Solutions. <http://www.cna.org/sites/default/files/research/non%20citizens%20in%20the%20enlisted%20us%20military%20d0025768%20a2.pdf>

PART II SECTION 3

1. See Part II Section 1 "Obscured for Centuries, the Nation is Bigger Than Ever"

2. MC5, 1997, *Imperialism and its Class Structure in 1997*, MIM.

3. See Appendix 3 for more on class definitions.

4. U.S. Department of Defense, 2012, "Demographics 2012: Profile of the Military Community," Office of the Deputy Under Secretary of Defense. <http://www.militaryonesource.mil/12038/MOS/Reports/2012_Demographics_Report.pdf>

5. U.S. Department of Defense, 2010, "Demographics 2010: Profile of the Military Community," Office of the Deputy Under Secretary of Defense. <http://www.militaryonesource.mil/12038/MOS/Reports/2010-Demographics-Report.pdf>

6. U.S. Department of Defense, 2009, "Demographics 2009: Profile of the Military Community," Office of the Deputy Under Secretary of Defense. <http://www.militaryonesource.mil/12038/MOS/Reports/2009-Demographics-Report.pdf>

7. U.S. Department of Defense, 2004, "Demographics 2004: Profile of the Military Community," Office of the Deputy Under Secretary of Defense. <http://www.militaryonesource.mil/12038/MOS/Reports/Combined%20Final%20Demographics%20Report.pdf>

8. Already, in 2015 a majority of youth in the United $tates are not white, while projections put whites losing their majority in the overall population around the year 2043. Census data from 2010 shows that while people over 85 in this country were 85% white that year, those under 5 were only 51% white. For "Hispanics" those numbers are 5% and 25% respectively.

9. AJ Vicens, 4 April 2014, "The Obama Administration's 2 Million Deportations, Explained," *Mother Jones.* <http://www.motherjones.com/politics/2014/04/obama-administration-record-deportations>

10. MIM(Prisons), November 2009, "National Oppression as Migrant Detention," *Under Lock & Key,* No. 11. <http://www.prisoncensorship.info/news/all/US/565/>

11. Jeffrey Passel, D'Vera Cohn and Ana Gonzalez-Barrera, 23 April 2013, "Net Migration from Mexico Falls to Zero – and Perhaps Less," Pew Research Center.

PART II SECTION 4

1. Rodolfo F. Acuña, 2006, *Occupied America: A History of Chicanos*, 6th edition, Longman Publishers, p. 275.

2. *CBS Nightly News*, 25 June 2012.

PART II SECTION 5

1. See MIM(Prisons)'s study pack on the Revolutionary Communist Party, U$A for an in-depth critique of the rcp=u$a's line on political economy, united front theory, homophobia and other issues <http://www.prisoncensorship.info/archive/>

2. RCP-USA, 2001, *The Chicano Struggle and Proletarian Revolution in the U.S.* <http://revcom.us/margorp/chicano.htm>

3. RCP-USA, October 2010, *Constitution for the New Socialist Republic in North America (Draft Proposal)*, Chicago, Illinois: RCP Publications.

4. RCP-USA, 1 May 2012, "Letter to Participating Parties and Organizations of the Revolutionary Internationalist Movement."

5. Raymond Lotta, 10 June 2012, "Everything You've Been Told About Communism is Wrong: Capitalism Is a Failure, Revolution is the Solution" from a series of speeches given by Lotta during a U.$. campus speaking tour in 2009-10, published in *Revolution* newspaper No. 217.

6. MIM, 2003, "MIM Accused of 'Anti-Americanism': What Americans?," 2003 MIM Congress. <http://www.prisoncensorship.info/archive/etext/wim/cong/noamericans.html> reads in part: "The Maoist Internationalist Movement is not anti-American, because there aren't any Americans to be against. The term 'American' should refer to all the people of America, but in practice in English the word 'American' has been misappropriated by philistines. 'America' refers to a geographic entity that includes Mexico and even 'Latin America.' The majority of people there are exploited and super-exploited who MIM champions as the social forces of progress."

7. J. Sakai, 1989, *Settlers: The Mythology of the White Proletariat*, 3rd edition, Morningstar Press.

8. RCP-USA 2001, p. 30.

9. Karl Marx, 1887, *Capital: A Critique of Political Economy*, Vol. I, Book One: The Process of Production of Capital, Ch. 31: Genesis of the Industrial Capitalist.

10. Zak Cope, 2012, *Divided World Divided Class: Global Political Economy and the Stratification of Labour Under Capitalism*, Canada: Kersplebedeb, p. 12.

11. RCP-USA 2001, p. 3.

12. RCP-USA 2001, p.16.

13. RCP-USA 2001, p.17.

14. Mario Barrera, 1989, *Race and Class in the Southwest: A theory of racial inequality*, University of Notre Dame Press, p. 128.

15. RCP-USA 2001, p. 30.

16. RCP-USA 2010.

17. J.V. Stalin, 1920, *Marxism and the National-Colonial Question*, Proletarian Publishers (1975), p. 46-74.

18. See Appendix 5.c on New Democracy and the Joint Dictatorship of the Proletariat of the Oppressed Nations

19. RCP-USA 2012.

20. V.I. Lenin, 1916, "The Socialist Revolution and the Right of Nations to Self-Determination."

21. Stalin 1920.

PART II SECTION 6

1. *Democracy Now*, 7 August 2012.

2. Dennis Cauchon and Paul Overberg, 17 May 2012, "Minorities are now a majority of births", *USA Today*.

3. *CBS Nightly News*, 17 May 2012.

4. Joe Hagan, 16 August 2012, "The long lawless ride of Sheriff Joe Arpaio," *Rolling Stone*.

5. Rodolfo F. Acuña, 2006, *Occupied America: A History of Chicanos*, 6th edition, Longman Publishers, p. 213.

6. J. Sakai, 1989, *Settlers: The Mythology of the White Proletariat*, 3rd edition, Morningstar Press, p. 60.

7. Kwame Nkrumah, 1970, *Africa Must Unite*, International Publishers, p. 1.

8. See Appendix 3 for class definitions

9. Mao Zedong, 1946, "Talks with the American correspondent Anna Louise Strong," *Selected Works of Mao Tse-Tung*, Vol. IV, p. 100.

PART III BURNING CHICAN@ BOOKS

1. Dennis J. Bernstein, 20 January 2012, "Carlos Muñoz interview," *The Progressive*.

PART III REVIEW: MEXICO'S REVOLUTION THEN AND NOW

1. See Appendix 3.b Labor aristocracy

PART III REVIEW: YOUTH, IDENTITY, POWER

1. Carlos Muñoz, Jr., Fall 1970, "On the nature and cause of tension in the Chicano community: A critical analysis," published in summary form in *Aztlán*, Vol. 1, No. 2, pp. 99-100.

2. See Appendix 1.b on United Struggle from Within (USW)

3. See Appendix 2.b on the United Front for Peace in Prisons (UFPP)

PART III REVIEW: CHICANO LIBERATION AND SOCIALISM

1. MC5, 1995, "On the Internal Class Structure of the Internal Semi-Colonies," *MIM Theory 14: United Front*.

2. Mao Zedong, 1937, "On Contradiction," *Selected Works of Mao Tse-Tung*.

3. Editor's note: Though the seal of parasitism was initially a phenomenon bestowed upon the white working class, the United $tates has stolen and plundered so much loot from the Third World that they have even found it in their coffers to now bribe sections of the oppressed nations, thus incorporating sections of the oppressed nation petty-bourgeoisie into the Amerikan labor aristocracy as a whole. Therefore, while the mass of oppressed nations in the United $tates were once the potential vehicles for revolution within the United $tates, this split in the working class has caused the oppressed nation lumpen (and migrant workers) to inherit the task of revolution. See Appendix 3.

4. Vicki L. Ruiz (editor), July 2000, *Las Obreras: Chicana Politics of Work and Family*, UCLA Chicano Studies Research Center.

5. Loïc Wacquant, 2001, "Deadly symbiosis: When ghetto and prison meet and mesh", *Punishment & Society*, Vol. 3, No. 1, pp. 95-133.

6. Bruce Franklin (editor), 1972, *The Essential Stalin: Major Theoretical Writings 1905-52*, Anchor Books.

7. See Appendix 1 for more information on these organizations

PART III LABOR, FAMILY, FEMINISM, AND REVOLUTION

1. Vicki L. Ruiz (editor), July 2000, *Las Obreras: Chicana Politics of Work and Family*, UCLA Chicano Studies Research Center.

2. See Appendix 4.b on United Farm Workers

3. João H. Costa Vargas, 2006, *Catching Hell in the City of Angels:Life and Meaning of Blackness in South Central Los Angeles*, Minneapolis: University of Minnesota Press.

4. See *MIM Theory 2/3: Gender and Revolutionary Feminism*

5. Misty Rojos, 26 September 2014, "Gov. Jerry Brown signs SB 1135, Prison Anti-Sterilization Bill," *San Francisco BayView*. <http://sfbayview.com/2014/09/gov-jerry-brown-signs-sb-1135-prison-anti-sterilization-bill/>

6. G.L. Romero and L. Arguelles, 1991, "Culture and Conflict in the Academy," *The California Sociologist 14*.

APPENDIX 3.B LABOR ARISTOCRACY

MIM trashes the myth of white exploitation

1. Seymour Melman, 1987, Profits Without Production, Philadelphia: University of Pennsylvania Press, p. 38.

2. Melman 1987, p. 34.

3. Revolutionary Communist League, *Class Struggle*, Vol. 15, No. 6-7, p. 11.

4. Maoist Internationalist Movement, 20 September 1987, *MIM Theory* No. 9, 10. (the old school *MIM Theory* journal)

5. *Pulse of Capitalism*, No. 91-3, p. 4.

6. Statistical Abstract of the United States 1991, p. 548.

7. William Domhoff, 1983, *Who Rules America Now? A View for the '80s*, New York: Simon & Schuster.

8. For a review of the avenues of exploitation of the Third World, read Alain de Janvry, *The Agrarian Question and Reformism in Latin America*, especially pp. 50-60. Chapter I provides a state-of-the-art and more thorough answer to the questions raised here.

Raise the Minimum Wage to $2.50

1. Jonathan Nack, 5 December 2015, "Protest Rocks Oakland McDonalds – Part of nationwide day of actions," *indybay.org*. <https://www.indybay.org/newsitems/2013/12/05/18747325.php>

2. Brian Tumulty, 28 December 2013, "NY, Dozen others raising minimum wage in 2014," *Poughkeepsie Journal*. <http://www.poughkeepsiejournal.com/viewart/20131228/NEWS12/131228001/NY-dozen-others-raising-minimum-wage-2014>

3. Jeffrey Dean, 27 December 2013, "300,000 Cambodian garment workers join anti-government protests," *Systemic Capital.com*. <http://www.systemiccapital.com/cambodia-protests-rage-for-second-day-police-fire-on-workers/>

4. Wiawimawo, May 2013, "Big Fat Elephant in the May Day Dialogue,"

MIM(Prisons). <http://www.prisoncensorship.info/news/all/US/1657/>

5. *Wikipedia*.<https://en.wikipedia.org/wiki/List_of_minimum_wages_by_country>

6. Wiawimawo, August 2013, "Rashid's Empty Rhetoric on the Labor Aristocracy," *Under Lock & Key*, No. 34. <http://www.prisoncensorship.info/news/all/US/1771>

7. Wiawimawo, July 2013, "Election Begs Question of the Road to Dual Power in New Afrika," *Under Lock & Key*, No. 33. <http://www.prisoncensorship.info/news/all/US/1679/>

8. Why $2.50? Some rough calculations done by comrades have shown that an equal distribution of wealth would put the hourly wage around $5 per hour. See: Soso, March 2013, "Identifying the U.$. Lumpen Starts with Understanding the First World Petty Bourgeoisie," *Under Lock & Key*, No. 31. <http://www.prisoncensorship.info/news/all/US/1609/> Since we're talking about a reform under capitalism we cannot have complete equal distribution or the profit motive would be gone and the economy would stop functioning. That's not a realistic reform to demand under capitalism. Setting the minimum wage at $2.50 per hour would leave the world's capitalists half of the money (after accounting for reinvestment, infrastructure etc.) to use as economic incentives. Of course, after we overthrow imperialism, under socialism we would be able to truly equalize wages globally as we eliminate capitalist profit.

APPENDIX 3.D FASCISM AND ITS CLASS NATURE

1. Georgi Dimitroff, 1935, "Working Class Unity - Bulwark Against Fascism."

2. Editor's note: See J. Sakai's article "The Shock of Recognition" from the book *Confronting Fascism: Discussion Documents for a Militant Movement* which is also available online at <http://www.kersplebedeb.com/mystuff/books/fascism/shock.html>. Note that our co-publisher, Kersplebedeb, also published *Confronting Fascism* and agrees with Sakai that revolutionaries should be combating imperialism and what they see as fascist movements among the oppressed nations at the same time. Our line is that fascism must be imperialist. As all fascist movements attempt to appear independent to gain popular support, this may not always be a simple delineation to make. But where Sakai writes about Osama bin Laden's al Qaeda being a fascist force in the book above, MIM disagreed and criticized any implications that they were an enemy of higher priority than the imperialists (see "Osama Bin Laden and the Concept of 'Theocratic Fascism'" from MIM's 2004 Congress <http://www.prisoncensorship.info/archive/etext/wim/cong/fascismcong2004.html>).

APPENDIX 4.B ON CESAR CHAVEZ

1. Recommended reading:

- Miriam Pawel, 2014, *The Crusades of Cesar Chavez: A Biography*, Bloomsbury Press. The beginning of ch. 25 addresses the beating and turning into authorities of Mexican migrants by UFW.

- "Union Vice President Speaks Out: The Union and the Green Carder," *El Malcriado: The Voice of the Farm Worker*, 15 June 1968, Vol. II, No. 8. This article more fully explains the UFW position, from their own newspaper. More primary source documents can be found in collection at <http://thinkmexican.tumblr.com/post/80947508130/cesar-chavez-uft-racist-language-against-own-people>.

Other potential sources which have not been thoroughly investigated by MIM(Prisons) but which have been cited by other sources:

- David G. Gutiérrez, 1995, *Walls and Mirrors: Mexican Americans, Mexican Immigrants, and the Politics of Ethnicity*, University of California Press.
- Frank Bardacke, 2012, *Trampling Out the Vintage: Cesasr Chavez and the Two Souls of the United Farm Workers*, 1st edition, Verso Books.

APPENDIX 5.A CELL STRUCTURE, VANGUARD PARTIES, AND MASS ORGANIZATIONS

1. MIM(Prisons), July 2011, "Building New Groups Vs. Working with USW and MIM(Prisons)," *Fundamental Political Line of the Maoist Internationalist Ministry of Prisons* (March 2012), p. 11.

2. MIM(Prisons), September 2010, "Self-Criticism on Relations with New Afrikan Ujamaa Dynasty," *Under Lock & Key*, No. 16. <http://www.prisoncensorship.info/news/all/US/793/>

APPENDIX 5.B UNITED FRONT

How to Build a United Front

1. MIM differs from other communist groups on three main questions: (1) MIM holds that after the proletariat seizes power in socialist revolution, the potential exists for capitalist restoration under the leadership of a new bourgeoisie within the party itself. In the case of the USSR, the bourgeoisie seized power after the death of Stalin in 1953; in China, it was after Mao's death and the overthrow of the "Gang of Four" in 1976. (2) MIM upholds the Chinese Cultural Revolution, 1966-1976, as the farthest advance of communism in human history. (3) MIM believes the North American white working class is primarily a non-revolutionary worker-elite at this time; thus, it is not the principal vehicle to advance Maoism in this country. (*MIM Theory* magazine)

The Questions of Independence and Initiative Within the United Front

Scanned and formatted by the Maoist Documentation Project

1. A quotation from Mencius.

2. V. I. Lenin, 1958, "Conspectus of Hegel's Book Lectures on the History of Philosophy", *Collected Works*, Russian edition, Moscow, Vol. XXXVIII, p. 275.

3. "The doctrine of collaboration between labour and capital" is the reactionary doctrine of the Second International, which advocates such collaboration in the capitalist countries and opposes the revolutionary overthrow of bourgeois rule and the establishment of the dictatorship of the proletariat.

APPENDIX 5.C NEW DEMOCRACY AND THE JOINT DICTATORSHIP OF THE PROLETARIAT OF THE OPPRESSED NATIONS

In Support of Self-Determination and New Democracy

1. Eldridge Cleaver, 1969, Post-Prison Writings and Speeches, Random House: New York, p. 69.

2. Cleaver 1969, p. 187.

Glossary

Amerikkka (Amerika): The white settler nation which has occupied North America since the 1600s

anarchism: Anarchists aim for a classless society free of oppression. They differ from communists in that they don't support the strategy of building a party based on democratic centralism to end oppression and they disagree that there will be a necessary stage of dictatorship of the proletariat before communism can be achieved. Although they have a hatred for oppression and authority, the groups are principally a First World phenomenon and have never won a revolution. (Source: *MIM Theory 8: The Anarchist Ideal and Communist Revolution* by MIM)

anti-imperialism: The belief that nations have the right to struggle for liberation when faced with oppression by other nations. Opposing imperialism means opposing the system where some nations use their power to exploit other nations' wealth. Imperialism stifles all indigenous economic and political activity in the oppressed nations. Anti-imperialists work to end the system of imperialism which allows a few nations to profit at the expense of the majority.

anti-imperialist united front: The loose alliance of classes and organizations that work to undermine imperialist domination. To achieve our principal task, we must unite all who can be united on the side of the oppressed against imperialism. Developing an anti-imperialist united front is facilitating the growth of the winning side of the principal contradiction in the world today. See also: principal contradiction

assimilation: Adopting on the part of members of oppressed nations the culture, custom, identity and outlook popular amongst oppressor nations. Assimilation occurs at the expense of national liberation and revolutionary internationalism. (Source: Revolutionary Anti-Imperialist Movement Glossary)

Aztlán: The name of the Chican@ nation's national territory, more commonly known as the "Southwest United $tates." Aztlán is also the word used to identify an internal semi-colony that has been and continues to be oppressed. The Chican@ nation of Aztlán developed in the territory of Aztlán during the Amerikan capitalist-imperialist stages of development.

Before the concept of Aztlán was ever used by Chican@ revolutionaries as representative of our struggle against imperialism, Aztlán was originally conceived in the 1960s as a propaganda tool used by cultural nationalists.

basic contradiction/fundamental contradiction of capitalism: social production vs. private ownership (Source: *Fundamentals of Political Economy* by Shanghai Press, Chapter 5)

Boriqua (Boricua): Derived from Borinquin, the indigenous Taíno term for the island named Puerto Rico by the Spanish colonizers, this term is used to denote a member of the nation that is now a colony of the United $tates.

bourgeois nationalism: Ideological expression of the upper and middle classes of oppressed nations, often implicitly identified with the capitalist-imperialist system yet dissatisfied with the current order and their place within. Bourgeois nationalism can play both a progressive role, insofar as it can be incorporated in the broad united front against imperialism, or a reactionary role based in its tendency to capitulate to imperialism and impose its own system of oppression. (Source: Revolutionary Anti-Imperialist Movement Glossary)

bourgeoisie: The bourgeoisie is the exploiter class most characteristic of the capitalist system. Their wealth is obtained from the labor of others, in particular the proletariat.

The term "bourgeoisie" now usually refers to the capitalist class in common usage. The capitalist class is that class of people who own enough property that they would not have to work to make a living. The capitalist class only works if it wants to. Also included in the term are people with very powerful positions in production or government generally. A ruler may or may not have great assets on hand, but if s/he really wanted them, s/he has the power to get them. For example, Ronald Reagan made a speech in Japan with a $1 million fee after he retired from the presidency. If he had been "poor" during the presidency, he still would have been part of the "capitalist class." What he was doing was central enough to the ruling class of capitalism that he had de facto access to the means of production, even if he had gambled away his ranch and other assets in Las Vegas while he was in the White House.

An overly restrictive definition of "capitalist" is someone who owns the means of production – factories, tools and patents for example. What is important is not the literal ownership of means of production but access to those means of production. Such access could be merely the ability to get a loan so large that it is possible to live off the business connected to such a loan. Access to political information in the military, intelligence or executive branch would make it possible to be rich making a speech like Reagan did or by selling secrets to foreigners. People with such access to information also may be bourgeoisie. For example, Reagan could take his $1 million speech fee and convert it into means of production such as ownership of tools and factory buildings. Whether he does that or not, we can say he has "access" to the means of production.

There is another common and critically important usage of the term "bourgeoisie." Technically the bourgeoisie includes other sections, including those more numerous than the capitalist class. The "petty-bourgeoisie" or "petit-bourgeoisie" refers to people who are exploiters but not on the scale of the capitalists. The petty-bourgeoisie often owns its own means of production or professional skills but does not hire enough workers to be able to quit working and still live a life of leisure. There are other categories of bourgeoisie that are not capitalist, such as what Mao called the "comprador bourgeoisie" which owes its existence to imperialist capitalists and cannot function on its own as a capitalist class. See also: capitalism

bourgeoisification: The process by which a group's class status becomes more allied with that of the bourgeoisie; in the imperialist countries, the so-called "workers" have such access to the means of production and consumption that that they have become bourgeoisified. See also: bourgeoisie

cadre: Literally, a frame or framework; a nucleus of trained, experienced activists in an organization capable of assuming leadership and/or training and educating, (instructing) others to perform functional roles. (Source: Black Liberation Army Political Dictionary)

cadre organization: In contrast to a mass organization, a cadre organization recognizes the importance of a worked out ideology to decide its line and actions. They strive to play a vanguard (leadership) role within a movement. Membership requires a higher degree of ideological unity and standard of discipline than a mass organization. See also: mass organization

capital accumulation: When a capitalist invests surplus value into means of production, rather than using it for persynal consumption. (Source: *Fundamentals of Political Economy* by Shanghai Press, Chapter 5)

capitalism: Capitalism is a mode of production, or economic system, where the bourgeoisie or capitalist class owns the means of production and exploits the labor of the proletariat. Because the proletariat owns nothing, they are forced to sell their labor power on the market in exchange for what they need to survive. When they work for the capitalist, the capitalist owns the value that they create and only pays them the portion of this value to sustain themselves. The rest is called surplus value, or the profit exploited from the worker, which is the basic law of capitalist economic relations.

Everything that has a use value and exchange value becomes a commodity under capitalism, including labor power. This allows for exchange to occur on a scale far beyond anything humyns have done before capitalism, because exchange values of any two commodities can be quickly compared from anywhere in the capitalist world. Capital itself is a value that can bring about surplus value, exploiting the workers. Capital includes machines, tools and raw materials as well as the labor power of the workers. Commodities and capital are unique to the capitalist mode of production and embody the exploitative relationship of the bourgeoisie to the proletariat. In contrast, bourgeois economists would have us believe that these are eternal things, and ignore their relationship to exploitation.

Capitalism exists where non-workers control the production of wage-workers, even if private property is officially state property. Under capitalism, democracy for the working classes is undermined through people's lack of control of their own workplace and society as a whole. Workers have little say in how their workplace is organized or what will be produced. In the United $tates, people in the inner cities have little control over their environment. They do not control the police or the spending of their tax money. And certainly the "justice" system is out of control. (Source: *Fundamental Political Line of the Maoist Internationalist Ministry of Prisons* by MIM(Prisons), Section 2)

chauvinism: Selfish prejudice, narrow-mindedness or bias; for example the First World-chauvinist belief that First World workers are better workers than Third World workers. (Source: *MIM Theory 1: A White Proletariat?* by MIM, p. 4)

Chican@: Of or belonging to the nation of Aztlán. Chican@s are generally of Mexican descent and citizens of the United $tates, but also include many people of Central and South American descent who have migrated to North America and integrated into the Chican@ nation. These Raza from outside of Mexico are living in Chican@ barrios and have developed to be a part of this nation in spite of their distinct national origin.

The origins of "Chicano" comes from the word "Mexica." If you were a Mexica then you became a Mechicano. "Mechicano was the original name the Spaniards first called our Mexica ancestors mispronouncing their Mexica name and it was used as a way to refer to all of Anahuac (Meso-America, i.e. Mexico) which at the time included what is today known as Central America and Aztlán-Chicomoztoc (the so-called U.$. southwest and beyond). Chicana and Chicano are just shortened and Spanish language versions of Mexica... Chicana and Chicano have long been considered perfectly acceptable variations on Mexica." We have chosen to use the gender-neutral spelling, Chican@. (Source: "Mexica Movement, An Indigenous Guide to the 21st Century" by Ol) See also: Aztlán

class: A group of people with a common relation to the means of production, to the distribution of the means of consumption, and to other classes of people (Source: *MIM Theory 2/3: Gender and Revolutionary Feminism* by MIM, p. 72) See also: means of production

class consciousness: The understanding by members of particular classes that they represent a certain class, that their class interests may intersect or oppose those of others classes, and of their agency when collectively organized for class struggle. Typically, class consciousness is used to describe the most broad, clearest perspective of either the proletariat, the bourgeoisie or their sub-classes. (Source: Revolutionary Anti-Imperialist Movement Glossary)

COINTELPRO: short name for the CounterIntelligence Program of the United $tates Federal Bureau of Investigation, which was used to refer to specific secret and typically illegal government operations; more generally used to refer to systematic campaigns directed by the Bureau against a wide array of selected domestic political organizations and individuals, especially during the 1960s. (Source: *Agents of Repression: FBI Secret Wars Against the Black Panther Party and the American Indian Movement* by Ward Churchill and Jim Vander Wall, pp. 37-38)

colonialism: Foreign domination of a country or people where the economic, political and military structure is controlled and run by the occupying force. The primary motivation of colonialism is generally the economic benefit of the "mother" country at the expense of the colony. (Source: Black Liberation Army Political Dictionary)

Comintern: (1919-1943) founded in Moscow following the 1917 Bolshevik revolution, the Communist International (Comintern) was formed to fight "by all available means, including armed force, for the overthrow of the international bourgeoisie and for the creation of an international Soviet republic as a transition stage to the complete abolition of the State." The founding of the Comintern was defined by a strong line on the labor aristocracy being the enemy class within the proletarian movement, following the pro-war nationalism that marked much of the Second International. The end of the Comintern came with similar experiences as the social democratic parties of Europe, representing labor aristocracy interests, put up no resistance to fascism, and earned the epithet social-fascists. The Comintern's heavy hand in China led to setbacks for the Chinese Communists at the hands of the Guomindang, demonstrating the incorrectness of one international body leading the world revolution and the correctness of Stalin's line of building socialism in one country at a time. In China Mao Zedong struggled against the Wang Ming-line of following foreign authorities to develop a strong indigenous revolution. (Source: *Labor Aristocracy, Mass Base of Social Democracy* by H.W. Edwards, Chapter XXIX)

communalism: A small scale, classless society. Communism is an advance over communalism in the organization of society on a larger scale. Afrocentric communists who have little to say about Marx, the Soviet Union, or China often romanticize pre-colonial communalist societies in Africa as their model. They ignore the contradictions that led to communalism's end, including their inability to defend themselves from larger, better organized societies that enslaved them. (Source: *How Europe Underdeveloped Africa* by Walter Rodney, p. 80)

communism: Communism is the abolition of power of people over people. This means abolishing "oppression," whether the oppression be of nations by nations, classes by classes, women by men or any other division in society. Communism is based on mutual cooperation, peace and justice instead of oppression.

Long-run goals of communism include the abolition of classes and organizing society without governments or borders. As in certain tribal societies in the past and living still today, communists believe that it is possible for humyns to organize themselves without war, crime, starvation and homelessness. When there are social problems, communists blame those problems on how society is organized. They seek to organize society to bring out the best in people, however flawed the species may be. No communist leader has ever claimed that a society has achieved communism yet. That means the industrial societies of our time have either lived in capitalism or socialism.

Many people have communist intentions. They want to abolish oppression and claim work towards communism. Because MIM(Prisons) judges political movements based on their long term effects relative to other real-life movements, we encourage people with communist intentions to study and apply Marxism-Leninism-Maoism, which we believe has proved the most effective path towards communism.

MIM(Prisons) reserves the term "communist" for those who share our views on the historic attempts in foreign countries to move toward communism and apply the method of dialectical materialism to current problems. The dividing line questions for communists involve an understanding of the two largest, most advaned socialist experiments: China and the Soviet Union. MIM(Prisons) believes communists must agree on six important questions, which are listed on page 2 of recent issues of *Under Lock & Key* or on our About page at http:// prisoncensorship.info/faq. See also Appendix 1.c for more on MIM(Prisons).

Finally, communists believe that a communist party – not just ad hoc or individual organizing – is necessary to seize state power from the oppressors. Within the party members carry out democratic centralism on all issues other than these six key points. This means struggling over disagreements internally, while upholding the organization line in public.

People working to end oppression who do not agree with MIM(Prisons) on these six questions or do not believe in the necessity of a party belong in other organizations – organizations MIM(Prisons) believes belong to political trends that are historically proven to be less effective in bringing about the end of oppression.

MIM(Prisons) expresses general unity with all other groups and outbreaks against imperialism; mass movements against oppression have as many forms as forms of power. In this spirit, we insist on telling people the uncompromised truth and discussing and criticizing the strategy and tactics of any given action. MIM(Prisons) encourages everyone, communist or not, to be involved in the struggle against imperialism. (Source: *Fundamental Political Line of the Maoist Internationalist Ministry of Prisons* by MIM(Prisons), Section 2)

comprador bourgeoisie: In colonized nations this class acts as junior partners to the imperialists in exploiting the colonized people. As a class, their interests are tied closely to those of the imperialists even if they have a national interest in independence. They sell out their nation for persynal benefit.

crypto-Trotskyism: Term used to refer to organizations that exhibit Trotskyist tendencies but which don't admit to being Trotskyist. Most significantly they suffer from the same great-nation chauvinism as the other Trots, over-emphasizing the role of the oppressor nation working classes and under-emphasizing the role of the liberation struggles of the oppressed nations. See also: Trotskyists

cultural nationalism: this is an idealist form of nationalism, which looks to the past to establish a national identity rather than taking destiny into our own hands and creating a new future.

"Cultural nationalism, or pork chop nationalism, as I sometimes call it, is basically a problem of having the wrong political perspective. It seems to be a reaction instead of responding to political oppression. The cultural nationalists are concerned with returning to the old African culture and thereby regaining their identity and freedom. In other words, they feel that the African culture will automatically bring political freedom. Many times cultural nationalists fall into line as reactionary nationalists." – Huey P. Newton, 1968 (Source: The Black Panthers Speak by Philip S. Foner (editor), p. 50) See also: idealism

democratic centralism: A system of organization where all members of an organization are able to participate in the formulation of policies, goals, programs and procedures. After a decision has been made regarding policies, goals, programs and procedures, all members are expected to publicly uphold the decision (line) that was made, even if they disagree with it, until the next opportunity arises to debate the issue further. In addition, higher committees are elected by broader levels of the organization and higher and lower levels are interdependent and accountable to each other.

dialectical materialism: The world outlook first developed by Marx and Engels by combining a dialectical approach with a materialist study of the world. The dialectical-materialist theory of knowing and doing is a constant cycle of knowledge development. Perceptual knowledge is used to make judgements and inferences, from which one forms rational knowledge, which one redirects to social practice. This revolutionary practice produces objective and subjective results, which become additional perceptual knowledge. (*MIM Theory 9: Psychology & Imperialism* by MIM, p. 92) See also: dialectics, materialism

dialectics: The study of contradictions within the very essence of things. The scientific analytical approach to studying contradictions within nature taking into account the historical development and the interaction of related things. Dialectics holds that nothing exists independent, isolated or unconnected, but that all phenomena are connected and part of the whole. They are dependent upon and determined by each other.

    Dialectics also holds that all things are in a constant state of motion, i.e. changes. They move from a quantitative level with constant small changes to a qualitative level with their very essence or character make a giant leap to a new existence. These changes follow a definite pattern determined by the external and internal contradictions within themselves. This being that all phenomena are made up of opposite forces, i.e. internal contradictions, which are the basis for change and that all external forces, i.e. external contradictions, interact and become the conditions or impetus to change. (Source: Black Liberation Army Political Dictionary)

dictatorship of the proletariat: A state in which the bourgeoisie has been toppled from power and the proletariat has taken control. Rule by force of the entire proletarian class and their allies over the bourgeois class and their allies. The dictatorship of the proletariat is an organized force to protect the non-negotiable interests of the majority of the world's people for food, clothing, shelter, medicine, and a pollution-free and militarism-free environment – survival rights. It represses those who put property or profit rights or other exchange value goals above survival rights. It also represses those who seek to cause strife within the dictatorship of the proletariat, by, for example, agitating for violence against the party. The development of the dictatorship of the proletariat marks the stage of struggle between capitalism and communism. (Source: *MIM Theory 14: United Front* by MIM, p. 38)

dogmatism: The belief in, or promotion of, ideas without basis in fact or without depth. Dogmatists are stubborn, and view things arrogantly and narrow-mindedly.

economic substructure: Production relations; determines superstructure. (Source: *Fundamentals of Political Economy* by Shanghai Press, page 8) See also: superstructure

economism: Reformism focused on improvements in wages or other economic demands without proposing a change in the economic system that creates inequality in the first place. (Source: *Labor Aristocracy, Mass Base of Social Democracy* by H.W. Edwards, Chapter XXI)

elite: A small group of people who have power over a larger group of which they are a part, usually without a direct responsibility to that larger group and often without their knowledge or consent. (Source: "The Tyranny of Structurelessness" by Jo Freeman)

exploitation: The appropriation of surplus labor from workers by capitalists. The main exploited classes in the world today are the peasantry, proletariat and lumpen-proletariat – almost wholly found in the Third World. A worker is exploited if s/he earns less than the value of h labor power.

fascism: "A movement of mixed elements, dominantly petit-bourgeois, but also slum-proletarian and demoralized working class, financed and directed by finance-capital, by the big industrialists, landlords and financiers, to defeat the working-class revolution and smash the working-class organizations." (Source: *Fascism and Social Revolution: How and Why Fascism Came to Power in Europe* by R. Palme Dutt)

feminism: The belief that no gender group should have power over any other gender group. Internationalist feminism seeks to end gender oppression for people all across the world, and develops strategy using dialectical materialism.

Internationalist feminism is in opposition to First World pseudo-feminism, which limits its scope to increasing the benefits of the gender aristocracy of First World wimmin. First World pseudo-feminist benefits are typically gained through increasing oppression of Third World wimmin. For example, First World wimmin enjoy a greater variety of relatively inexpensive birth control methods because of non-concensual drug testing on Third World wimmin.

feudalism: The mode of production in which the aristocracy owns the land and serfs work on it giving a portion of the proceeds to the owners. Characterized by a landlord system, found in agrarian societies. Under feudalism, land is the primary means of production and landless or semi-landless peasants are the primary producers. Social relations under feudalism are usually based on tradition.

The social order which preceded capitalism, its main characteristic being the exploitation of the mass of peasantry by the feudal nobility. Feudalism prevailed throughout the Middle Ages, undergoing various forms of development in different countries. Its final stage, caused by the advance of commodity exchange, was serfdom, in which exploitation of the peasantry was of the severest kind, little different from slavery. "The basis of the relations of production under the feudal system is that the feudal lord owns the means of production and does not fully own the worker in production, i.e. the serf, whom the feudal lord can no longer kill, but whom he may buy and sell." (Source: *History of the Communist Party of the Soviet Union* by CPSU(B) Central Committee 1939)

Existing side by side with feudalism, and presaging its later replacement by the capitalist mode of production, were such social elements and forces as guilds, growth of the towns, advance of commerce, establishment of the banks, emergence of the bourgeoisie (burghers, burgesses), the appearance of manufactories alongside the handicraft workshops. (Source: *Marxist Glossary* by L. Harry Gould, p. 48)

financial capitalist: Those capitalists who lend temporarily idle money capital to other capitalists in need of this money. Money capital is lent for a share of the surplus value the borrowing capitalist extracts, and this share is called interest. (Source: *Fundamentals of Political Economy* by Shanghai Press, Chapter 7)

First Nation: Indigenous population which has been colonized by, but not integrated into, an invading settler nation.

First World lumpen: The class of people in the First World who are excluded from the productive process. By virtue of living in the First World this class, on average, receives more material benefits from imperialism than the global proletariat. As such their interests are not the same as the exploited classes and we do not include them in the "lumpen-proletariat." But their conditions in many ways parallel those of the lumpen-proletariat standing in stark contrast to the majority of the First World populations. (Source: *Fundamental Political Line of the Maoist Internationalist Ministry of Prisons* by MIM(Prisons), Section 2) See also: lumpen-proletariat

First Worldist: An attitude that is chauvinist in favor of the people of the First World. See also: chauvinism,

focoism: The belief that small cells of armed revolutionaries can create the conditions for revolution through their actions. Demonstrated revolutionary victories, the successes of the foci, are supposed to lead the masses to revolution. Focoism often places great emphasis on armed struggle and the immediacy this brings to class warfare. Focoism is different from people's war in that it doesn't promote the mass line as part of guerrilla operations. (Source *What is MIM?* by MIM)

gender: One of three strands of oppression, the other two being class and nation. Gender can be thought of as socially-defined attributes related to one's sex organs and physiology. Patriarchy has led to the splitting of society into an oppressed (wimmin) and oppressor gender (men).

Historically, reproductive status was very important to gender, but today the dynamics of leisure-time and humyn biological development are the material basis of gender. For example, children are the oppressed gender regardless of genitalia, as they face the bulk of sexual oppression independent of class and national oppression.

People of biologically superior health-status are better workers, and that's a class thing, but if they have leisure-time, they are also better sexually privileged. We might think of models or prostitutes, but professional athletes of any kind also walk this fine line. Athletes, models and well-paid prostitutes are not oppressed as "objects," but in fact they hold sexual privilege. Older and disabled people as well as the very sick are at a disadvantage, not just at work but in leisure-time. For that matter there are some people with health statuses perfectly suited for work but not for leisure-time. (Source: "Clarity On What Gender Is" by MC5, from 1998 MIM Congress)

gender aristocracy: Those who are not part of the patriarchy but who enjoy gender privilege so that their interests in leisure-time and in relation to pleasure align with the patriarchy. The gender aristocracy in the First World is often focused on ways to expand or justify their privilege while ignoring the plight of the truly gender oppressed (e.g. campaigning to legalize sex work, as opposed to campaigning to end the conditions that drive gender oppressed wimmin into sex work). (Source: *MIM Theory 2/3: Gender and Revolutionary Feminism* by MIM) See also: patriarchy

genocide: The deliberate eradication of part or all of an ethnic group or nation.

hegemony: Domination, especially in a national context.

humyn: Alternate spelling of "human" to oppose seeing people as predominately men, who are the oppressor gender.

hypothesis: A supposition or proposed explanation made on the basis of limited evidence as a starting point for further investigation. See also: law (scientific)

idealism: The concept that mind is primary and matter is secondary. Idealists believe that all things originate from the idea and that matter is only a reflection of what exists in the mind, as one perceives it. The physical world can only be conceived as relative to, or dependent on the mind, spirit or experience. (Source: Black Liberation Army Political Dictionary)

identity politics: The idea that a persyn or group's political analysis and practice is less important than their identity. Identity politics is a pre-scientific way of thinking that leads people to follow others for reasons like where they are from, their appearance or other cultural cues, regardless of the correctness of their political line.

ideology: A systematic set of principles and beliefs relating to life, culture, politics, etc. Integrated assertions, theories and aims that constitute a socio-political program. Generally our political ideology is used to create our political line. (Source: Black Liberation Army Political Dictionary)

imperialism: Imperialism is an economic system that V.I. Lenin defined as the "highest stage of capitalism." It became well pronounced in the early 1900s, and is defined by the globalization of capital, the dominance of finance capital and the division of the world into imperialist and exploited nations; the latter Maoists see as the principal contradiction in the world today.

As the economic system that dominates the world, imperialism determines much of the material reality that all inhabitants of planet Earth face today, including war, poverty and environmental destruction. This means that the status quo promoted by imperialist interests is the biggest hindrance to change. As the dominant imperialist power, both financially and militarily, the United $tates generally serves as the primary target of our attacks as anti-imperialists. (Source: *Fundamental Political Line of the Maoist Internationalist Ministry of Prisons* by MIM(Prisons), Section 2)

individualism: A narrow selfish approach or outlook based upon putting oneself before the interests of the people, organization, and comrades. A bourgeois tendency expressed in the "pull yourself up by your bootstraps" theory. (Source: Black Liberation Army Political Dictionary)

integrationism: The political strategy of incorporating into the oppressor nation as equals rather than struggling for self-determination; for example, the idea that the oppression of New Afrikans can be ended by having more New Afrikan cops, lawyers and politicians. See also: revolutionary nationalism

internal colony: A colony contained entirely within the borders of a colonial power, e.g. the First Nations of North America or Aboriginal Australian nations. See also: colonialism

internationalism: The ethical belief or scientific approach in which peoples of different nations are held to be equal. Internationalism is opposed to racism and national chauvinism. (Source: MIM FAQ: What is Internationalism?) See also: chauvinism

labor: The expenditure of humyn labor power; physical action with the intention of meeting a material need or want. Work done as part of the basic economic process of a society.

Labor power is what the workers sell to capitalists for a money wage. Labor is the actual work. "On the one hand all labor is, speaking physiologically, an expenditure of human labor power." (Marx, *Capital Vol. 1*, New York: International Publishers, 1967, p. 177; *MIM Theory 1: A White Proletariat?* by MIM, p. 5) See also: labor power

labor aristocracy: Unlike the traditional petty bourgeoisie, they do not own their own means of production and so must work for others. But unlike the proletariat and semi-proletariat the labor aristocracy in the First World earn more than the value of their labor and therefore have interests that fall in the bourgeois camp allying with imperialism.

In Lenin's day the Labor Aristocracy was the "upper strata of the proletariat." Lenin wrote that he was "obliged to distinguish between the 'upper stratum' of the workers and the 'lower stratum of the proletariat proper.'" (*Imperialism, the Highest Stage of Capitalism*) "The capitalists *can* devote a part (and not a small one, at that!) of these superprofits to bribe *their own* workers, to create something like an alliance (recall the celebrated 'alliances' described by the Webbs of English trade unions and employers) between the workers of the given nation and their capitalists *against* the other countries." (*Imperialism and the Split in Socialism* by V.I. Lenin, Lenin's emphasis).

In the First World today we define this group as the lower segment of the petty-bourgeoisie, working for a wage and earning more than the value of their labor but without the means to get a loan to start a small business themselves. This group benefits from the imperialist world's superexploitation of the Third World. They are bought off by the imperialists with these superprofits. In the First World this group is not exploited and so not part of the proletariat. On the contrary, their incomes are often higher than those traditionally classified as the petty bourgeoisie in the Third World, further demonstrating their bourgeois character. (Source: *Fundamental Political Line of the Maoist Internationalist Ministry of Prisons* by MIM(Prisons), Section 2) See also: petty bourgeoisie, proletariat

labor power: "The capitalist buys labor power in order to use it; and labor power in use is labor itself." (p. 177) Labor power is the ability to do labor. Labor power is what the workers sell to capitalists for a money wage. Labor is the actual work. "On the one hand all labor is, speaking physiologically, an expenditure of human labor power." (p. 46) The value of labor power is "the cost of producing or reproducing the laborer himself." (p. 538) Quotes from Karl Marx, *Capital Vol. 1*, New York: International Publishers, 1967. (*MIM Theory 1: A White Proletariat?* by MIM, p. 5)

Labor Theory of Value: Labor is the sole source of value. The worth of a product is determined by the amount of work required to create it. (Source: *Fundamentals of Political Economy* by Shanghai Press, Chapters 3 and 4)

lackey: A flunky. Footman. To wait upon or serve slavishly. Also lacquey. (Source: Black Liberation Army Political Dictionary)

law (scientific): A scientific idea that stands the test of time, often without change; experimentally confirmed over and over; can create true predictions for different situations; has uniformity and is universal. See also: hypothesis

left wing of white nationalism: We often refer to the left wing of white nationalism when talking about the self-proclaimed communist, anarchist and radical reformist groups that help prop up imperialism by making it seem more benign. They are characterized by an integrationist approach towards the oppressed nations, in their efforts to preserve white dominance in the imperialist system. (Source: "The real lessons of the Chicano Moratorium and the high treason against Maoism" by MIM) See also: white nationalism

Leninism: Ideology rooted in following the theories of V.I. Lenin, leader of the Russian revolution until his death in 1924. Includes ideas regarding the nature and significance of imperialism, the role of the state and support for the theory that a disciplined vanguard party is essential to a successful socialist revolution leading to a dictatorship of the proletariat and the peasantry. Generally considered to be an advance on Marxism, also called Marxism-Leninism. Dogmatic Leninists do not believe that there have been significant advances in revolutionary theory since the death of Lenin. We see Maoism as the next stage of development of Marxism-Leninism.

liberal bourgeois: The free-thinking section of the bourgeoisie who believe in individual freedoms for all while at the same time holding tight to the bourgeois way of life. Liberalism is a capitalist ideology, which had progressive features in feudal societies that were authoritarian. See also: Liberalism

Liberalism: There is a distinction between "liberalism" and "Liberalism." Liberalism as a proper noun prioritizes individual rights and choice. It may attack the state and other organizations claiming privileges higher than individual rights. The doctrine of "laissez-faire" (or non-interference) economics belongs in Liberalism, which is one reason that many conservatives are also Liberals, if they live in societies where they believe they have a "free market" worth defending. The individual right to trade and conduct business without state interference is common to much conservatism and Liberalism. Many other people believe they have individual "free speech" rights that they want to maintain as part of the status quo. Hence, we say there can be conservative Liberals and liberal Liberals. Within Maoism, Liberalism refers to tolerance for things that violate our political principles. (Source: "What is the difference between Liberalism and Communism?" by MIM)

line: Line is generally a belief, but line can also be a goal. For instance, our belief is that only through communism can we abolish the oppression of groups of people over other people. At the same time it is our goal to abolish the oppression of people over other people.

lumpen-proletariat: In a world where the vast majority must sell their labor power to survive, the lumpen-proletariat are those who are not able to sell theirs due to the limitations of capitalism at providing full employment. This class is rarely employed, often living as parasites on other proletarians. A small portion of the proletariat in Europe when Marx first wrote about them, the lumpen-proletariat has become an important class in itself. With the rise of mega-slums in the Third World following the period of neo-colonialism, this class has surpassed 1 billion people. (Source: *Fundamental Political Line of the Maoist Internationalist Ministry of Prisons* by MIM(Prisons), Section 2) See also: First World lumpen

Manifest Destiny: In the 19th century, Manifest Destiny was a widely held belief in the United States that American settlers were destined to expand throughout the continent. Historians have for the most part agreed that there are three basic themes to Manifest Destiny:
 * The special virtues of the American people and their institutions;
 * America's mission to redeem and remake the west in the image of agrarian America;
 * An irresistible destiny to accomplish this essential duty. (Source: *Native America, Discovered And Conquered* by Robert J. Miller, p. 120)

Maoism: Maoism is the writings of Mao Zedong – or the doctrine which guided the first successful Third World peasant revolution that liberated China in 1949. Maoism is famous for land reform, collectivization of agriculture in what was then a poor country, ejecting both foreign occupiers and pro-landlord elements with the strategy of "People's War" against numerically, financially and technically superior enemies, abolishing China's huge drug addiction, ending pornography and prostitution, eliminating the practice of breaking wimmin's feet (footbinding) to make them smaller and supposedly cuter, establishing China's first law allowing divorce and eventually instituting worker-run industry without private property in the means of production.

Complete revolution is fundamental to Maoism. This means that all social, cultural, political and economic relations must be revolutionized and that people will not be liberated by simply breaking the state or smashing capitalism. Groups, individuals or ideologies which choose one issue – imperialism, racism, capitalism, sexism – as central typically cede the other areas to the status quo. Maoism dictates that while struggling against the state, the Party must establish a new and revolutionary culture not based on ideologies of domination and greed. The Party must lead a revolution against class, gender and national chauvinisms within its ranks and against the state. Maoism accepts Lenin's concept of a vanguard party.

Mao proved that it was possible to lead socialist revolution in a poor and backward country with the main forces coming from the peasantry in the countryside led by the political ideology from the city called "proletarian ideology" and this point remains controversial in the imperialist country so-called communist movement. Even more importantly and dividing supposed communists everywhere, Mao was the first communist leader to argue that class struggle continues under socialism and that such struggle must go on within the the communist party and against the bourgeoisie inside that party. Mao warned that without successful struggle against the bourgeoisie in the party, there would be a restoration of capitalism done in the name of socialism at first – as in fact happened in the Soviet Union and China. Since much of Mao's writing merely continues previous Marxism-Leninism or because many of the new parts of Marxism-Leninism contributed by Mao are now widely accepted, it is Mao's doctrine on the bourgeoisie in the party above all which continues to separate Maoism from other varieties of supposed communism to this day.

In a historical sense, Maoism as a doctrine liberated China, influenced all the subsequent anti-colonial struggles in Africa and Asia and inspired many other revolutionary movements including ones inside the United $tates. (Source: *Fundamental Political Line of the Maoist Internationalist Ministry of Prisons* by MIM(Prisons), Section 2)

Marxism: an integrated body of revolutionary science based on an objective understanding of the laws of capitalist social relations, the application of a materialist world view towards history and social development and the perspective of the modern proletariat. Marxism is not a defined, ahistoric world-view or ideology, but a living, radical field of scientific inquiry into social change, oppression and struggle. (Source: Revolutionary Anti-Imperialist Movement Glossary)

mass organization: A group of people without a specifically worked out universal ideology (such as Maoism) leading it. Membership requirements are less strict than for a cadre organization, as a mass organization's aim is to unite as many people as possible, often around a single issue.

materialism: The doctrine that matter is the basis of reality. A method of philosophic inquiry which sees material and social circumstance as paramount in shaping individual and social consciousness. Materialism developed in opposition to philosophical Idealism, which saw consciousness and ideas as the force giving order to the physical world. Materialist philosophy tends to look at how the social relations of production in a society give shape and form to the society and its members, i.e. how production and economic activity tend to determine laws, values, ideology, forms of government, etc. (Source: Revolutionary Anti-Imperialist Movement Glossary) See also: idealism

McCarthyism: The practice of making accusations of subversion or treason without proper regard for evidence. It also means "the practice of making unfair allegations or using unfair investigative techniques, especially in order to restrict dissent or political criticism." (Dictionary.com) The term has its origins in the period in the United States known as the Second Red Scare, lasting roughly from 1950 to 1956 and characterized by heightened political repression against communists, as well as a campaign spreading fear of their influence on American institutions and of espionage by Soviet agents. Originally coined to criticize the anti-communist pursuits of Republican U.S. Senator Joseph McCarthy of Wisconsin, "McCarthyism" soon took on a broader meaning, describing the excesses of similar efforts. The term is also now used more generally to describe reckless, unsubstantiated accusations, as well as demagogic attacks on the character or patriotism of political adversaries. (Wikipedia: McCarthyism)

means of production: The tools humyns use to transform nature to meet their needs. (Source: *Fundamentals of Political Economy* by Shanghai Press, p. 5)

metaphysics: That which exists outside of reality and cannot be perceived by the five senses. This concept states that ideas are the only true and permanent reality and so knowledge derived from acceptance of pre-existing ideas is the only genuine and valid wisdom, ie. religion, which is based on belief in Divine Word. (Source: Black Liberation Army Political Dictionary) See also: idealism

militant: Aggressively active in the service of a cause. (Source: *Labor Aristocracy, Mass Base of Social Democracy* by H.W. Edwards, Chapter XXI)

militarism: The development and process of increasing military aggression as part of capitalist oppression. An economic system that centers around development of a country's military forces. It includes war-mongering or the advocacy of war or actual carrying out of war or its preparations. Militarism is inherent to imperialism because of 1) the need to use force to exploit other nations' labor and natural resources; 2) war is a solution to imperialism's perennial crisis of overproduction; 3) it falsely increases demand, thereby circulating capital that has become over-concentrated in the imperialist core. Oppressed nations can engage in militarism in a flawed effort to advance their economic systems as well.

mode of production: Unity of the productive forces and the relations of production; an economic system such as feudalism, capitalism or socialism. See also: productive forces, production relations

monopoly: complete control of the supply of goods or services in a specific market. This results in a market in which there is only one seller of a commodity from which others can buy goods/services.

nation: "A nation is a historically evolved, stable community of language, territory, economic life, and psychological make up manifested in a community of culture."
Nation is the predominant form of organization of humyn beings in the era of imperialism. As national markets and borders became important to the economic destiny of a region, the nation-states of Europe took form first. For the exploited, the national project is taken up in resistance to imperialism because it hinders their economic development. (Source: "Marxism and the National Question" by J.V. Stalin)

national liberation: The intellectual, political, social and military movement of oppressed nations to gain autonomy from their oppressors. (Source: Revolutionary Anti-Imperialist Movement Glossary)

national minority: A group of people from a nation residing in the territory of another nation. For instance Filipinos living within U.$. borders are still a part of the Filipino nation as a whole and have not developed into a distinct nation separate from the Philippines. As a result they are part of the Filipino national liberation struggle. This is in contrast with New Afrikans in the U.$. who have formed a distinct nation, no longer a part of the nations from which they came. (Source: "Marxism and the National Question" by J.V. Stalin)

national oppression: The exercise of power by one national group over another. The contradiction that defines the economic system of imperialism is that between the oppressor nations and the oppressed nations. This oppression comes about primarily as a means of one nation to exploit value from another.

nationalism: An ideology based around the identity of a nation. The character of this ideology will depend on the position of that nation in the global economic system and the political development of the people of that nation. Nationalism has been part of both the most oppressive and most liberatory social movements in the era of imperialism. See also: cultural nationalism, nation, revolutionary nationalism

neo-colonialism: A covert form of colonialism, in which the colonizing countries transfer wealth from the colonized countries without explicitly taking over political control of the subjugated nations. (Source: *MIM Notes 115*, p. 4) See also: colonialism

neo-Trotskyism: Trotskyists with at least a little connection to reality begin to realize that effective reformists accomplish reforms; effective bourgeois politicians get elected and Maoists carry out People's Wars and seize power. However, Trotskyists have done none of these things in the last 75 years on a global scale, so inevitably there is pressure on them to take up reformist theses or to abandon select Trotskyist tenets. That's not to mention the intense competition amongst their organizations all vying for basically the same social material. When it comes to the on-the-street activist in Amerika, you will find his/her heart in neo-Trotskyism. It's a situation found only in the imperialist countries, where the petty-bourgeoisie pines for a "perfect" socialism or none at all (which in practice means none at all), and thus declaims Stalin as much or more than Bush. (Source: "What's your line?" by MIM) See also: Trotskyists

New Afrikan: Our Afrikan ancestors landed on these shores as Ashanti, Ibo, Fula, Moors, etc. We didn't have a collective identity, language, culture, tradition, etc. But thru our collective oppression and our collective resistance to that oppression, we developed a collective language, culture, and so on in the southern part of what is now known as the U$A. We developed into a "new" Afrikan people, a people who are separate and distinct from all other people on planet Earth. Thus, we claim the national identity of New Afrikan and claim as our national territory the states Louisiana, Mississippi, Alabama, Georgia and South Carolina. Our national territory has been named the Republic of New Afrika.

We uphold the usage of New Afrikan as opposed to "Black" and "African-American." "Black" implies the fictitious categorization of "race." African-American implies that we have fully integrated into this country as full citizens. (Source: "On the Term New Afrikan" by Royal Council of the Black Order Revolutionary Organization) See also: nation

New Democracy: A post-revolutionary government which is led by the proletariat and unites the popular classes of oppressed and exploited nations with the aim of achieving national unity and autonomy against imperialist exploitation and building the prerequisites for socialism and communism.

Land is central to the New Democractic phase. In semi-feudal societies, the popular classes along with the national bourgeoisie destroy the feudal powers and redistribute land more democratically, unleashing the productive forces of the nation. In all cases, the oppressed nation establishes the integrity of its territory free of imperialist occupation during the New Democratic phase.

Mao Zedong distinguished New Democracy from the old bourgeois democratic revolutions that overthrew feudal systems in parts of Europe. In a world dominated by imperialism the bourgeoisie is no longer a progressive force that can lead a successful revolutionary transformation of the economic substructure of society. That is why New Democracy requires proletarian leadership in a united front with all anti-imperialist classes, including the national bourgeoisie. (Source: Revolutionary Anti-Imperialist Movement Glossary)

opportunism: in the process of political struggle we find unprincipled people sometimes taking up the cause of communism. In general this is the policy and practice of subordinating the real interests of the proletarian revolutionary movement to that of one's sect or oneself.

"Right opportunism" underestimates what the revolutionaries can accomplish, while "ultraleft opportunism" or "left opportunism," overestimates what can be accomplished in the given conditions. On the basis of both "right opportunism" or "left opportunism" it is possible to attack the correct road, the political path that yields the fastest way out of oppression and exploitation.

oppressed nation: Imperialism is defined by the principal contradiction between oppressed nations and oppressor nations. The oppressed nations are those whose destinies are determined by the oppressor nations, and suffer under their domination. The oppressed nations are the world's majority, roughly equivalent to the countries making up the Third World, but also including internal colonies. See also: internal colony, oppressor nation

oppression: The exercise of power by one group over another. (Source: *MIM Theory 2/3: Gender and Revolutionary Feminism* by MIM, p. 50)

oppressor nation: Imperialism is defined by the principal contradiction between oppressed nations and oppressor nations. The oppressor nations are those who control and oppress other nations for their own benefit. Oppressor nations are the dominant imperialist nations, such as Amerika, Britain, Japan, Australia, France, Germany, etc. They are the minority of the world's people. See also: oppressed nation, principal contradiction

parasitism: Living off of the products and work of others. (Source: *Fundamentals of Political Economy* by Shanghai Press, Chapter 11)

patriarchy: The manifestation and institutionalization of male dominance over wimmin and children in the family and the extension of male dominance over wimmin in society in general; it implies that men hold power in all the important institutions of society and that wimmin are deprived of access to such power (Source: *The Creation of Patriarchy* by Gerda Lerner, Appendix, p. 239) See also: gender

peasantry: The class of people who labor on the land and possess their means of production: tools and the land itself. A defining characteristic of the peasantry is that it must pay rent or a tribute to maintain its possession of the land. Members of this class are peasants. (*A Dictionary of Marxist Thought* by Tom Bottomore) See also: feudalism

petty bourgeoisie (petit-bourgeoisie): Generally the petty bourgeoisie is the group between the bourgeoisie and the working class, sometimes called the "middle class." They are economically self-supporting or even earning more than they consume for their own support. This class includes those who own their own means of production and work for themselves. They cannot generate sufficient surplus value from exploitation of others to live without working themselves, so they are not primarily exploiters, unlike the bourgeoisie. Two sub-groups:

    1. Owners of Capital (small businesses, real estate, stocks, etc.): Owns their own business or has means to, or has ability to get loan to start a small business. The pure petty bourgeois class is separated from the labor aristocracy by their ownership of wealth.

    2. Labor Aristocracy: Unlike the traditional petty bourgeoisie, they do not own their own means of production and so must work for others. But unlike the proletariat and semi-proletariat the labor aristocracy in the First World earn more than the value of their labor and therefore have interests that fall in the bourgeois camp allying with imperialism. (Source: *MIM Theory 1: A White Proletariat?* by MIM, p. 5) See also: labor aristocracy

phenomenon: Any observable fact or event; includes matter and ideas. Every phenomenon is a product of a subject (observing) and an object (appearing). (plural is phenomena) (Source: *The Nature of Brain Work* by Joseph Dietzgen, p. 21)

philosophy: World outlook; how one perceives, understands and interprets life in general. Method of understanding the world history, contradictions and the development of things. (Source: Black Liberation Army Political Dictionary)

pig: One who oppresses the people in the name of the state; "an ill-natured beast who has no respect for law and order." (Source: *The Black Panther* newspaper by the Black Panther Party for Self-Defense)

political error: All Maoists make errors. Those who think they do not are probably not doing anything and counting that as not making an error. Another common cause of believing one makes no errors is Christianity or other forms of metaphysics. Those who take action realize that they are going to make errors. Our best leaders simply make the fewest. (MIM FAQ) See also: opportunism, revisionism

post-modernism: A trend in academia and teaching which says there is no truth and everything is relative. Post-modernism opposes a scientific approach to humyn society.

power: In the context of liberation struggles this term means the ability of people to define a phenomenon and make it act in a desired manner. (Source: Interview with Huey Newton 1968) See also: self-determination

pragmatism: The philosophy of being practical without regard for larger issues. Pragmatism calls on its participants to grope through experience for the correct course of action. Sometimes appears as not "thinking outside the box" because one ignores greater principles and scientific knowledge. Can also be seen as the error that is opposite of idealism, which puts political ideals in place of real world conditions and possibilities. (Source: *MIM Theory 10: Labor Aristocracy* by MIM, p. 70) See also: idealism

pre-Columbian: The pre-Columbian era incorporates all period subdivisions in the history and prehistory of the Americas before the appearance of significant European influences on the American continents, spanning the time of the original settlement in the Upper Paleolithic period to European colonization during the Early Modern period. While the phrase "pre-Columbian era" literally refers only to the time preceding Christopher Columbus's voyages of 1492, in practice the phrase usually is used to denote the entire history of First Nation cultures until those cultures were significantly influenced by Europeans, even if this happened decades or centuries after Columbus's first landing. (Wikipedia: Pre-Columbian era)

primitive accumulation: The process by which large swathes of people are violently disposed of their traditional means of production in service to capital. It is generally assumed that the origins of capitalism lie in England and were brought about through the violent concentration of capital through domestic policies of dispossession and concentration of land (which also had the effect of creating from the peasantry a domestic class of "free" laborers dependent on working for a wage) and returns on slave trade (which had the effect of creating import markets of raw materials and export markets for finished goods). This initial concentration of land and wealth was invested into factories and new technologies, increasing the productivity and hence profitability of the latter mode of production. Today, primitive accumulation still occurs, whereas people are physically or socially dispossessed to make way for the further expansion of monopoly capital. (Source: Revolutionary Anti-Imperialist Movement Glossary)

principal contradiction: The highest priority contradiction that communists must focus their energy on for a long period of time – a strategic period. The concept of the principal contradiction comes from dialectical materialism, which says that everything can be divided into two opposing forces. These contradictions are the basis for any changes that thing goes through. Every phenomenon or problem has a principal contradiction within it. Defining the principal contradiction in humyn society is a crucial step in transforming it.

The principal contradiction in the world today is between the imperialist countries and the countries they oppress and exploit. Based on this fact, we say the principal task is to build public opinion against imperialism and to build institutions of the oppressed that are independent of imperialism, in order to seize power from the imperialists. See also: dialectics

production relations: Mutual relationships formed in the process of providing food, clothes, and shelter for ourselves as a species. In class society, these relationships are ultimately reflected in class relationships. (Source: *Fundamentals of Political Economy* by Shanghai Press, p. 4)

productive forces: The power which humyns use to transform nature for their use, includes tools (means of production) and humyns. (Source: *Fundamentals of Political Economy* by Shanghai Press, p. 5)

proletarian feminism: Feminism which gives preference for the revolutionary struggle of the oppressed and exploited masses as the means of abolishing patriarchy. (Source: Revolutionary Anti-Imperialist Movement Glossary) See also: feminism

proletarian internationalism: Today, there are two kinds of internationalism, bourgeois internationalism and proletarian internationalism. In the proletarian internationalist view, exploitation inevitably leads to violent conflict, so peace amongst nations depends on a global view not defending private property.

"There is one, and only one, kind of real internationalism, and that is – working whole-heartedly for the development of the revolutionary movement and the revolutionary struggle in one's own country, and supporting (by propaganda, sympathy, and material aid) this struggle, this, and only this, line, in every country without exception." - V.I. Lenin, about World War I in "The Tasks of the Proletariat in Our Revolution" (Source: MIM FAQ: What is Internationalism?) See also: internationalism

proletarian morality: What the proletariat determines to be right and wrong, good and bad. A thing is good or bad depending on whether it serves humyn need. In class society, different classes often have opposing interests, therefore what is right to one class is wrong to another. Pacifists apply an idealist form of morality by saying that violence is never justified. Similarly, anarchists denounce hierarchy and oppression in the hands of the oppressed, even if used as tools to destroy hierarchy and oppression in the bigger picture. Proletarian leadership must abide by proletarian morality in order to maintain the active support of those they are leading to action. See also: proletariat

proletariat: The group of people who have nothing to sell but their labor power for their subsistence. The proletariat does not draw any profit from any kind of capital because they have none. There are several groups that fall within the proletariat:

1. The working proletariat are exploited by others who make a profit off of their labor.

2. The non-working proletariat make up the reserve army of the proletariat. In current times this group is usually temporarily unemployed and seeking employment. The long-term unemployed usually fall into the lumpen-proletariat.

3. The lumpen-proletariat, a group of people who are unable to sell their labor power in the long term and so end up living as parasites on other proletarians. This group is found in the Third World, and is distinct from the First World lumpen.

Proletarians are propertyless and thus have "nothing to lose but their chains." The proletariat is the least conservative element of society. (Source: *MIM Theory 1: A White Proletariat?* by MIM, p. 5) See also: lumpen-proletariat

pseudo-feminism: An ideology that promotes the interests of biological wimmin of the First World while claiming to represent the interests of the gender oppressed. The ideology of the gender aristocracy, which shares in male privilege rather than challenging it. See also: gender aristocracy, feminism

racism: MIM observes scientifically that race does not exist and that what really happens in the United States is national oppression, not racial oppression. "Racism" does exist as an element of the superstructure of society, that is to say the ideas and culture, but "racism" is a product of national oppression, including the exploitation and enslavement of various nations by others. Racism can only be disguised, never eliminated, by propagating politically correct attitudes, because racism is just a justification for exploitation and enslavement. To rid the world of this exploitation and enslavement, and hence racism, requires armed struggle against the imperialists.

For more on racism's inherent presence in capitalism, see *Labor Aristocracy: Mass Base for Social Democracy* by H.W. Edwards. (Source: *MIM Theory 1: A White Proletariat?* by MIM, Appendix 3)

rate of profit: s/(c+v), which stands for surplus value divided by the sum of constant capital plus variable capital (labor) involved in production of a commodity. The capitalist uses rate of profit instead of rate of surplus value to conceal the fact that all value comes from the worker. However, rate of profit is also relevant to the capitalist in that his return on capital investment declines as the rate of profit declines due to the development of the mode of production under capitalism. The rate of profit declines, even if the rate of surplus value increases as production becomes more capital intensive with advanced technology. (Source: *Fundamentals of Political Economy* by Shanghai Press, Chapter 7)

Raza: The Spanish word for race, or people; *Raza* (or *la Raza)* is used as a catch-all term to describe the people of so-called "Latin America."

reactionary: Characterized by tendencies toward backward and repressive status-quo. Those forces which oppose revolutionary change and actively work to prevent or destroy any progressive movement, country, etc. (Source: Black Liberation Army Political Dictionary)

reformism: Working within the current system to make changes without fundamentally changing the current system through revolution.

relative surplus population: Unique to capitalism, there is always a portion of the population excluded from production as a result of capital accumulation. (Source: *Fundamentals of Political Economy* by Shanghai Press, Chapter 5)

revisionism: Revisionism refers to political views that claim to be Marxist yet revise Marx's work fundamentally by failing to apply the scientific method of dialectical materialism. Revisionists commonly downplay class struggle, overplay the struggle to increase production and technical progress compared with political matters, don't believe imperialism is dangerous, advocate reformist means of change and don't uphold the dictatorship of the proletariat. Revisionism is bourgeois ideology, enemy politics. (Source: *Fundamental Political Line of the Maoist Internationalist Ministry of Prisons* by MIM(Prisons), Section 2) See also: opportunism, political error

revolution: A complete and radical change from one social system into another. The violent and complete struggle waged by the people to rid themselves of an oppressive system of government into a more progressive and humane society. This includes not only the political structure, but also the philosophy and ideology, mode of production, and relations of production as well as the social mentality and outlook of society. (Source: Black Liberation Army Political Dictioanry)

revolutionary nationalism: an ideology that sees the solution to the plight of the oppressed nation in liberating itself from the global imperialist system to attain self-determination. Revolutionary nationalists see the struggle of the nation as primary; they may or may not be communists. See also: cultural nationalism, integrationism

right wing of white nationalism: The right wing of white nationalism prioritizes the preservation of Western culture and white racial purity. They are unwilling to integrate other nationalities into the imperialist countries, even to preserve the system that they benefit from. (Source: "The real lessons of the Chicano Moratorium and the high treason against Maoism" by MIM) See also: left wing of white nationalism, white nationalism

sectarianism: The tendency to place the interest of one's particular organization above that of the revolutionary struggle.

self-determination: In reference to oppressed nations and people, the principle of or ability to choose the course of future development free of reactionary, outside interference. (Source: Revolutionary Anti-Imperialist Movement Glossary)

semi-colony: An oppressed nation that is colonized by an oppressor nation, but does not exhibit all of the characteristics of a traditional colony. Within the United $tates we speak of the internal semi-colonies of New Afrika, Boricua, Aztlán and various First Nations. As imperialism has advanced, the Amerikans no longer depend on these nations as sources of new wealth as they do the Third World nations that we would call colonies, or, most likely, neo-colonies. See also: colonialism, internal colony, neo-colonialism

semi-proletariat: Portions of the semi-proletariat are similar to the petty-bourgeoisie in that both groups are gaining material benefit from ownership of some capital. These semi-proletarians are distinguished from the petty-bourgeoisie in that they work for themselves, but earn income similar to exploited workers. In the Third World this includes semi-owner peasants, street vendors, and small handicrafts workers. In the First World we see those self-employed in small businesses in the ghetto, barrio or reservation (i.e. cutting hair in their home).

The semi-proletariat also includes portions of the proletariat who must sell their labor to survive but work outside of the productive sector. These workers are exploited by others, unable to earn the value of their labor. These non-productive workers mostly exist in the Third World as shop assistants, poor peasants on semi-feudal farms, technicians, and civil servants. The non-productive sector in the First World is dominated by petty-bourgeois labor aristocrats, so to distinguish between these two groups we draw the line at the international average value of labor.

Full time minimum wage workers in the United $tates today are above this level and so not part of the semi-proletariat. The international average value of labor has been conservatively estimated around $5 per hour in 2014. Those only earning enough to average $5/hour or less in a 40 hour work week, outside of the industrial proletariat, would be representative of those who do not own their own capital, do not work in production, and so would be included in the semi-proletariat. See also: proletariat

settler: Foreign invader who establishes permanent residence in an occupied land.

socialism: When Maoists use the term socialism we are referring to the transition stage between the capitalist mode of production and communism. This involves organizing society with the goal of meeting people's needs, not making profit. History shows that a dictatorship of the proletariat (the people instead of the capitalists) is necessary to make socialism work and maintain democracy in a socialist society. (Source: *Fundamental Political Line of the Maoist Internationalist Ministry of Prisons* by MIM(Prisons), Section 2) see also: dictatorship of the proletariat

state: Social institution through which a class or classes legitimize and maintain their rule over others. From Engels: "The state is, therefore, by no means a power forced on society from without; just as little is it 'the reality of the ethical idea', 'the image and reality of reason', as Hegel maintains. Rather, it is a product of society at a certain stage of development; it is the admission that this society has become entangled in an insoluble contradiction with itself, that it has split into irreconcilable antagonisms which it is powerless to dispel. But in order that these antagonisms, these classes with conflicting economic interests, might not consume themselves and society in fruitless struggle, it became necessary to have a power, seemingly standing above society, that would alleviate the conflict and keep it within the bounds of 'order'; and this power, arisen out of society but placing itself above it, and alienating itself more and more from it, is the state." (Source: *The Origin of Family, Private Property and the State,* Sixth Edition by Frederick Engels, p. 177-178; *The State and Revolution* by Lenin, V.I.)

strategy: Long-term plans to achieve various goals on the way to communism. For every stage in the revolutionary struggle, there is a strategy. (Source: *MIM Theory 5: Diet For a Small Red Planet* by MIM, p. 50) See also: line, tactics

subjectivism: The belief that what one feels or likes is true or supreme. (Source: "Combating subjectivism in all arenas, from cigarettes & drugs to sectarianism and white chauvinism" by MIM)

superexploitation: A worker who receives wages less than the value of her/his labor power is superexploited. This means the worker is paid less than what is necessary for subsistence. (Source: *MIM Theory 1: A White Proletariat?* by MIM, p. 5) See also: labor power

superprofits: These are profits derived from workers paid less than what is necessary for their subsistence – workers that are superexploited. (Source: *MIM Theory 1: A White Proletariat?* by MIM, p. 5) See also: exploitation, superexploitation

superstructure: Includes national government, army, law, and other political systems and their corresponding ideological forms, such as philosophy, literature, and fine arts. (Source: *Fundamentals of Political Economy* by Shanghai Press, p. 8)

surplus value: The difference between the value of work done and the wages paid for that work; this is the original source of all profits. Note that only productive labor produces value/surplus value.

tactics: Short-term plans, some of which may be used again and again in slightly different circumstances. Tactics are short term and flexible based on day-to-day changes in the situation. (Source: *MIM Theory 5: Diet For a Small Red Planet* by MIM, p. 50) See also: line, strategy

terrorism: The use of violence or threats of harm against a civilian population for social, political or economic ends.

theory: A scientific idea that uses many observations and has much experimental evidence; can be applied to unrelated facts and new relationships; flexible enough to be modified if new data/evidence is introduced. See also: law (scientific), hypothesis

Third World: The portion of the geographic-social world subjected to imperialist exploitation by the First World. (Source: Revolutionary Anti-Imperialist Movement Glossary)

Trotskyists: Supporters of Leon Trotsky, the Russian Menshevik leader who opposed V.I. Lenin until the Soviet victory in 1917. Trotsky broke with Stalin over the feasibility of socialism in one country which Trotsky said was impossible. Orthodox Trots believe that the working classes of the advanced capitalist countries are the best vehicle for worldwide revolution and downplay the anti-feudal and anti-imperialist struggles of the oppressed nations. (Source: *On Trotskyism: Problems of theory and history* by Kostas Mavrakis; "What's Your Line?" by MIM)

ultra-leftism: Ultra-leftists will tend to judge real-world revolutionaries in the light of principles that only Jesus/Moses/Muhammad-type figures could implement. Ultra-leftism thus smacks of religion/idealism. The ultra-left also tends to go to unsustainable extremes to achieve their objectives. Note: rightism and ultra-leftism are both errors WITHIN the revolutionary movement. We are not talking about the "right" and "left" wings of the Amerikan government commonly referred to in the bourgeois press. (Source: *Fundamental Political Line of the Maoist Internationalist Ministry of Prisons* by MIM(Prisons), p. 45)

underdeveloped: Modern underdevelopment expresses a particular relationship of exploitation: namely, the exploitation of one country by another. All of the countries named as 'underdeveloped' in the world are exploited by others; and the underdevelopment with which the world is now pre-occupied is a product of capitalist, imperialist and colonialist exploitation. African and Asian societies were developing independently until they were taken over directly or indirectly by the capitalist powers. When that happened, exploitation increased and the export of surplus ensued, depriving the societies of the benefit of their natural resources and labour.

... For economic development it is not enough to produce more goods and services. The country has to produce more of those goods and services which in turn will give rise spontaneously to future growth in the economy. For example, the food-producing sector must be flourishing so that workers would be healthy, and agriculture on the whole must be efficient so that the profits (or savings) from agriculture would stimulate industry. Heavy industry, such as the steel industry and the production of electrical power, must be present so that one is capable of making machinery for other types of industry and for agriculture. Lack of heavy industry, inadequate production of food, unscientific agriculture – those are all characteristics of the underdeveloped economies.

It is typical of underdeveloped economies that they do not (or are not allowed to) concentrate on those sectors of the economy which in turn will generate growth and raise production to a new level altogether, and there are very few ties between one sector and another so that (say) agriculture and industry could react beneficially on each other.

Furthermore, whatever savings are made within the economy are mainly sent abroad or are frittered away in consumption rather than being redirected to productive purposes. Much of the national income which remains within the country goes to pay individuals who are not directly involved in producing wealth but only in rendering auxiliary services – civil servants, merchants, soldiers, entertainers, etc. (Source: *How Europe Underdeveloped Africa* by Walter Rodney)

united front: The strategy of uniting various organizations and individuals for cooperation towards a common goal, while maintaining the independence of initiative of each organization within the united front.

Historically the most important application of this strategy has referred to uniting the popular classes for the struggle against imperialism. As Mao wrote about the united front in the war against Japan: "To sustain a long war by long-term co-operation or, in other words, to subordinate the class struggle to the present national struggle against Japan – such is the fundamental principle of the united front. Subject to this principle, the independent character of the parties and classes and their independence and initiative within the united front should be preserved, and their essential rights should not be sacrificed to co-operation and unity, but on the contrary must be firmly upheld within certain limits." (Source: "The Question of Independence and Initiative Within the United Front" by Mao Zedong)

unity-criticism-unity: A process implemented by revolutionary organizations to strengthen organizational unity and individual and group practice. Members of a group united on a set of principles and objectives struggle internally behind closed doors among themselves by working (practice) together, observing and analyzing each others' errors and then offering constructive criticism to each other to correct errors and overcome any shortcomings in order to strengthen each other and thus advance the group towards its stated objectives.

This is a process of transforming old unities to new ones, in a continuous cycle. This is principled unity and struggle of theory and practice, which any organized body must engage in if it wishes to succeed in accomplishing its stated objectives.

vanguard: The party (group or individual) with the most advanced political line.

white nationalism: An ideology that serves the interests of the white nation to the exclusion of the world's majority, marked principally by a belief that whites or Amerikans deserve more wealth and resources than other peoples. White nationalism is also defined by the denial of the existence of internal semi-colonies in settler states.See also: left wing of white nationalism, right wing of white nationalism

womyn (wimmin): Alternate spelling of woman (women) removing the word "man" ("men") to oppose seeing wimmin as derived from men. Specifies wimmin as a social group/gender, not as a biologically determined group. See also: gender

Index

for	ATM	*see*	August 29th Movement
	BB-PC		Brown Berets - Prison Chapter
	BC		Barrio Committee
	CASA		El Centro de Acción Social Autonoma
	CIA		Central Intelligence Agency
	COINTELPRO		Counter Intelligence Program
	Comintern		Communist International
	El Comité		El Comité Estudiantil del Pueblo
	FBI		Federal Bureau of Investigation
	GPCR		Great Proletarian Cultural Revolution
	ICE		Immigration and Customs Enforcement
	ILPS		International League of Peoples' Struggles
	INS		Immigration and Naturalization Services
	LO		lumpen organization
	LULAC		League of United Latin American Citizens
	MASA		Mexican American Student Association
	MAYO		Mexican American Youth Organization
	MEChA		El Movimiento Estudiantil Chicano de Aztlán
	MIM(Prisons)		Maoist Internationalist Ministry of Prisons
	MLM		Marxism-Leninism-Maoism
	NAFTA		North American Free Trade Agreement
	NAMP		New Afrikan Maoist Party
	PLP		Progressive Labor Party
	rcp=u$a		Revolutionary Communist Party, U$A
	RUP		Raza Unida Party
	SB1070		Senate Bill 1070
	SNCC		Student Nonviolent Coordinating Committee
	UCLA		University of California Los Angeles
	UFW		United Farm Workers
	UFPP		United Front for Peace in Prisons
	UMAS		United Mexican American Students
	USSR		Soviet Union
	YCCA		Young Citizens for Community Action
	YLP		Young Lords Party

Acevedo, Joe 169
African-American 156, 166, 304
Agreement to End Hostilities 8, **233**
Alabama 73, 304
The Alamo **30**, 181
Alianza Federal de Mercedes **49**, 181
Alta California 29
Alurista (poet) 57

Anasazi 93-94
Argentina 96, 118-120
Arizona 21, 29, 31, 39, 57, 73, 114-115,
   169-172, 177-178, 180, 219
Arpaio, Joe 171
August 29th Movement 48-49, 131, 193, 281
Austin, Stephen 30, 181
Aztec 22, 32, 57, 71-72, 83-84, 94

Aztlán as myth 156

Barela, Francisco 31

Barrio Committee **87-92**, 102

Belize 120

Black Berets 181

Black Panther Party for Self-Defense 45, 50, 53-54, 102, 135-136, 195, 197-198, 209, 251-252, 256, 273-274, 294-295, 305

Bolivia 61, 120

Boriqua (Boricua) 62, 73, 81, 110, 113-118, 129, 224, **291**, 309

Bracero Program **42-44**, 66

Brazil 120

Brown Berets 47, **50**, 102, 181, 191, 193, 222

Brown Berets – Prison Chapter 6, 191, **221-222**

California 8-9, 23, 29, 31-34, 46-47, 57, 100, 104, 114-115, 118, 168, 177, 188, 209, 212, 219, 221, 233
  Anaheim 168-169
  Los Angeles 46-47, 53-54, 118, 132, 140, 205, 207, 210
  Santa Barbara 47

Camino Real 23-24

capitalist crisis 11, 43, 77, 140, 255-256, 302-303

Castro, Julian 47, 150-153

La Causa 50

cell structure 87-92, 201, 229-230, **262-267**

Central America 11, 14, 22, 57, 75, 113-124, 144, 293

Centro de Acción Social Autonoma **53-55**, 209

Central Intelligence Agency 151

Chican@ nation
  language 11, 15, **58**, 99-100, 121-123, 126, 159, 162, 177, 217, 284
  population growth 113, 160

Chicanismo 8, 12, 17, 48, **98**, 211-213

Chicano Moratorium 131-141, 143

Chican@ Student Movement 47-48, 136, 188, 193, 281

Chicano Youth Liberation Conference 51, 57, 156

Chile 22, 118-120

China 38, 45, 53, 68, 78, 100, 102, 125-126, 148, 154, 158, 164-165, 191, 197, 208, 218, 231, 270, 272, 281, 283, 290, 295, 301-302

Chinese Revolution 78, 200, 268

Cleaver, Eldridge 195, 273

Clinton, Bill 146

Cold War 44

Colombia 109, 120

Colorado 29, 31, 39, 46, 51, 57, 114-115, 219
  Denver 51-52, 198
  Ludlow 39

Colorado Fuel and Iron Company 39

Comité Estudiantil del Pueblo **48-49**, 193

communalism 80, 172, 217, **294**

Communist International 14, 43, 253, 257, **294**

Communist Manifesto 77, 245

Cortez, Gregorio 31, 34

Cortina, Juan "Cheno" 31, 34

Costa Rica 120

Counter Intelligence Program 55, 88, 151, 153, **293**

Crockett, Davy 30

Crusade for Justice **50-52**, 150, 181

Cuauhtemoc 71-72

Cuba 45, 53, 60, 68, 82, **113-115**, 119, 218

democratic centralism **88**, 223, 263-264, 291, **295**

Diaz, Manuel 168-169

East Los Angeles 13 - 47

Ecuador 118-120

Egypt 77, 158

El Salvador 113, 118, 120, 124

Engels, Frederich 14, 77, 191, 198, 231, 258, 295, 309

ethnic studies 13, 188, 203, 211-212

farm workers 259-261

fascism 43, 138, 140, 232, **257-258**, 289, 294, 296

Federal Bureau of Investigation 45, 47, 51, 139, 293-294

feminism 17-18, 53, 98, 202-213, **297**, 307
  First World pseudo-feminism 203, 206, 297, 307
  proletarian feminism 17, 307
  reproductive rights 53, 208-209

First Nations 14, 32, 40, 51, 65, 73, 79-81, **93-94**, 110, **119-120**, 129, 143, 157, 161-164, 215, 219, 274, 297, 299, 306, 309

First World 13, **62-64**, 90, 196, 204, 206, 217, 231, 239-242, 245-246, 249, 253-256, 258, 262-263, 289, 291, 293, 297-300, 305, 307, 309-310

Flores Magón, Enrique 34

Flores Magón, Ricardo 34

Foreign Miners Tax 33

El Gallo: a Voz de la Justicia 50

Gang of Four 231, 290

gangs (see also pandillas) 64, 99-101, 105, 174, 233

Garza, Catarino 34

gender aristocracy 202, **297-298**, 307

El Grito del Norte 50

Gonzalez, Rodolfo "Corky" 50, 52

Las Gorras Blancas 31, 34, 187, 281

Great Depression 39, 43

Great Proletarian Cultural Revolution 78, 197, 231

Guatemala 71, 118, 120, 124

Guyana 120

Hernandez, Sergio 67

Hijas de Anahuac 35

Hispanic 12, 113-121, 145, 152, 171, 214, 218, 285

Ho Chi Minh 200

Honduras 120, 124

Hoover, J. Edgar 45, 47

Huerta, Dolores 96

Illegal Immigration Reform and Immigrant Responsibility Act 138, 146

Immigration and Customs Enforcement 20, 44, 66, 69, 73, 86, 177

Immigration and Naturalization Services 44

International League of Peoples' Struggles 138-140

internationalism 17, 37, 40, 48, 68, 84-85, 131, 133, 136, 164-165, 224, 236, 291, 294, **299**, **307**

La Junta 50

Kansas 57

King, Martin Luther 136, 138, 151, 189

Knights of Labor 281

Korea 45, 60, 68, 245

labor aristocracy 14, 43, 63-64, 82, 128, 141, 144, 184, 195, 198, 231-232, 240-241, **243-249**, 253-254, 258, 277, 287, 294, **299**, 305, 309

Latin America **15-17**, 45, 61, 68-69, 128, 195, 200, 282, 286, 288, 308

Latino 12, **16**, 42, 60, 79, 95, 116-123, 132, 135, 145, 160, 166-167, 171, 192, 205, 214, 218, 223-224

League of United Latin American Citizens **42**, 44, 74, 187, 214

Lenin, V.I. 14, 37, 48, 53, 64, 68, 77, 80, 130, 136, 155, **165-166**, 183, 191, 195, 198-200, 219, 231-232, 241, 251, 258, 281, **298-301**, 307, 309-310

Liberalism 13, 149, 264, 300-301

Los Angeles County General Hospital 53

Los Angeles Times 39, 47

Ludlow Massacre 39

lumpen 10-11, 14, 17-18, 20, 54, 61, 64, 70, 89-92, **99-106**, 110, 136, 144. 169, 206-207, 218, 229, 287, 289, **297**, 307
   First World lumpen 64, 242, **255-256**, 297, 307
   lumpen organization 53, 89, 92, 99-103
   lumpen-proletariat 184, 241-242, 296-297, **301**, 307

lynching 25, 33, 35, 49, 67, 83, 187

machismo 11, 209

Magonistas 183

Malcolm X 132, 151

La Mano Negra 34, 187

Mao Zedong 21, 38, 45, 48, 53, 72, 78-79, 85-86, 100, 102, 104, 131, 136, 154-156, 164-165, 173, 191-192, 196, 199-201, 219, 223, 231-232, 270, 279, 281-282, 290, 292, 294, **301**, 304, 311

Maoist Internationalist Movement 14, 81, 88-90, 109, 131, 133, 135-136, 143, 145, 197-198, 202, 208, 230-232, 243, 245-247, 249-250, 253-254, 256, 258-259, 262-263, 268-269, 273-274, 277-278, 281, 286, **290**

Maoist Internationalist Ministry of Prisons 6-7, 9, 88, 90, 109, 143, 201, **226-232**, 237, 250, 253, 255-258, 260, 262-264, 267, 286, 294-295

Martin, Trayvon 15

Martinez, Elizabeth "Betita" 50, 52, 96

Marx, Karl 20, 48, 53, 74, 77, 106, 136, 183, 191, 219, 231, 242-245, 249, 255, 257-258, 294-295, 301, 308

Marxism 16, 37, 53, 72, 80, 98, 155, 158, 162, 173, 191-192, 194-195, 199, 206, 217, 248, 255, 258, 270, 300, 302, 308

Marxism-Leninism-Maoism 18, 47, 53, 64, 164, 217, 229, 274, 276, 281, 294

McCarthy era 44, 302

Mercado, Victoria 96

Mestizo 22-25, 29,121-123, 128

Mexican-American **11-12**, 42-43, 59, 86, 131, 156, 161, 189, 210

Mexican American Student Association 181

Mexican American Youth Organization 181

Mexican Revolution
   of 1810 - 25, 181, 186
   of 1910 - **35-37**, 75, 150, 183-184

Mexico City 23, 71

Mora, Magdalena 96

Moreno, Luisa 42, 96

Movimiento Estudiantil Chicano de Aztlán 47-49, 181

multicultural 6, 13, 85, 109, 129-130, 192, 212

multinational 49, 69, 80-83, 132-133, 137, 141, 155, 164, 167, 193, 201, 281

corporations 149, 246

Muñoz, Jr., Carlos 46-47, 178, 188-193

Murrieta, Jaoquin 33-34

National Guard 39, 43

national minority 15, 18, 59, 62, 64, 113, 127, 155-156, 166, 249, **303**

nationalism 51, 53, 82, 84-86, 102, 129, 131, 133, 136, 143, 155, 158, 164, 166, 195, 199, 254, 294, 303

    bourgeois nationalism 61, 85, 151, 191, **291**

    Chican@ nationalism 17, 69, 130, 133, 157, 195, 198, 295

    cultural nationalism 83-85, 166, 191, **210-212**, 217, 295

    narrow nationalism 83-84, 166, 219

    proletarian nationalism 110, 165

    revolutionary nationalism 17, 48, **83-87**, 109, 130, 191, 196, 217, 219, 308

    white nationalism 86, 110, 134-135, 146, 149, 156-157, 300, 308, **312**

Nationalist Party of Puerto Rico 43

Nebraska 33

New Afrika 15, 33, 38, 40, 47, 53, 73, 80-81, 102, 110, 115, 128-129, 143-144, 150, 152, 156, 159, 162, 164, 169, 191, 207, 252, 256, 278, 299, **303-304**, 309

New Afrikan Black Panther Party (Prison Chapter) 251

New Afrikan Maoist Party 267

New Deal 43

New Democracy 87, 154, 164-165, 198, **273-278**, 304

New Mexico 23-29, 31-32, 34, 49-50, 57, 94, 114-115, 219

    Dawson 39

    Santa Fe 25

    Tierra Amarilla 49

Newton, Huey 195, 295, 306

Nevada 29, 31, 41, 57, 114-115

Nicaragua 118, 120

Nkrumah, Kwame 68, 172

North American Free Trade Agreement 75

Oklahoma 31, 57

Operation Fast and Furious 66

Operation Wetback 44-45

Order of the Sons of America 42, 187

Panama 120, 124

pandillas 99-102

Paraguay 119-120

Paris Commune 76-77, 80, 91

Partido Liberal Mexicano 34-35, 183

patriarchy 11, 18, 50-51, 53-55, **95-98**, 197, 203-211, 225, 298, 305, 307

Patriot Act 45, 139

peace 8-9, 13, 37, 47, 49, 193, **234-237**, 267, 294, 307

Peru 82, 118, 120, 208

Pine Ridge reservation 94

Plan de San Diego **40-42**, 181

El Plan de Santa Barbara 47

El Plan Espiritual de Aztlán **51**, 156

Polk, James 30-31

post-modernism 109, 129, **305**

pre-Columbian 16, 181, 217, **306**

prisons 6, 8-11, 35, 45, 47, 49, 63-64, 70, 77, 83, 88-90, 96, **99-106**, 110, 124, 138, 146, 152, 154-155, 169-171, 174, 178-179, 187, 191-193, 199, 201, 209, 218, 221-226, 229-237, 251, 253, 256, 267, 282

    long-term isolation 8, 104

    prison population 104, 146, 224

    SHU 104-105, 221-225, 233-234

Progressive Labor Party 131, 135-137, 276

Puerto Rico 43, 53, 60, 62, 113, 115-117, 119, 195, 291

Raza Unida Party 52, 150-153, 188, 198, 211

reformism 43, 51, 55, 80, 138, 146, 148-149, 152, 198, 204, 207, 250, 265, 288-289, 296, 300, 303, **308**

    immigration reform 137, 141-149, 259, 261

    land reform 36, 61, 204, 301

Regeneración 34-35, 39

revisionism 61, 80-81, 136, 166, 196, 198, 211, 217, 281, 305, **308**

Revolutionary Caucus 52

Revolutionary Communist Party, U$A 137, **154-167**, 188, 196-197, 217, 276, 286

The Revolutionary Congress Created by the Plan de San Diego 41

Rockefellers 39

Roosevelt, Franklin D. 43

Russia 37, 60, 77, 162, 191, 199, 251, 310

Russian Revolution 77, 82, 199, 300

Santa Fe Trail 28, 125

security 87-90, 262-264, 267

Sediciosos 40-41

Senate Bill 1070 - 169-171

September 11, 2001 - 45

Sison, Jose Maria 137-141

Socialist Workers Party 196

South Africa 172, 244

South America 14, 57, 60, 113, 118-119, 121, 123, 159, 218, 293

South Carolina 304

South Dakota 94

Soviet Union 77-78, 200, 208, 231, 294-295, 297, 301-302, 310

Stalin, Joseph 14, 33, 48-49, 56, 58, 65, 77, 100, 129-130, 136, 155, 162, 165-166, 191, 199-201, 223, 231, 254, 257-258, 281, 290, 294, 303-304, 310

Student Nonviolent Coordinating Committee 50

superexploit 13, 67, 159, 195, 243-244, 246, 248-250, 254, 276, 299, **310**

superprofits 13, 64, 140, 144, 184, 195, 198, 241, 247-249, 299-300, **310**

superwages 13

Taos Revolt 31

Talamante, Olga 96

Tenochtitlan 22, 57, 71

Texas 25, 30-32, 34, 41-42, 45-46, 57, 114-115, 118, 150, 152, 159, 174, 181, 186, 210, 219

    Austin 30

    Brownsville 34

    El Paso 204

    San Antonio 150

Texas Rangers 32, 42, 49

Third World 114, 17, 30, 48, 53, 61-64, 73, 79, 82, 84, 91-92, 115, 128-129, 133-134, 146, 160, 192, 198, 205, 208, 212, 224, 229, 231, 240-252, 255, 258, 276, 287-288, 293, 296-297, 299, 300-301, 304, 307, 309-310

Tijerina, Reies Lopez 49

Treaty of Guadalupe Hidalgo 31-33, 52, 181

Article X 31

Trotsky, Leon 136, 183, 199-200, 310

Trotskyism 82, 109, 136, 189, 194-195, 198, 201, 269, 276, 295, 303, 310

    crypto-Trotskyism 81, 189, 196-197, 276, **295**

    neo-Trotskyism 196, **303-304**

United Farm Workers 204, 260, 289-290

united front 18, 40, 49, 68, 79, 83, 86, 91-92, 94, 136, 165, 193, 224, 230-232, 236-237, **265-272**, 281, 286, 291, 304, **311**

United Front for Peace in Prisons 193, **236-237**, 267

United Mexican American Students 46, 181

United $tates-Mexico border 30, 38-39, 48, 58-59, 66-68, 134, 138-139, 146, 148-149, 152-153, 156-160, 184, 186, 217, 244-245, 259-260

United $tates War on Mexico 25, **30-32**, 49, 61, 66, 158, 186-187

University of California Berkeley 188

University of California Los Angeles 177, 192, 203

Uruguay 119-120

Utah 29, 31, 41, 57, 114, 218-219

value of labor 144, 240-241, 246, 299-300, 305, 309-310

vanguard party 79, **87-92**, 98, 154, 201, 209, 292, 300-301, 311

Vasquez, Tiburcio 34

Venezuela 118-120

Vietnam 45-46, 53, 60, 68, 82, 125-126, 131-132, 145-146, 284

Villa, Pancho 36-37

World War I 40, 42-43, 244, 307

World War II 43, 78, 103, 113, 244, 254-255

Wyoming 29, 31, 33, 57

Young Citizens for Community Action 50

Young Lords Party 53, 102, 197, 209

youth 15, 20-21, 30, 32, 46-47, 50-51, 53, 59, 70-72, 74-75, 83, 99-103, 132, 145, 152, 168-169, 177-178, 180, 197, 205, 285

Zapata, Emiliano 34, 36-37

Zoot Suit Riots 4

Stop Torture in Prisons!

Reel Soldier Productions presents:

UNLOCK THE BOX

MOVIE DOCUMENTING THE STRUGGLE TO SHUT DOWN PRISON CONTROL UNITS

Stop Torture in U.S. Prison

"The purpose of the Marion Control Unit is to control revolutionary attitudes in the prison system and in the society at large."

-from Warden Ralph Arons's testimony in federal court

Unlock the Box is a movie documenting the struggle to put an end to long-term isolation in u.$. prisons that has been waged by prisoners and activists for decades. Starting from the premise that long-term isolation is a form of torture that serves no purpose except the state's oppressive aims at social control, Unlock the Box documents the many forms of struggle that this movement has taken over the years.

Each narrative is highlighted by the voices and artwork of current and former prisoners who have done time in control units. Also featured is new research on the growth and extent of the use of long-term isolation in the united $tates. Throughout the movie there is a focus on lessons from struggle and analysis of the relationship between the prison movement and the global effort to put an end to imperialism in all its forms. The desired purpose of the movie is to continue to bring the realities of the torture going on in these prisons to a broader audience and to help create greater clarity on what needs to be done to replace a system of torture with a system that works in the interests of humynity.

Reel Soldier Productions

www.abolishcontrolunits.org

114 minutes • 2008 • color • stereo

*intellectual property is one means of exploitation under imperialism

ALSO FROM KERSPLEBEDEB

Eurocentrism and the Communist Movement
by Robert Biel

978-1-894946-71-1 • 215 pages • $17.95

A work of intellectual history, Eurocentrism and the Communist Movement explores the relationship between Eurocentrism, alien-ation, and racism, while tracing the different ideas about imperial-ism, colonialism, "progress", and non-European peoples as they were grappled with by revolutionaries in both the colonized and colonizing nations. Teasing out racist errors and anti-racist insights within this history, Biel reveals a century-long struggle to assert the centrality of the most exploited within the struggle against capitalism.

Amazon Nation or Aryan Nation: White Women and the Coming of Black Genocide
by Bottomfish Blues

978-1-894946-55-1 • 168 pages • $12.95

The two main essays in this book come from the radical women's newspaper Bottomfish Blues, which was published in the late 1980s and early '90s; while a historical appendix on "The Ideas of Black Genocide in the Amerikkkan Mind" was written more recently, but only circulated privately. These texts provide raw and vital lessons at the violent crash scene of nation, gender, and class, from a revolutionary and non-academic perspective.

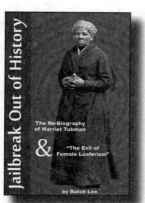

Jailbreak Out of History: the Re-Biography of Harriet Tubman
by Butch Lee

978-1-894946-70-4 • 169 pages • $14.95

The anticolonial struggles of New Afrikan/Black women were central to the unfolding of 19th century amerika, both during and "after" slavery. The book's title essay, "The Re-Biography of Harriet Tubman," recounts the life and politics of Harriet Tubman, who waged and eventually lead the war against the capitalist slave system. "The Evil of Female Loaferism" details the pivotal New Afrikan women's class struggles against capitalists North and South, and the creation of a neocolonial Black patriarchy, whose task was to make New Afrikan women subordinate to New Afrikan men just as New Afrika was supposed to be subordinate to white amerika.

WWW.KERSPLEBEDEB.COM /// WWW.LEFTWINGBOOKS.NET

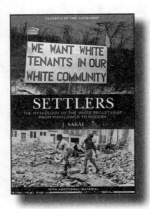

Settlers: The Mythology of the White Proletariat from Mayflower to Modern

by J. Sakai

978-1-62963-037-3 • 456 pages • $20.00

J. Sakai shows how the United States is a country built on the theft of Indigenous lands and Afrikan labor, on the robbery of the northern third of Mexico, the colonization of Puerto Rico, and the expropriation of the Asian working class, with each of these crimes being accompanied by violence. In fact, America's white citizenry have never supported themselves but have always resorted to exploitation and theft, culminating in acts of genocide to maintain their culture and way of life. This movement classic lays it all out, taking us through this painful but important history.

Basic Politics of Movement Security
"A Talk on Security" by J. Sakai &
"G20 Repression & Infiltration in Toronto: An Interview with Mandy Hiscocks"

978-1-894946-52-0 • 2014 • 72 pages • $7.00

There are many books and articles reporting state repression, but not on that subject's more intimate relative, movement security. It is general practice to only pass along knowledge about movement security privately, in closed group lectures or by personal word-of-mouth. Adding to the confusion, the handful of available left security texts are usually about underground or illegal groups, not the far larger public movements that work on a more or less legal level. Based on their own personal experiences on this terrain, these two "live" discussions by radical activists provide a partial remedy to this situation.

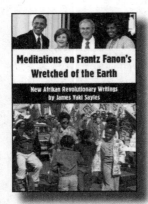

Meditations on Frantz Fanon's Wretched of the Earth:
New Afrikan Revolutionary Writings

by James Yaki Sayles

978-1-894946-32-2 • 399 pages • $20.00

"This exercise is about more than our desire to read and understand Wretched (as if it were about some abstract world, and not our own); it's about more than our need to understand (the failures of) the anti-colonial struggles on the African continent. This exercise is also about us, and about some of the things that We need to understand and to change in ourselves and our world." James Yaki Sayles (Atiba Shanna)

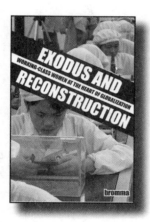
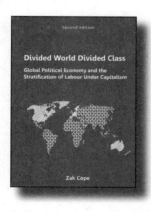

KER SPL EBE DEB

Since 1998 Kersplebedeb has been an important source of radical literature and agit prop materials.

The project has a non-exclusive focus on anti-patriarchal and anti-imperialist politics, framed within an anticapitalist perspective. A special priority is given to writings regarding armed struggle in the metropole, and the continuing struggles of political prisoners and prisoners of war.

The Kersplebedeb website presents historical and contemporary writings by revolutionary thinkers from the anarchist and communist traditions.

All books and pamphlets published by Kersplebedeb are available from AK Press, Amazon, and Baker & Taylor.

Kersplebedeb can be contacted at:

Kersplebedeb
CP 63560
CCCP Van Horne
Montreal, Quebec
Canada
H3W 3H8

email: info@kersplebedeb.com
web: www.kersplebedeb.com
            www.leftwingbooks.net

Kersplebedeb